PRAISE FOR *THE TRAUMA CLEANER*

'*The Trauma Cleaner* is a disturbing and fascinating
read with a heavy, beating heart at its centre.' *Australian*

'One of the most arresting works of biography
you will read in a long time.' *Guardian*

'A book as multifaceted as its subject…a wondrous
portrait of an inspiring character.' *Saturday Paper*

'She lets Pankhurst's courage, humanity and sheer
decency shine through. It's a fascinating read.' *SA Weekend*

'An anomalous, indelible treasure…Krasnostein allows
Sandra's story room to breathe and expand, to quietly
but confidently stake its claim to the reader's heart.'
*Kill Your Darlings*

'Written with sensitivity, insight and warmth…
Krasnostein has pieced together a compelling history.'
*Books + Publishing*

'Krasnostein is an astute observer of human nature and her
understated yet elegant prose is reminiscent of Helen Garner.'
*Readings*

'[Pankhurst's] story is probably one of the most touching,
thoughtful and thought-provoking you will ever read…Sarah
Krasnostein tells it with moving compassion, even love.'
*New Zealand Herald*

'Brutal, heartbreaking and utterly moving.' *Better Reading*

'Superbly sensitive…both confronting and edifying.'
*Toowoomba Chronicle*

9      D0238158

Sarah Krasnostein was born in America, studied in Melbourne and has lived and worked in both countries. Earning her doctorate in criminal law, she is a law lecturer and researcher. Her essay 'The Secret Life of a Crime Scene Cleaner' was published on *Longreads* and listed in *Narratively*'s Top 10 Stories for 2014. She lives in Melbourne and spends part of the year working in New York City. *The Trauma Cleaner* is her first book.

sarahkrasnostein.com
@delasarah

# The Trauma Cleaner

One woman's extraordinary life in death, decay & disaster. By Sarah Krasnostein

TEXT PUBLISHING MELBOURNE AUSTRALIA

textpublishing.com.au
textpublishing.co.uk

The Text Publishing Company
Swann House, 22 William Street, Melbourne, Victoria 3000, Australia

The Text Publishing Company (UK) Ltd
130 Wood Street, London EC2V 6DL, United Kingdom

First published in 2017 by The Text Publishing Company
Reprinted 2019

Cover design by W. H. Chong
Page design by Text
Typeset in Bembo 12/17 by J&M Typesetting

Printed and bound by CPI Group (UK) Ltd, Croydon, CR0 4YY.

National Library of Australia Cataloguing-in-Publication entry:
Creator: Krasnostein, Sarah, author.
Title: The trauma cleaner: one woman's extraordinary life in death, decay & disaster.
ISBN: 9781925498523 (paperback)
ISBN: 9781925410761 (ebook)
Subjects: Pankhurst, Sandra.
Cleaning personnel—Biography.

Before I go on with this short history, let me make a general observation—the test of a first-rate intelligence is the ability to hold two opposed ideas in the mind at the same time, and still retain the ability to function. One should, for example, be able to see that things are hopeless and yet be determined to make them otherwise.

F. Scott Fitzgerald, *The Crack-Up*

# AUTHOR'S NOTE

Some names—along with details of character, incident and place—have been changed. Those changes were kept to the minimum required to protect the privacy of certain individuals in this book.

The challenges posed by Sandra's memory loss mean that parts of her biographical story have required imaginative reconstruction. All dialogue and characters are, however, based on what she does remember and, where possible, interviews with third parties or historical records.

Nothing has been exaggerated.

This is what it says on the back of Sandra Pankhurst's business card:

'Excellence is no Accident'
Hoarding and Pet Hoarding Clean Up ★ Squalor/Trashed
Properties ★ Preparing the Home for Home Help Agencies
to Attend ★ Odour Control ★ Homicide, Suicide and
Death Scenes ★ Deceased Estates ★ Mould, Flood and Fire
Remediation ★ Methamphetamine Lab Clean Up
★ Industrial Accidents ★ Cell Cleaning

I first saw Sandra at a conference for forensic support services. A gaggle of public servants, lawyers and academics had just emerged from a session on offenders with acquired brain injuries to descend on urns of crappy coffee and plates of sweating cheese. I passed a card table in the lobby where brochures were spread out next to a sign inviting you to drop your business card into an ice bucket for a chance to win a bottle of shiraz. Next to the ice bucket— silver, with a stag's head on either side—a tiny TV played scenes of before and after trauma-cleaning jobs (which brought to mind the words 'faeces' and 'explosion'). Sitting behind the table a very tall woman, perfectly coiffed and tethered to an oxygen tank, fanned her hand out and invited me to enter my card. Hypnotised by her smile and her large blue eyes and the oxygen mask she wore like jewellery and the images on her TV, I haltingly explained that I don't have business cards. I did, however, pick up one of her brochures, which I read compulsively for the remainder of the day.

Sandra is the founder of Specialised Trauma Cleaning (STC) Services Pty Ltd. Each day for the past twenty years, her job has led her into dark homes where death, sickness and madness have suddenly abbreviated the lives inside.

Most people will never turn their mind to the notion of 'trauma cleaning'. But once they realise that it exists—that it obviously has to—they will probably be surprised to learn that the police do not do trauma clean-up. Neither do firefighters or ambulances or other emergency services. This is why Sandra's trauma work is varied and includes crime scenes, floods and fires. In addition, government housing and mental health agencies, real estate agents, community organisations, executors of deceased estates and private individuals all call on Sandra to deal with unattended deaths, suicides or cases of long-term property neglect where homes have, in her words, 'fallen into disrepute' due to the occupier's mental illness, ageing or physical disability. Grieving families also hire Sandra to help them sort, disperse and dispose of their loved ones' belongings.

Her work, in short, is a catalogue of the ways we die physically and emotionally, and the strength and delicacy needed to lift the things we leave behind.

*We specialise in the unpleasant tasks that you need to have taken care of.* Performing a public service as vital as it is gruesome, Sandra is one of the world's unofficial experts on the living aspects of death. So much is clear from her brochure, which also showcases her intense practicality. Quoth the Brochure of Pankhurst:

People do not understand about body fluids. Bodily fluids are like acids. They have all the same enzymes that break down our food. When these powerful enzymes come into contact with furnishings and the like, deterioration is rapid. I have known enzymes to soak through a sofa and to eat at the springs, mould growing throughout a piece of furniture, and I have witnessed the rapid deterioration of a contaminated mattress.

Most of us will never realise how many of these places there are or that they can be found in every neighbourhood, regardless of socio-economics. We will never see them or smell them or touch them. We will not know these places or lament them. But this is the milieu in which Sandra spends much of her time; it is where she works and takes phone calls and sends emails, where she laughs and makes the office small talk most of the rest of us roll out in the office elevator; it is where she passed into early and then late middle age.

STC services have the compassion to deal with the residents, a very underestimated and valued requirement by its cus-tomers.

Her advertising materials emphasise compassion, but that goes far deeper than the emotional-intelligence equivalent of her technical skill in neutralising blood-borne pathogens. Sandra knows her clients as well as they know themselves; she airs out their smells, throws out their weird porn, their photos, their letters, the last traces of their DNA entombed in soaps and toothbrushes. She does not, however, erase these people. She couldn't. She has experienced their same sorrows.

•

'Hi Sarah, it's Sandra. I believe you contacted me for an interview. If you could call me back on [number] it would be appreciated, but possibly not today as I'm just *inundated* at the moment and I'm on my way to a suicide. So if you could just call me back tomorrow, maybe, on [number], thank you. Bye for now.'

When I return her call, I learn that Sandra has a warm laugh and that she needs a lung transplant. She asks me when I would like to meet. I tell her that I can work around her schedule. So she says, 'Okey dokey,' and flips open her diary. 'How about the cafe at the Alfred Hospital?' she suggests, explaining parenthetically that she has a couple of hours next week before she sees her lung specialist.

It struck me then that, for Sandra Pankhurst, death and sickness are a part of life. Not in a Buddhist koan sort of way, but in a voicemail and lunch-meeting sort of way. Over the next few years, she would reveal to me how this unrelenting forward orientation, fundamental to her character, has saved her life.

During my time with Sandra, I met a bookbinder, a sex offender, a puppeteer, a cookbook hoarder, a cat hoarder, a wood hoarder and a silent woman whose home was unfit for her many rabbits and whose skin was so swollen that I thought at any moment it would burst like a water balloon. I heard Sandra bend and flex language into words and idioms she made her own: 'supposably', 'sposmatically', 'hands down pat!'. I had the rapturous experience, many times, of simply listening to her swear. I saw wonders of the dark world, as true of our collective human life as radio stations and birthday cards: walls that had turned soft from mould, food that had liquefied, drinks that had solidified, flies raised on human blood, the pink soap of the recently deceased and eighteen-year-old chicken bones lying like runes at the bottom of a pot.

I listened to Sandra's news like it was the middle of the Han dynasty and she had just returned west from the Silk Road, except that she was really just telling me about her morning or her afternoon—about waiting for the psych team to collect the man who killed his dog so that she could clean its blood off his floors; about a 'love triangle stabbing'; about the man who died in the ceiling of his home while spying on his family; about the dead hermit eaten by his dog; about the 240-litre container of syringes she filled and removed from a drug house; about the man who threw himself on a table saw and the mess he left for his family to find.

I learned the many sides of Sandra: the social commentator ('We've some areas where no life skills are taught; we are getting generation after generation that are slovenly.'); the bawdy ('I've had more cock than I've had hot dinners.'); the confident ('If I had better health I'd run for government and I'd be a kick-arse person.'); the self-compassionate ('I have no shame of what I had to do to get to where I needed to go.'); the philosophical ('Everything happens for a reason and it's really hard to say why it happens at the time.'); the perfectionist ('I've always set tough standards. As a prostitute, I was a great prostitute. As a cleaner, I'm a great cleaner. Whatever I do, I do to the best of my ability.') and the positive ('This year is going to be my best year ever.').

Which is all to say, I learned that Sandra is at once exactly like you or me or anyone we know and, at the same time, she is utterly peerless.

One thing Sandra is not, however, is a flawlessly reliable narrator. She is in her early sixties and simply not old enough for that to be the reason why she is so bad with the basic sequence of her life, particularly her early life. Many facts of Sandra's past are either entirely forgotten, endlessly interchangeable, neurotically ordered, conflicting or loosely tethered to reality. She is open about the fact that drugs have impacted her memory ('I don't know, I can't remember. The lesson to be learnt is this: Do not take drugs, it fucks your brain.'). It is also my belief that her memory loss is trauma-induced.

But there is something else of which I have become convinced over my years of speaking with her. Most people Sandra's age can tell you in detail about how they came up, about the excitements and tragedies of being a young adult out in the world for the first time. This isn't because their brains are any better than Sandra's or because they did less drugs or drank less or had kinder childhoods. It is because they've told their stories more often. Because they were consistently surrounded by friends or parents or partners or children who were interested in seeing them as a whole person.

This is how true connection occurs. This is how events become stories and stories become memories and memories become narratives of self and of family from which we derive identity and strength. Part of the reason the timeline is never clear for Sandra, no matter how many times we go over it, is that, until now, she has never had any reason to repeat it honestly or in full.

'A lot of people know some of the story, but they do not know all of the story.' And here it hits me what it is we are doing by telling this story. It is something at once utterly familiar and completely alien to Sandra: we are clearing away the clutter of her life out of basic respect for the inherent value of the person beneath.

Using words as disinfectants, we are trauma cleaning. Word by word, sentence by sentence, we are reuniting fragments scattered by chaos to create heat and light. We cannot always eliminate what is bad or broken or lost but we can do our best to put everything in its place, such Order being the true opposite of Trauma.

And so your story is imperfect, Sandra, but it is here, made complete, and it is my love letter to you.

# Kim

A short drive north from Geelong, a woman lives in a house with broken windows and dark words sprayed across its exterior in writing that looks like it came from the hand of a giant. It says I HATE YOU and BRAIN and WELL BEING? and HUMANITY and THE SHAME. The windows facing the street are covered, variously, with blankets, a battered blind held in place by a blue plastic flute and a sheet of cardboard. On the lawn, random mounds of large rocks, bricks, wooden planks, metal grilles and wires dot the dying grass. A large handwritten sign that says HYPACRITES is balanced across two of the mounds. There are a couple of sun-bleached garden gnomes and an industrial-sized bag of mulch on which more words have been scrawled in black paint: SAME SONG, SWORDS, HOMELESS.

Sandra is sitting in an immaculate white SUV with a large white sticker stretched across the back window that says MISSIBITCHI. She is scheduled to do a cleaning quote at 9 a.m. As always, she is early and she is on her phone. Someone from the Salvation Army inquiring about laundry costs for a client with bedbugs. Sandra replies that it's thirty-five dollars per bag, plus pick-up and delivery.

She covers the phone and whispers guiltily, 'I just started charging for that.' Wrapping up the call, she pops her door open and unfolds her long, slim legs from the car. Sandra is wearing bright pink lipstick, a navy blouse, dark skinny jeans and pristine white ballet flats. As always, her platinum blonde hair is perfectly blow-dried and it floats slowly around her as she turns in the morning light.

The tenant at this morning's job is named Kim. Sandra has been briefed that Kim describes herself as a puppeteer, a magician and a pet trainer and that, though she is 'a smart woman', she becomes extremely suspicious of those trying to help. She will talk about her self-diagnosed conditions which include bipolar disorder and a tumour in her head. Kim is 'very angry' because the previous cleaner got rid of her pets, 'thirty rats, all dead'. I'm still processing the image of thirty dead rats as we walk towards the house. Sandra starts explaining that the goal is to make Kim sufficiently comfortable with the cleaning process so that the job causes her minimal distress.

To reach the short flight of stairs leading up to Kim's front door, Sandra walks down a cracked concrete driveway, around the colossal bag of mulch, past a red sombrero and under a low-slung makeshift hammock full of water. Though Kim opens her front door, she remains hidden deep inside while Sandra explains that she is here to help but first needs to have a look around.

'I'm from a private enterprise,' Sandra explains, breathless from the strain the small climb has placed on her deteriorating lungs. 'We do organisation. We work *with* you, looking after your stuff and making sure it's safe and sound. We do it in conjunction with you, *we work together.*' She is fighting for breath, audibly sucking it in where she can between words. After a beat, peering up at Sandra, Kim seems to accept this and steps back, allowing her in.

You could easily mistake Kim for a young boy but she is a mother in her early forties. She is short, she is fine featured and small boned and bloated. She has pale skin and blue eyes that are darting and swooping like swallows. She is wearing heavy black work boots, baggy khaki pants, a big black T-shirt and a long black scarf; also a fingerless black glove on one hand. There is an old black blanket wrapped around her waist like a skirt. Her blonde hair has been hacked into a bob and a white road of scalp shines out where a strip has been randomly shaved through it. She has homemade tattoos on one arm. A long wooden spoon has been tied with rope around her shoulders. Standing in her doorway, emerging from the cavernous darkness of her home, she would present as some type of troglodytic warrior but for the fact that she is radiating fear so vibrantly that it is contagious.

'Can you just watch where you walk?' Kim asks. 'I've made it as safe as possible.' Her voice, too, is that of a young boy, piping but gruff, trying to be brave. She gestures towards a box and says in an off-handed way, 'I study magician stuff, not that I'll ever do it.'

Stepping inside, Sandra puts her hand on Kim's shoulder and says, 'I hear that you're an animal trainer. I need help with a dog. Here, look at this.' She starts swiping through photos on her phone, her long red nail clicking crisply on the screen until she gets to a shot of her Lana, small and white, staring at the camera mid-shiver. 'She's Lana Turner and I'm Bette Davis,' Sandra explained the first time I met that damaged and diminutive creature, who barked continuously at a pitch that made me squint. 'She's my security girl. I got her from the animal shelter, but she rescued me.'

Sandra explains to Kim how Lana was probably abused because she cowers at any quick movement, how the dog still refuses to be picked up and runs off, which is real rough because of her lung problem, you see? Kim cracks a half-smile and drops suddenly onto all fours before explaining from down there that Sandra simply needs to adopt a 'submissive permissive physical language' with the dog. Sandra nods at the words with vague interest, not conscious of the fact that she has just intuitively executed that same move with Kim, who—even in explaining this—is mirroring it right back at Sandra.

'Right. You can help me, I can help you,' Sandra says. 'We'll work together.' She looks at her surrounds, raring to begin.

What Sandra does here is magnificent. Beautiful. If we all talked to each other in this way, with warm camaraderie and complete non-judgment, much pain would be spared and happiness generated. And though I will not say that it is entirely altruistic—that so unselfconsciously does she handle her wounded clients that she appears, from where I stand, like Saint Francis of Assisi cooing at an anguished dove—it is still absolutely heartening to watch.

One of Sandra's talents is that she is superb at—I won't call it small talk because, though that too is true, it is the form rather than the function—she is superb at instantly conveying a bespoke blend of respect, warmth, humour and interest that establishes a basic human equity and makes nearly everyone comfortable enough to immediately return the favour. This gesture is the opposite of the shaming to which she has been subjected consistently throughout her life, and it is lovely to witness its salutary effect on the whole spectrum of humanity.

Of course, Sandra's skill at making others feel secure also eliminates a whole host of threats to herself and optimises her ability to move forward with her work and with her life, because Sandra is a virtuoso at survival. As she said to me once, 'What I feel that I'm good at is that I can talk to Mrs Rich Bitch, Mr Penny Pauper. I can put myself on any level, because I'm probably an actress, you know what I mean? I can then deal with *who* I need to deal with and *how* I need to deal with.'

The house is dark, though some light filters in through the cracks around the window coverings. A wooden marionette dangles by the front door. Different-coloured words are written all over the walls. 'This is the Hilton compared to what it was,' Kim says, explaining that she's been up cleaning for two days without sleep. She itches at one of the open sores on her arm.

'What I'm thinking of doing here so that we can clean it all out for you—tell me what you think—is we're going to bring a safe container in for all your stuff,' Sandra explains softly, before being interrupted by her phone. She takes the call, turning herself towards the wall. The timing is agonisingly awkward but there are extremely few, perhaps no, conversations Sandra won't interrupt to take a phone call. And it's no use getting terribly offended over it because, in the Great Karmic Cycle of Pankhurst, there are extremely few, perhaps no, conversations that she won't interrupt to take *your* call. She briskly deals with whatever it is before returning to focus on the conversation.

Kim is waving at the outside of the house. 'That was just my outcry. It's done now, it's finished,' she says quickly, explaining how she tried to paint over the words, even though the paint wasn't an exact match, as a gesture of goodwill towards the landlord. Inside, though, she insists that the writing on the walls is therapeutic.

'I've got lots of trauma, right? And what I'm doing here is running what is called a domestic violence hypnotic behavioural therapy lab.'

'Right,' Sandra murmurs, encouraging.

'OK, so that on the wall'—Kim motions around the room—'is to do with shock, it's to do with trauma. I started this myself. I was traumatised. I'm only just walking around this complete house myself, 'cause the garage burned down and set…things…off. Very bad.' Kim's voice quivers and she explains that the garage caught fire four years ago.

Motioning to the makeshift splint around her shoulder, Kim says, 'I've got…really…bad muscles. I think it's to do with my tumours that're causing bad signals in my body. This time I've done a lot of work and my shoulder is very sore, so it's a reminder not to use it.' She sets her mouth in a stoic line and looks down at the floor.

'I want to get your opinion about how you want it to be here, because that's what my goal is,' Sandra says soothingly.

A small dog scratches at the screen door and Kim warns Sandra not to let it in because her rats, who act as 'door security', are not in a cage. 'They live in a chair,' she explains, motioning to a large armchair with a blanket puddled on the seat. 'And they walk around the house. But they won't move. They're actually shit-scared at the moment.'

'How would a compromise be, if we got this cleaned up and we got you canvases that you could do the exact artwork on for your therapy treatment? I think that's the best way, don't you?' Sandra looks down earnestly at Kim.

'It is, it is,' Kim agrees, sighing deeply. 'But do you know what it is…I draw. It's my therapy or whatever. But I've been locked up, institutionalised, shackled illegally. Mate, to look at white walls…'

'I understand that,' Sandra cuts in. 'But if we could make it like a gallery, with your proper artwork, we'd be killing two birds with one stone.'

As part of her quoting process, it is Sandra's custom to take photos on her small camera. Kim advises against using the flash too close to the fireplace where a heater has been ripped out. 'It'll aggravate them,' Kim explains, referring to the rats. Then she starts insisting that this clean cannot be like the last attempt. The previous cleaner stole her DVD player. 'But possessions are nothing. What's really cut me up is that I come home'—she is indignant, incredulous—'and he's chucked these rats out all over the backyard.'

'Unacceptable,' Sandra barks.

'Yep. Not only that, I had to agree to euthanasia. The oldest rats I had—I actually spent twenty-four seven with them, I was making a Christmas video at the time, it was absolutely beautiful—I come home and they're poisoned. And that was *not* the agreement. It's not right. It's not right.' She is getting visibly furious.

Sandra puts a hand on Kim's shoulder. I wonder how long it has been since Kim has been touched in this way. 'Let's have a look around, shall we?'

I hang back, sapped for a moment by the smell. Hanging over everything is one of two smells (the other being death) that I will discover and come to know during the time I spend watching Sandra at work: human dirt at close quarters over time. We have no single word for it, this smell. We have no adjective to describe how profoundly repulsive and unsettling it is. It's not just human effluence or rot, nor is it a simple matter of filth or grime or feculence or unwashedness. It's not merely nasty or gross or disgusting, or the 'FEH!' of my grandmother. I wonder if, in less hygienic times, we did have a word for it or whether there is one in other languages. Or whether, in fact, the absence of this word communicates something more effectively than language ever could—that such a smell is verboten because it signifies a fundamentally destabilising taboo: a level of disconnection and self-neglect that is, essentially, a living death.

Standing in the hallway, I imagine the smell settling like snow on my hair and my skin, breathing it like smoke into my nose and mouth; how it curls its way into the fibres of my clothing and the hollows of my ears. Like death, it is an old smell; so fundamentally human that it can only be disavowed. You avoid this smell each time you take a shower and each time you wash your hands. Each time you brush your teeth or flush the toilet, or launder your sheets and towels. With every plate you scrub clean, every spill you mop up and every bag of rubbish you tie up and throw out. Every time you open a window or walk outside, breathing deeply, to stretch your legs and stand in sunlight. This smell is the lingering presence of all the physical things we put into and wash off ourselves. But it is equally the ineffable smell of defeat, of isolation, of self-hate. Or, more simply, it is the smell of pain.

Instructively, however, over our time here Sandra whispers to me that 'this house doesn't smell' and also that it 'smells strongly of rats'; a startling and only superficially paradoxical observation that tells you much about the things she encounters in her work on a daily basis.

I walk out of the living room and into a smaller room that feels like a closet due to the fact that most of the walls and ceiling have been painted black. There is a naked mattress propped up against one wall and a couple of wooden chairs, but most of the space is taken up by piles of random items tied together to form strange teepees or stacked like kindling around the room: knotted shirts, ropes, pipes, a ukulele, a lawn torch, hats, wires, sticks.

I stop and stand, transfixed, before a mural in crayon and chalk and paper that dominates one of the black walls. It is vital, beautiful. It depicts the night sky, thick lines of psychedelic colour swirling in on themselves and around a young girl holding a flaming torch. The girl has been torn from a book, pasted to the wall and seamlessly integrated into the larger cosmos of this image. She stands there, staunchly balanced between a lemon yellow dagger and the word 'Knowledge'. Perfectly primitive, the image is, at the same time, powerfully allegorical and somehow, though of course this seems insane, it appears to thrum on the dark wall with some talismanic promise of power. Also, it conveys as starkly as a road sign the thousand, thousand miles between where Kim is now and where she should have been. With all the appliances ripped out, it takes me a while to realise that this room was once the kitchen.

Sandra enters the room with Kim and compliments the mural while thinking aloud how she can advocate on Kim's behalf to preserve it under the terms of the tenancy. Perhaps, she muses, they can mount a frame around it, directly on the wall. Kim immediately tries to have another painting in a different room thrown into the deal. I follow them slowly down the hall, passing a graffitied bookshelf stocked with VHS tapes and DVDs. *Bugs Bunny. Peter Pan. Aladdin. Mary Poppins.* Propped up against the tapes is a photo of twin boys in their school uniforms, maybe ten years old. The same face as Kim except lovely and full of life.

I listen as Kim explains another large image on the wall to Sandra.

Executed with the same talent as the first image, it is chilling and predominantly black. It depicts a dark figure, the type a child would draw, with spiky hair and uneven limbs, but it has been elongated, distorted as though seen in a fun-house mirror. It stands in sharp relief against an indigo sky in which float numbers and letters. There is a roiling hole or bright burning furnace in the centre of the figure. And scratched into the black paint, over and over and over again, are the lines of another figure: the shadow of this shadow man. This is a perfectly realised human world of crisis and isolation as effective as any Giacometti or Bacon or Munch. Except that it is not hanging in the Tate or MoMA, it is painted on a dirty wall next to a free-standing wardrobe with the doors ripped off.

'This is from when my mother was involved in a murder–suicide. I was five years old,' Kim explains, leaning against a door on which are scrawled the words TRAUMA and PUNISH and MIND/COST in pea-green crayon. (In different handwriting, a child's handwriting, are the words 'incy wincy' in careful orange script.) 'I don't need medication. It's trauma. It needs to come out. My brain has nightmares which are horrific.' She explains how she woke up from a nightmare and just started drawing on the wall, because she had to, and I think of her alone in this dark house in the dark night. Exorcising this image onto the nearest wall.

The bedroom. Kim sleeps on the top level of a bunk bed next to a broken chest freezer with the word CUNT scrawled on it in large brown letters. There is an accordion in the middle of her bed. A web of cellophane and rope has been twisted around the bed posts; various funeral booklets are stuck here, suspended like flies. Upstairs, in the other two bedrooms, piles of clothes and sheets, everything the colour of newsprint. Also, an electric guitar with strings missing and a toy helicopter, its blades smeared with crayon.

'I can get you a fridge,' Sandra says casually to Kim as they descend the stairs. 'And a washing machine, a fancy new one. And a dryer.' When Sandra does a deceased estate and there is no next of kin to take the bed linen or TV or furniture, she stores these orphaned items and waits for the right fit, then she installs them for free into the freshly cleaned homes of her hoarding and squalor clients.

With an autistic client who had been sleeping on the cement floor of his bare apartment, she once explained, 'The TV came from a murder, I stored it so it was aired out and ready to go, there was a lounge and I had a table, so I gave him that.' She gave another client, going through a divorce, 'a proper lounge suite with a recliner, a foldout bed, a vacuum cleaner, kitchen stuff, a whole range of linen, and I've got pillows for him. This is going to be a major transformation for this guy.'

She does this because she is deeply generous but that's not the entire explanation. There's also her drive to execute each job as perfectly as possible, which sets her apart from the other industrial cleaners who are happy with doing adequate work. But that's not the whole story either. She has been intuitively righting her environment—cleaning it, organising it, coordinating it, filling in gaps where she can, hiding them where she can't—since she was a child. It is her way of imposing order on her world and it brings her profound satisfaction.

Kim walks out of her bedroom and into the small laundry room which leads outside. She is volatile, emitting instability like radio waves, and I too feel jumpy, nervous. While the type of high energy that Sandra gives off always feels warm, like a car engine that's been driving for hours, Kim crackles. Suddenly, she shoots back out of the room and runs circles around us, bent low at the waist. I startle and, without thinking, grab Sandra's arm.

'It's the dog,' Sandra says lightly. Kim's dog managed to get inside and she is chasing it back out so that it doesn't attack the rats. We continue into the laundry room where a screen door leads to the backyard. There is no washing machine, no dryer. Just taps on the wall. There is a low table covered in a bedsheet with a velour pillow in the centre, on which various items are stored in boxes that once held tea-light candles and rolling papers. There is a crayon-streaked kettle and toaster, empty packets of chips, bread, tea bags. A small picture of the Virgin Mary hangs high on the wall of this makeshift kitchen. Also, a small postcard of Einstein. The dirty floor is carpeted with a brown blanket on which pink-handled cutlery appears to have been deliberately positioned. There is a toilet in a tiny room off to the side; the floor there is strewn with ten volumes of the *World Book* and the walls are painted bright blue and covered in green writing: OOH PUNCH & JUDY SHOW!, SUICIDE TAB 111 11, MARY HAD A LITTLE LAMB. A frying pan lies at the base of the toilet, a crucifix dangles from the toilet-paper holder.

Surveying the dining situation, Sandra asks Kim if she would like a microwave. 'I, uh, I...uh...I would do that...' Kim replies quietly, then pins a coffee can between her feet and hops it to the other side of the room.

The backyard is vast. A Hills hoist is stuck like a cocktail umbrella in the dead centre of the dead lawn; debris everywhere in the spongy yellow grass. Despite it being the end of summer, the bushes and trees along the fence line are devoid of leaves. An entropic mound of trash and broken furniture oozes towards the house from the far corner of the yard. This is where Kim deposited the stuff that was crowded up to the ceiling inside the house during the last inspection.

I hear Kim telling a story inside like she's at a bar with friends;

Sandra breaks out into long laughter with her. Then they come outside and Kim, frowning, squats and lights a cigarette butt. Sandra's phone rings. 'Good morning, Sandra speaking,' she answers pertly while sitting down on a milk crate and majestically crossing her legs. Balancing her clipboard on her lap, she listens while making notes. The little dog trots over and places its front paws on her leg.

'We might have to take up the carpet,' Sandra says, staring into the middle distance and stroking the dog's head. Her perfectly manicured nails are extra-long acrylics, sufficiently durable for her to participate (ungloved, as is her preference) in an all-day trauma clean and emerge looking as though she has just been at the manicurist. At least, if you don't peer too closely at the undersides. She favours juicy bright shades of cherry red or apricot or watermelon, or a glazed glitter baby pink. Intensely practical about her appearance, as she is about most things, she has opted for permanent eyeliner, lip liner and eyebrow liner so that she can throw on minimal make-up and be ready for the day. Her eyelashes and eyebrows, like her hair, are white blonde and her eyes are very blue, slightly wide-set and enormous. Regardless of what she is doing that day or how long she has been doing it for, she looks immaculate and smells lovely.

The dog jumps onto Sandra's clipboard, leaving brown paw prints on the paper. She reaches around it to continue making notes. 'See, that's because body fluids go through to the underlay. It can be the size of a coin, but spread out underneath,' she explains into the phone. 'You can surface clean it but if you have children crawl over it at some stage, you're likely to be sued later on. In my mind, I'm not happy with that. I'd rather you be safe, sound and it's sterilised. We can certainly look at that for you. That's the trauma side of things but there may be an industrial clean needed, like if the walls need to be washed down because the body fluids have evaporated in the heat or if there was gas in the room, I'm not sure how they killed themselves.' The dog launches itself off Sandra's arm, ripping

18

two puncture holes in her skin. They start to bleed more than you would think. 'It's my paper skin,' she whispers, covering the phone and then wiping at the blood. Her cortisone inhalers cause skin atrophy; just now it tore like wet tissue. 'Where's the house?' she asks. 'Ah, that's just a hop, skip and a jump for us.' Pleased, she finishes the call.

The dog nestles between Kim's knees. 'Aw, god, you want love,' she laments theatrically as she ties her black scarf around her head like a turban. And then, quietly, 'You want breakfast...' She leans her head back, the burnt-out butt dangling from her lip.

Staring at the mountain of junk in the back corner of the yard, I think of the photos on the bookshelf of the boys with Kim's face and the Disney VHS tapes and the two unused dark bedrooms. I watch as the old sink and the battered washing machine rise up from the pile and right themselves, the two tiny headboards snap back onto the two small bed bases and all the clothes shake themselves off, fold themselves up and assemble in piles. I watch as everything floats up across the lawn and back inside and back through time to before the garage burned, when the walls were white and blankets covered the beds instead of being worn as skirts or used as carpets. But I know that, while Mary Poppins may have sung out from the TV and clothes may have dried on the line, things were not OK. Things here were never OK.

We walk around to the front of the house on our way out. Sandra is professional and obsessively efficient in her work but she cannot stay entirely serious for too long without indulging a playful flirtiness which she fans out like a peacock's tail. When she does this her eyes gleam and she is very beautiful and very hilarious and I cannot help, always, just to be delighted by her. She points to Kim's headgear and says, 'You look like Taliban.'

'I can be,' Kim smiles shyly and then they both giggle.

Despite seeing the same old shit each day for twenty-one years,

Sandra treats each client as unique in their circumstance and equal in their dignity. I asked her, once, how she manages to maintain that attitude of compassion and absolute non-judgment. 'I think it's a drive for me that everyone deserves it because I deserve it as well,' she explained.

Back on the footpath, I look up and down the street. The neighbourhood is shabbier than it first appeared and the smell with no name is here too, high on the breeze, its meaning as public and as private as a song. I ask Kim how she got into puppeteering. She answers that it was a way of working through the things she couldn't speak about. How does she manage to work that marionette hanging inside without hopelessly twisting all the different strings like everyone else?

'It's like playing an instrument. It's like dancing,' she says simply.

Her house looks like the aftermath of a personalised earthquake visited by a vengeful god but even here, in the midst of such disturbing chaos, what Kim has elegantly just confirmed is the profound power of sequence; the beauty of order. Heartbeat, breath, ebb tide, flood tide, the movements of the earth, the phases of the moon, seasons, ritual, call and response, notes in a scale, words in a sentence. Human connection and security lie here. Sandra will start work at Kim's house next week.

# 2

It didn't start at the twenty-buck fuck shops. It didn't start in the barnlike brothel where the girls roosted like hens, wire on the windows and around the light bulbs to prevent the men from ripping them out of the ceiling. It didn't start with the boyfriends who stuck around only as long as her money lasted, or with the beatings from the cops who hated boys dressed like girls or with the women who wouldn't open the door when she stood outside pleading in the dark, naked and bleeding. It didn't start with any of that. It started when she was a little boy in a small house with a dirt driveway running up along the side.

Maybe his name was Glen. Maybe it was Daniel. Or John or Mark or Tim. The actual name matters only because it is a piece of information that Sandra chooses to keep for herself. Statistically, it's most likely to have been Peter. And although that was not his actual name, it is what he'll be called. Not for lack of imagination, but because he had the right to be treated like any other boy born that year, and he was not.

If his father drove in a straight line up the driveway, Peter knew he wouldn't be beaten. But if the car rolled in crooked, it meant his father had been drinking, which meant that he would wobble with purpose to the detached room out the back where his son lay, tensed, in whalemouth darkness. Then he would grab the boy and beat his thin body with the copper stick his wife used for stirring laundry.

'He's at it again, Pammy,' the neighbour would say to her daughter, drying her hands on a dishtowel before turning around to shut the kitchen window gently on the boy's cries. 'Better go and turn up your radio.'

Sandra's father, Robert, was born in 1923 and raised in Footscray. When my father-in-law talks about growing up in Footscray, he talks about the rope walk, long and narrow under its corrugated iron roof, and how the boys who worked at the rope factory became men who died early, their lungs full of resin and dust. Footscray is gentrifying fast now but this inner-city neighbourhood was a major industrial zone from the mid-1800s until the 1960s, when manufacturing began to decline, and a part of town where no one had it easy.

The Collins family lived on Droop Street initially, a road that drops obliquely, if not with melancholic defeat, away from West Footscray and sags towards Footscray proper as if gradually shoved out of place over time by forces beyond its control. Robert was eleven when his fourteen-year-old brother, Harold, died in 1934. In 1939, sixteen-year-old Robert Griffith Parker Collins carried his four names across state lines to Greta, New South Wales, to enlist in the Second Australian Forces, but by 1942 he was back home living with his parents and working as a labourer.

By then the family had moved to Birchill Street, which shows itself as a tiny T on the map of West Footscray; an oddly shaped street possessed of not one but two dead ends. It was, however, agreeably nestled within easy walking distance of Sims grocery store and St John's Primary School as well as the chemist, the post office, the Church of Our Lady of Perpetual Help and, were she to deny one's pleas for intercession, as she did regularly but through no fault of her own, Footscray Hospital. Seven years later, Robert was still living at home—now with his wife, Ailsa—and making a living as a grocer while she worked as a saleswoman.

By 1954 the couple had finally struck out on their own, at least as far as the small white cottage immediately opposite his parents. From here Robert, whom people inexplicably called Bill, would set out each day for his clerical role at the Royal Australian Air Force Base in Braybrook, followed by an evening shift at the Plough Hotel during which he would drink himself into a rage and then drive sloppily home to beat his wife and children. This was Peter's home, where he was brought after he was adopted through the Catholic Church in the early fifties. Six weeks old.

In the taxonomy of pain there is only the pain inflicted by touching and the pain inflicted by not touching. Peter grew up an expert in both. Malnourished, the skin on his thin neck perpetually covered in boils, he was as scarred as the surface of Mercury; a planet lacking atmospheric protection, exposed to the hurtling debris of space and wearing its history of collision and battery on its face.

The second child and the oldest son, he was adopted after Bill and Ailsa lost a son in childbirth and were told that they could have no more biological children. For about five years it was just Peter and his older sister, Barbara. But then Ailsa fell pregnant, first with Simon and two years later, Christopher. That's when they told Peter that he had been adopted as a replacement for the son they had lost. And that they had made a mistake because they now had not just Simon but also Christopher, you see? This was stated clinically, as a matter of fact, 'nothing bitter and twisted or anything'.

A few years later, they moved Peter out of the room he shared with his brothers, with its bunk beds and black walls and bright red bedspreads, and into a low shed his father built in the backyard.

•

Ailsa is the 'prima donna of sponges'. She loves to bake, and Peter's first memory is of hugging her leg in the kitchen. When he grows too tall for that, he never stops trying to be close to her. His eyes follow her around the kitchen, around the house, out the door. His eyes map her face. Is she angry? Is she sad? What can he do to make it better? To feel the weight of her hand pressing gently on the back of his shoulders; maybe even her warm cheek on his ear? Is there something he can help her with after his father leaves for work in the morning? Something he can do for her after school? He would give anything to sit quietly next to her while she talks on the telephone with her sister or flips through a magazine. If he is lucky enough to eat dinner with the rest of the family, he will check her face during the meal and again while he is cleaning up. When that is done, he will check once more just to be sure that nothing has changed, that there's nothing he might have missed. And then he will look at her, silently saying goodnight, willing her to come tuck him in, to stay next to his bed where he can see her outline in the dark and hear her breath while he falls asleep.

But though sometimes she seems less angry, or at least more distracted, he never finds what he is looking for. Instead, she busies herself with the house and the shopping and the cooking and cleaning and her church, and her other children as Bill beats Peter for their misdeeds.

'See? See what you'll get if you do it again?' his father, breathless and sweating, warns the other kids after he gets through with Peter. And then he locks his son outside to watch from his room in the yard as the house lights glow yellow and then go out.

Because Peter is not allowed into the family home after 4:30 p.m. each day he lives delicately, like lace, just at the edges. This presents a range of practical problems. First there is the food issue: he is always hungry. How does a starving child feed himself? If he is smart, he steals canned fruit or baked beans from the pantry when no one is looking. And that will work until he accidentally burns part of the house down.

One of Peter's chores is to light the hot water system and one day he forgets. He panics. He tries to fill it up with the petrol that goes in the lawnmower, and the laundry room catches fire. Strangely, he doesn't get beaten for the fire; he gets beaten for stealing food after his stash of crushed, empty cans is discovered hidden behind one of the walls that burns down.

The 'whole street is family'—both blood relatives and 'your close people' whom you would also call aunty and uncle. Aunty Dot lives right next door. Aunty Rosemary lives next door to Dot. Peter's paternal grandparents still live across the street; Grandma grows lilies in the front garden. His grandparents come over on Sundays for dinner and, while they know Peter has his own room out the back, to them it is just a practical measure in a small house. What they do not know, as they sit there at the table with their son and daughter-in-law and four grandchildren eating 'a roast and three veggies overcooked to the shithouse', is that this is the only night of the week that Peter is allowed inside the house, the only time he is given a meal.

Throughout the year, everyone carries their hard rubbish to the vacant patch of land at the end of the street. Here, as the seasons change, rises an increasingly sprawling pile: the chair missing a leg, nubs of brooms worn down with sweeping, wooden crates missing planks like teeth; all the broken things mixed together to form a jagged accumulation that is monstrous against the night sky, though its parts are as familiar as breathing. And then, on Guy Fawkes Day, it is lit and the children cheer.

Peter loves this time, when he feels included in something both ordinary and majestic. The adults stand around, chatting and drinking while they stare into the flames which burn themselves to death, leaving the ashes that will blow away over the coming days so that the next chair can break and be dragged down to start the pile anew.

Without regular nutritious food, Peter's teeth start snapping off at the gums. In a few years, he will break several teeth at once by biting into a banana sandwich. All his teeth need to be removed by the time he is seventeen. None of his siblings have similar problems. The gully trap by the side of the house where he squats over the drain for a drink is also the only place he can wash. He is not bathed regularly nor taught how to clean himself. There is an outdoor toilet he can use but the bathtub is inside and he has no access to it. His pale skin becomes red and inflamed; he is uncomfortable and embarrassed in his bubbling body.

The hours spent alone grind by in stupendous boredom but of greater import is the unfulfilled human need to belong, to be loved: to feel sufficiently safe that energy can then be directed towards learning and growing and loving others. The door to Peter's family shuts on him every day at 4:30 p.m. and therefore that door, along with so many others, never truly opens.

Though Peter does not like school, where he is regularly caned by the nuns and made to kneel in the corner for acting out, he enjoys the walk there each morning. Left on Blandford, then down an unmade road through the tip in order to bypass the house with the Alsatian, emerging onto Essex, past the house of the woman known only as the Witch and then straight down until Eleanor Street. He loves looking at the way the ladies do their gardens. He feels safe on the way to school, not because there are no dangers but because he knows clearly where they are and how to avoid them.

Forbidden to bring friends home, he starts visiting the nuns at St Joseph's Convent after school. He spends all his spare time there doing work for the sisters, who are cold but predictable, and whose small house across from the school is a sanctuary. When he knocks at their door, they put him to work with odd jobs or errands and in this way he is made to feel useful and accepted. Being of service is its own reward; it distracts him, fills him with purpose and pride. Also they feed him afterwards: a cup of tea, a slice of toast.

At thirteen he gets a job after school sweeping up hair at the barber shop. Someone comes in asking for French letters and: 'Do we sell French lettuce?' Peter politely inquires of his boss. The men in the shop disintegrate into barking laughter and never stop giving him shit about it. He spends his pay on toys and new clothes for his little brothers. He buys Simon a chemistry set and carries it proudly back to Birchill Street, where Bill throws it out of the window in a drunken rage, smashing it to pieces.

Bill continues to regularly attack Peter, his hot breath smelling of booze and his caterpillar eyebrows meeting in dark concentration as he sets about beating his child with his fists or the copper laundry stick. When he is feeling particularly sadistic he will tie the boy to the clothesline for better purchase. And though everyone turns away, and his mother's silence slices through him—still, Peter climbs in through the kitchen window every time he hears his father doing the same to her. But his parents always reconcile and then they both, somehow, just hate him more.

Peter avoids playing with other boys, prefers the company of the girls in his class, so Bill tries to toughen him up by forcing him to join the army cadets. Peter dreads the weekly session at the Drill Hall. To avoid going, he feigns ingrown toenails so painful he can't walk. At school, forced to play football, he stands apart from the team, eyes lowered, hands jammed deep in his pockets. He tries to act casually invisible, hoping the ball never comes near him and hopping out of its way when it does. He endures the jeering and wrath of the other boys.

And then, one day, a change. The family is going on holiday; they will take the overnight ferry to Tasmania and drive around the countryside for a week. Peter is not invited. Bill tells him to paint the house while they're gone; Ailsa says if he does a good job they'll bring him back something special, something he really wants. His siblings chatter excitedly in the back seat until his mother slams the door shut on their voices and he watches the car drive away.

After he finishes painting each day, Peter carefully rubs the white flecks off his skin with turpentine before walking down the road to the quarry next to the YMCA, where he picks through rocks and trash under the darkening sky. He selects the cleanest bricks and hauls as many as he can back home. Kneeling at the edge of the lawn, he arranges them with great care into a neat, scalloped border. The process of imposing beauty on the backyard is calming and his heart skips a little when he imagines the surprise, the appreciation on his parents' faces. He would do all this for them, happily, in the hope that it might be his key inside, but his mind does also wander to the gift his mother promised.

The house is freshly painted and the garden is perfect when the car pulls up a few days later and Peter runs out to greet them. Ailsa herds the younger children inside, Bill silently unloads the luggage and carries it in. And then Peter is just standing there, alone again in a tidy yard. His sister leans out of the screen door and shoves the small package at him: a pair of plastic cufflinks in the shape of Tasmania.

Sandra's voice gets tight with the memory of that day. 'They said to me that they would bring back something I really, really wanted, and all I really, really wanted was a transistor radio, so I could have some company.' She gets up from her large green sofa and walks into her kitchen where she reaches over the sink and grabs something off the window ledge: a small radio. 'I didn't get it off them, but I have this one now as a constant reminder.'

As she turns the dial back and forth between her long red nails, tinny voices swell and fade in the space around us and I remember reading that all static is radiation, still, from the Big Bang; a living memory, an echo.

Ailsa is at her cake-decorating class and it is raining on the night Peter is finally exiled from his family. Bill is barking at him, forcing him to get his hair shaved into a crew cut. This time Peter refuses and Bill throws him out. Seventeen years old. Peter will only see his father three or four more times before Bill dies of heart problems at the age of fifty-five. On one of these occasions Bill tries to run him over in the street with his car. And then there will be Peter's eighteenth birthday party, when Bill turns up drunk and wielding a knife to the tiny flat where Peter is living. Peter will have no idea what sparked his father's rage that particular night but will be forever grateful to his neighbour, a Hungarian single mother, who intervenes and drives the man away.

As an adult, Sandra knows nothing about her biological parents. Only that she was meant to die in her first weeks, sick perhaps, and that she was adopted through the Catholic Church, which sent her home with a florid and violent alcoholic. She has no desire to find out more information about her biological family. 'Especially now, 'cause like, how'd you be? Rocking up at the door and going: "Hi, I'm your son!" They'd have a fucking heart attack!' She laughs. 'You've gotta take the good with the bad, you know what I mean?'

Her younger brother, Simon, is the only family member she has maintained contact with throughout her life. But Simon, who was not spared Bill's violence by virtue of being his biological son—or less effeminate—would never talk about their childhood, cutting Sandra off when she tried. She did, however, go back to their old street when she was in her forties, to visit Aunty Dot, who still lived next door.

Sandra called her up and told her 'what the situation was' (that she was now living as a woman) and that she would love to pay her a visit. Aunty Dot invited her over. Sandra was emotional on the drive back to her old neighbourhood. She was trying not to cry because she had applied her make-up with extra special care that day and didn't want to look 'like a shitbox' by the time she arrived. Her desire to look respectable and successful and feminine magnified the silent struggle for dignity and autonomy faced by all adult children trying to go back home on their own terms. She knocked on the door and Aunty Dot welcomed her in.

'I always thought there was something different about you, Sandra, because you loved frilly curtains and you loved girlie things,' Aunty Dot said to the graceful woman sitting on her couch. They had a cup of tea and spoke lightly of easy things and for long moments Sandra let herself feel the impossible warmth of if *this* were her childhood home and Dot were *her* mother; wrapped herself in the feeling like a fur coat in a store and then cast it off before she got too comfortable.

Finally, Sandra said, 'I've got to ask you Aunty Dot, no one will validate that anything ever happened to me. I don't know whether I dreamed all this or I was imagining it 'cause no one would *talk* about it. Can you tell me, was it all in my mind or did things really happen, was I bashed like that…'

And Aunty Dot was probably speared by the question. She probably felt a maternal urge to protect Sandra by not pressing on the wound, felt her tongue falter under the golden rule against mixing in but also a justified anger at Bill's criminal violence. So she said to this lovely blonde lady, in whom she clearly saw the sweet face of the gentle boy she had known, 'Well, let me put it to you this way, my dear. It wasn't a very good life for you.'

Sandra walked back to her car in her good shoes, past her old house with the bungalow out the back and drove away. Not long after that, Aunty Dot died.

•

Sandra touches on a number of theories about her parents.

'I always thought that my mother was my mother, but my father wasn't my real father and that's why he hated me,' she says. But that theory went out the window when they told her she was adopted. So it led to a different idea.

'I can always remember being in the kitchen with my mother before I was seven and hanging on to her leg because I think all I ever wanted was to be loved by somebody and, by being an adopted child, there wasn't that love there,' she says, her voice quivering very slightly.

An aunt once told her that Bill was her biological father, and that her real mother was in fact Ailsa's sister Sheila, with whom Bill had been having an affair and who died in childbirth. She doesn't know what to believe.

'My father hated my guts. He made no bones about it. Look, they knew I was different but they just thought I was a gay person, I think. But *I* didn't know what I was myself! I just always knew… well…I don't really know.' She pauses to think. 'I just sort of felt different. I didn't feel normal.'

The key question in Sandra's cosmology is not to do with sexuality or gender or adoption or Catholicism or alcoholism. It is how a parent can shepherd any newborn through infancy and childhood into adolescence, and cease entirely to care about that child's way in the world.

You want to give everyone the benefit of the doubt. Imagine Bill and his self-loathing or trauma or mental illness; imagine his helplessness and rage every time he decides to raise another glass and throw another punch. Did he blame himself for the death of his brother all those years before? And find an echo in the death of his newborn son? Did he meet something in the army that ate away at him like mould, turning him dark and soft on the inside until he could not hold himself upright without a drink?

It is impossible for a parent to be an alcoholic without spreading their emotional isolation, like a disease, throughout the home. Imagine Ailsa, the girl who loves to bake, the woman whose cakes are light and high and whose dark religion tells her to fear her effeminate son. Imagine how every day she drags herself out of bed to wrestle with her dead baby and her newborn and her three other children and her husband who cannot stop drinking and beating her. Imagine her nausea rising from sheer exhaustion, the helplessness and fear and pain that bubble up to scald her and everyone she touches. Perhaps Ailsa and Bill are sufficiently hateful to deny us even the basic satisfaction of conceiving of them as villains.

And yet. Imagine the feeling of holding a six-week-old baby boy, using your arms for his bed and your hand for his blanket and your name for his name. Think of the way his heartbeat slows when you hold him close. Imagine that baby as a boy frozen in his bed, straining to read the sound of a motor in the driveway over the noise of his own racing heart. Think of the pain his father deliberately inflicts on him, think of his paralysis and how, in some universes, the Big Bang happens in reverse: an instant retraction of time and space to a point of singularity.

No longer allowed home, Peter went to stay with the McMahons, the family of his friend Mary who lived about five kilometres away. They took him in and included him as part of their family for six months until they left for a long holiday overseas. Before they went, they arranged for him to move in with their eldest son and the father connected him with his first real job.

Fitting and turning wasn't really his bag because he hated the greasy hands, but the security the job offered was a welcome relief. For the first time, Peter felt normal, even successful, turning up to work each day at Brunton's Bright Steel, freshly showered, always on time, a Vegemite sandwich shyly tucked in the small bag he carried with him on the train. He felt tall inside walking into the factory complex in the growing shadow of the Westgate Bridge, then being built. He was an efficient worker, too, and a quick learner and excellent with people, so he was quickly promoted to the laboratory where they started training him in metallurgy.

Peter was in the lab at 11:50 a.m. on 15 October 1970, when the steel girders on the bridge turned blue under pressure and collapsed with a roar that could be heard over twenty kilometres away, killing thirty-five construction workers. The light bulbs in the lab and on the factory floor burst out of their sockets, plunging the rooms into a darkness in which one worker became caught in a machine, screaming while the ground trembled. Over the factory's back fence, Peter watched emergency workers arrange their cars into a square where they threw body parts away from the crowds that had gathered nearby. It was his 'first seeing of death'. By the time construction on the bridge resumed in 1972, Peter had moved on to another job.

'I was married by then...I'd met a girl on the way to...'cause I lived at, um, I must've lived at Williamstown then, over the Mars Music Store...because on the Williamstown train, going to Spotswood, that's where I met this girl...'

Sometimes, listening to Sandra try to remember the events of her life is like watching someone reel in rubbish on a fishing line: a weird mix of surprise, perplexity and unexpected recognition. No matter how many times we go over the first three decades of her life, the timeline of places and dates is never clear. Many of her memories have a quality beyond being merely faded; they are so rusted that they have crumbled back into the soil of her origins. Others have been fossilised, frozen in time, and don't have a personal pull until they defrost slightly in the sunlit air between us as we speak. And when that happens there is a tremor in her voice as she integrates them back into herself, not seamlessly but fully.

Sometimes, though, the smallest particulars—names and feelings and exquisite details—are so quickly recalled and finely drawn that it is like she has been holding them, all this time, in the palm of her hand. She can sketch, at any moment, the floor plan of her childhood home and explain to you how the master bedroom was near the front door, which had a glass panel running down the side. How you stepped down into the lounge room and where her mother's display cabinets were built into the wall and how they were filled with the good crystal. Where Barbara's bedroom was and the boys' bedroom was. How you stepped outside into the backyard onto 'a patio-type affair' that eventually became the bungalow to which she was exiled. But the age at which that exile occurred changes drastically. Sometimes it is seven, then eleven, other times it is thirteen. No matter how many times we go over this and over this, it is never clear.

What I think is that there were two seismic shifts in the way Sandra was treated as a child. The first came when her younger brothers were born. From the age of seven, she was subject to significant neglect and abuse. However, she probably continued to live inside the house, sharing a room with her brothers, until she was around thirteen. I say this because the yard that she landscaped while her family was away on their Tasmanian holiday included a fishpond. The bungalow that Bill built for her to move into was placed over that fishpond. So she must have been sent to sleep out there when she was thirteen.

This might have been a practical measure to save space in a small house or maybe, like the army cadets and the crew cuts, it was the way the Collins boys were toughened up to become men, but it was also a continuation of the particular neglect and violence that she had been subjected to for most of her childhood.

So I tell the story here as Sandra remembers it most often—as an exile from the table and the home and the family at seven years

34

old—because all memory is a particular metaphysics in which our experiences of reality constitute our only reality. Regarding the question of historical truth, the answer is both that there must be one and that there is none. When it comes to Sandra's history, this problem is compounded: her reality is as conflicted as it is real.

# Girl, interrupted

I pull up in front of a complex of endless Soviet-style apartments and walk over to the immaculate travelling hardware store that is the STC van, where I am handed a white disposable jumpsuit. The package specifies the garment's 'application' as follows: Asbestos Removal, Abattoirs, Painting, Forensics, Insulation, Laboratories, Factories, Food Processing, Waste Control, Medical, Law Enforcement, Pesticide Spraying. I am also given a disposable respirator mask and a pair of blue rubber gloves. Four of Sandra's cleaners are there: Tania, Cheryl, Lizzie and Dylan, everyone reduced to a small cheery face sticking out of a white disposable hood. Dylan, tall and still baby-faced, hands me two flat white things that look like chefs hats but turn out to be shoe covers. I glance at the others to figure out how to put them on.

With our hoods up and our blue gloves on we stand there looking like something between Smurfs and astronauts. Except for Sandra. Sandra is wearing a slim-line purple parka—ironed—with jeans and spotless white canvas sneakers. Sandra looks like she should be enjoying a Pimm's after a walk along the beach. Instead she leads us through the security gates, into an elevator and up one floor to a flat where a young woman died of a heroin overdose and lay undiscovered for two and a half weeks in the summer heat. Sandra will collect the deceased's personal items for the family, appraise what needs to be done to rent the apartment again and supervise the cleaning.

A man on the ground floor looks up and asks what we are doing.

'Just some maintenance, darl,' Sandra reassures him, which, in its way, is the truth.

One of the cleaners unlocks the door. Sandra has a quick look inside. 'Ugh. Stinks,' she says. 'Right. Masks on, breathe through your mouth!' She warns everyone to watch out for syringes while helping Tania don her mask. Tightening it, Sandra says to her wryly, 'You may never breathe again, but don't worry about it.'

Cheryl takes out a small jar of Tiger Balm and rubs it into each nostril before slipping on her mask.

Sandra remains unmasked. 'Been doing it for so long, I don't bother...Grin and bear it!' she sings.

It is not her most visible trait—you would miss it altogether if you did not know her well, if she had not let you in sufficiently to welcome your calls with a sweetly rasping, 'Good morning my little dove'—but that is what makes it her strongest: a bodily fortitude so incredible that it cannot be ascribed to mere biology. Aside from carrying around with her a lime-coloured leather handbag of fine quality in which she keeps an electric-blue tin of mints, six lipsticks, three jail-sized key rings, tissues, a camera, a little black diary for notes, a pen to write them with, a Ventolin inhaler, a mascara, a bottle of water, her iPhone and a cord with which to recharge it, Sandra also carries the burden of lung disease so severe that she cannot take more than a few steps, however slowly, without fighting for breath. And though you will hear this struggle, and though the sound of it is excruciating (even if it doesn't descend into one of the frequent coughing fits so powerful it seems like it will turn her inside out), she will get on top of it as quickly as possible, accept no concern or special treatment, and resume whatever activity or conversation was interrupted with such competent dexterity that, if you remember it at all, the interruption will seem as significant as one sneeze in a cold.

It is, of course, not a cold. It is chronic obstructive pulmonary disease with lung fibrosis and pulmonary hypertension. It can be managed with daily oxygen use, rest and the avoidance of environmental threats, but it is incurable.

Sandra uses her oxygen tank sparingly because she believes that the more she uses it, the more she will need it and it is one of the Golden Rules of Pankhurst 'not to be reliant on any person or any thing'. So while she keeps the tank at the ready, it is more in the spirit of a safety net ('If I end up getting pneumonia, then I'm fucked.') rather than as a tool for daily living. As regards rest, she does not. She works at least six days per week and while she might make it home, some days, by four o'clock to watch *The Bold and the Beautiful*, it is not unusual for her to leave home at 6:30 a.m. and return at 7:30 p.m. She averages twelve hundred kilometres per week, driving to and between jobs across the state.

She will sometimes take perfunctory precautions against the environmental threats she encounters numerous times each day (sick clients, black mould spores, pathogens in accumulated biological material) by wearing a mask or gloves. But these are quickly cast off because they impede her ability to work efficiently, and because she does not want to alienate her already-distressed clients.

'I'm meeting someone there, quite often a family member, I don't want them to go into shock, like, "This person from outer space has come here." I grin and bear it and I go in,' she explained to me once.

In addition to severe pulmonary disease, Sandra also has cirrhosis of the liver. The causes of her conditions are various and not susceptible to confident isolation. The chemicals she used in the early years of her cleaning business may play a role; so too her decades of double-dosing female hormones. Then there are viruses and biology and a factor euphemistically known as 'lifestyle', which carries with it specious overtones of culpability. Her drinking, and her years of heavy drug use earlier in her life, conform with the fact that trans people have higher rates of self-medication.

I mentioned once to her how I read that, even on the normal dose of hormones, the medical recommendation is to stay as healthy as possible through diet, exercise and abstaining from cigarettes and alcohol. Her thoughts on this were expressed by a prolonged period of deep laughter and, as she finally dabbed at her eyes, the comment: 'Fuck me, that's a bit like a comedy routine.'

Sandra has not had a cigarette in ten years, but while she has abstained from alcohol during the periods in which her health has been particularly bad, she allows herself 'a [couple of] glass[es] of wine [and]/or Scotch' every evening—against medical advice, given the condition of her liver.

Every day she wakes up early to the drone of the television in order to drown out the demons that wake alongside her. And though it's only partly successful she gets up anyway and dresses nicely anyway and goes out to run a business anyway. She hustles for more work and repeatedly tears herself away from the Velcro of her mind to crack jokes and, after a long day of driving between jobs that range from the distasteful to the apocalyptic, she returns home to cook herself and Lana a fillet steak, administers that speedily nibbling dog a sliver of Prozac and pours herself her drinks after retiring to her couch to finally enjoy a few hours of peace.

Which is all to say that Sandra's diagnoses, while true, are not truer than her will. But she's long known that the body can be a liar. So when you ask her how she is doing, she will say, 'Oh, you know, mustn't grumble,' and then scoop you up and rush you through the latest updates on her plans for beauty treatments or expanding her business.

'Once I make up my mind to do something, I'm very powerful. Nothing can gild the lily. I'm very focused. It's like smoking. Since I was diagnosed with lung problems, I stopped like *that*.' Sandra snaps her fingers, and the gold heart dangling from her bracelet clinks against the chunky chain. 'There's no weaning or waning, it's *bingo*. I'm a firm believer that you're as powerful as your mind. Firm believer. Mmmm,' she growls in agreement with herself.

Thirteen-hour work days and six-day work weeks and forty-eight-hundred-kilometre months and deep laughter from the woman whose health was judged, by three different specialist panels, too risky to waste a lung transplant on. All agreed that she would not survive the surgery, in part because of the condition of her liver. She told them, 'I don't want to die grasping for air. It's better that I have the operation. I'm in a win–win: I either get the operation and I live, or if I die, I go out trying.' Still, she was denied.

Her outrage at this was expressed once when she told me that one of her hoarding clients, an elderly man whose oxygen bottles were sitting in a pile of his own faeces, had mentioned that he had been offered a lung transplant but wasn't sure he wanted it. She was utterly enraged recounting this to me: '*He* gets a chance and I don't?!' She could understand neither how he was a better candidate nor how one could be ambivalent about the proffered organ. 'You take opportunities when you get them, baby!'

When I asked Sandra's doctor what the average patient with her comorbid conditions would be doing each day, he replied that they would be at home, resting. I mentioned how much she takes on and her seemingly infinite energy, and he responded drolly but with clear fondness and admiration: 'She should just be tired *all* the time. I can't *imagine* what she would have been like without this.' He stopped to ponder the counter-factual scenario for a moment before shaking his head. 'It's just incredible.'

Sandra's lifestyle is not what runners would call a suicide pace.

From left: Barbara, Peter, Simon

Sandra's father, Bill, with an unidentified child,
possibly Peter

Peter and Linda's wedding day

Simon's christening: Peter, Bill, Ailsa, Linda

On the contrary, it is deeply sustaining. 'I like to keep busy,' I heard her explain to a client once. 'Having a terminal illness, I find that it keeps my mind busy, I don't think about it, and I stay positive.' She has no more chances for a lung transplant. 'None at all. Signed, sealed and delivered. How many times have they had me dead and buried? They should name me Lady Lazarus,' she laughed. I had seen for myself the months of deep depression that followed the panel's final decision. The months when she found that the less she did, the less she wanted to do, until she was, yes, willing herself to die.

'Breathe through your mouth! Concentrate on it!' Sandra commands as she turns the doorknob and leads the charge straight ahead into the dim apartment.

The first thing I notice is the flies. Their papery corpses are crisp underfoot. I wouldn't say that the place is carpeted with flies, but there is a pretty consistent cover of them on the tiles. It is a small apartment. The laundry cupboard is located in the tiny foyer and the dryer door is opened wide. A basket of clean clothes is on the floor beside it.

I walk past a bathroom and two small bedrooms and into a living room–kitchen area. The TV has been left on and is playing cartoons. There is a balcony at the far end of the apartment; a breeze blows in through the open sliding door and over the sofa, which has been stripped of its cover but not the person-shaped rust-red stain spread across the seat nearest the window. The stain is shocking and frightening but not as frightening as the tableau of life suddenly interrupted.

Cheryl is in the main bedroom guessing about the face of the woman whose underwear drawer she is emptying. Tania is making an inventory of the kitchen. She opens drawers and cupboards, taking photos of everything inside. The top drawer has the full complement of cooking utensils owned by high-functioning adults. The cupboard has a big box of cereal, a jar of Gatorade powder. A grey plastic shopping bag of rubbish is suspended from the handle of the cupboard under the sink.

'Everything has to go,' Sandra says, striding through.

'The fridge comes with the apartment,' Lizzie reminds her.

'Ah.' Sandra is dismayed. I watch her mentally flick through the library of disinfectants in her van. 'What else comes with the apartment? We need to be clear or else we'll throw everything out.'

The lone magnet on the fridge says: *If your doctor is closed, we're open. After hours medical helpline…*

On one side of the kitchen sink is a pile of clean syringes. On the other side, an unopened box of organic cotton tampons, tossed there like they were purchased an hour ago and are waiting for the milk to go into the fridge before they are taken to the bathroom cupboard. Tania photographs a drawer full of grey plastic bags.

Everyone has gathered around a few framed photos of the deceased woman with friends or family.

'What a waste, hey,' someone says, peering into it rabbinically.

'Pretty girl,' another says. I wonder if that's what she looked like when she died, or at the time in her life she would forever try to return to.

The cleaners are quiet and efficient; quick and respectful. They remind me of nurses. Black mounds of dead flies are pooled in the light fixtures. I scan the bookshelf. There is *Narcotics Anonymous*. There is *The Secret of Attraction. Taking Care of Yourself and Your Family* and *When Everything Changes, Change Everything*. There are DVDs. There is *Bridesmaids*. An ad for Big Hugs Elmo, the toy that hugs back, comes on the TV. I go into the main bedroom.

A copy of *The Instant Tarot Reader* holds a piece of black fabric in place over the window near the bed. There are bottles of Ralph Lauren perfume and a pink salt lamp and an organic lip balm from Miranda Kerr's line.

'Anything that's personalised, anything that's got her handwriting, her name…' Cheryl reminds Lizzie as they squat to sort through the desk at the foot of the bed. They are winding up her phone charger and putting her handbag near the front door.

Sandra instructs Dylan to take the clean syringes and seal up the yellow plastic container of dirty syringes on the coffee table for the police 'as evidence of drug activity'. Although the police do not disclose investigative details to Sandra, she knows this death is not being treated as a homicide. Still, she suspects the woman was not alone when she died. 'You do your own Sherlock Holmes. You play detective all day long,' she told me once.

I cross the hall. The bathroom cupboards are open. There are the usual creams and appliances. Fake tan. The brand of exfoliator I use.

I go back into the living room and force myself to look around slowly. I see two scattered bed pillows covered with the same red-brown stain as the one on the couch. Drying blood. I see a viscous smear of human shit on the floor under the couch. I see a big bottle of Pepsi Max, still full, and a pack of cigarettes on the coffee table, also full. I do not see any living flies. The apartment is simultaneously so full and so empty; absence is a presence like dark matter and black holes.

Sandra places a birthday card with a sassy cat on it into a white rubbish bag full of personal items and then instructs Dylan to look carefully through all the books to see if there are any photos between the pages. The family want anything that's personalised. It's important.

The four small rooms are an encyclopaedia of striving and struggle. The basket of clean laundry. The elliptical machine painted thick with dust. The kitchen drawer of grocery bags at the ready for reuse. The Narcotics Anonymous handbook and the *Secrets of Attraction*. The clean syringes. The smell of death, unnoticed for two and a half weeks at the height of summer, which is seeping through my mask and into my mouth.

We step outside for a moment. There is blood on Lizzie's gloves; redder—fresher—than the blood on the fabric of the couch. Someone asks Sandra where it came from if the house was locked up.

'Maggots,' she replies dryly. 'Cycle of life. It's quite amazing.'

While Sandra teaches Dylan how to double-bag the personal items so they don't smell, how to wrap tape around the top in a way that is easy for the family to open, I stare across into the windows of the identical apartments surrounding us.

This is how it ends, sometimes, with strangers in gloves looking at your blood and your too-many bottles of shampoo and your now-ironic Make Positive Changes postcard of Krishna and the last TV channel you flipped to on the night you died and the way the sun hits the tree outside your bedroom window that you used to wake up looking at. This is how it ends if you are unlucky, but lucky enough to have someone like Sandra remember to go through your books for pieces of you to save before strangers move their furniture into the spots where yours used to stand.

# 4

Peter is introduced to Linda by a mutual friend one morning on the train to work. She flirts with him, this tall, gentle boy who is brilliantly blond in the morning light. She is short. She is a year or two older. She has beautiful eyes and long black hair and a cheeky smile and he likes the way he feels when she looks up at him. They chat shyly, swaying from side to side as the crowded carriage is pulled down the rails.

Later, when he is taunted by the men he dates about the little woman waiting at home, he will launch into a jeremiad about how it wasn't supposed to be that way. *We sorta become friends while we spoke on the train but, like, I weren't interested in anythink really, just in someone to share a house with, you know?* He will explain that the deal was: she had her room and he had his room. That things went fine there for a little while, until the Sunday morning she violated their agreement by entering his private sanctuary to serve him breakfast in bed, and then fucking *seduced* him.

And that is how he will always remember it: slightly wounded and wondrous, mainly for theatrical effect but also truly marvelling about how naive he was to think that just because he could complete the physical act of sex with her, he was meant to marry her. Still. He felt proud—for a time only, but even so, yes, very proud—to be doing what normal people did. He had something they had. He was, finally, inside.

Though he is nineteen, Peter needs his parents' consent before he can marry Linda in the little bluestone Catholic church in the city. So he returns to Birchill Street, the papers folded crisply in his pocket like a bureaucratic exemption from his father's violence and his mother's contempt.

He stands in the living room and explains to them how he proposed to Linda and how she said yes and how he's already asked her father for permission (leaving out the part about how he did so despite being frightened of her family—the father, the brothers; their hard drinking, their roughness).

Bill does not look up from his paper. Ailsa leans against the kitchen doorway listening, tongue cocked. 'Look, we know what you are,' she shoots, squinting at him over her long nose through ice-light eyes so close together they always seem crossed. 'We know this won't work.' She agrees to sign the papers anyway.

And then there is nothing more for him here, in this house where he learned to walk. So he mumbles his thanks and leaves feeling heavier with each step as the full weight of his mother's words lands on him and he realises there is nothing he can do to make them love him.

He won't, for many years, realise the glorious corollary of this: that there is nothing he can possibly have done to make them *not* love him. And although he will come to know this over the next forty years, to hold the dry thought in his mind, he will never come to feel it in that part of him below the neck, where true security resides. This will leave him prone to the dark like a light bulb loosely screwed into its socket and flickering.

•

46

Why, at nineteen, would Peter have required parental permission to marry? Perhaps it was an administrative quirk at that particular church? Perhaps the parental consent Sandra remembers obtaining was in fact for something else entirely, the lease on her first flat, maybe? Or perhaps it wasn't a permission form at all but rather, simply, a wedding invitation? Sandra does not remember. Like the year of her marriage or whether she had a wedding reception or the births of her children or the details of her divorce or the year of her sex reassignment surgery, she simply, genuinely, does not remember.

'It's a complete blackout.'

'I don't know, isn't that weird?'

'I'm not that good with dates and remembering.'

'I've lost a couple of years. It doesn't add up to me. It just doesn't add up.'

'I don't really know, to be honest with you. I've just cut it all out.'

The things Sandra doesn't remember could fill this book, could fill many books, could fill a library. Sometimes I imagine those books. They are unlike the books I grew up around: soft, yellowed bricks smelling of home. Instead they have immaculate spines and uncut pages. I hear the crisp crack they make on first opening. Some of the books are part of a series (*Peter Collins: Early Years, Lives of Birchill Street, Peter Collins: Lost Years, 1973–89*). Others are monographs (*Adoption and the Catholic Church in Victoria*). There is memoir (*Early Influences, Rooms I Lived In*), cooking (*Cake Icing & Decorating for All Occasions* by Beryl Guertner), history (*A Social History of the Western Suburbs*). This library of things Sandra doesn't remember includes works in other media: a watercolour of Birchill Street at dusk, road maps, photographs, a shopping list scribbled on the back of a phone bill (eggs, flour, bread, milk, gin).

The library they fill, dark and silent as a crypt, exists as much as it does not: it has a shape. In this way, the things Sandra has forgotten are as telling as the things she remembers and this helps me make

47

sense of a life that has left such light traces on the historical record. The dates and facts that can be externally verified are the stars I steer by. Much has been lost, but I have studied you for years now, Sandra P. You are my Talmud, my Rosetta Stone, my Higgs boson. Where my research runs dry, I can offer only educated deductions and informed imaginings, but what is the alternative?

Whatever its name, I refuse it. Sandra, this is your story. You exist in the Order of Things and the Family of People. You belong, you belong, you belong.

Bill drops Ailsa off at St Augustine's and then he drives away. Anticipating that his mother might loudly proclaim her objection to his marriage, Peter has arranged with his friends Ian and Freda to sit near her during the ceremony and escort her out should this happen. And although Ailsa keeps quiet, her objection is still within the range of human hearing. Seeing her sitting there, silently smouldering, Peter knows that while his mother hates him for being different, and would abhor him more had he confirmed her clear conviction regarding his homosexuality, equally she doesn't want this for him—the best chance at repressed normality offered by Melbourne in 1972.

He will never be sure why she comes that day. Perhaps it is for appearances, so that people won't talk more than she thinks they already are. Perhaps it is staking her claim to some measure of the pride she is entitled to in raising a child to adulthood. Perhaps it is punitive or retributive or an act of witness to the injustice she sees in the ceremony, sitting there in silent incantation as if to say, 'It's bad enough that you are an abomination, but now you will drag this poor girl down with you.' The three possibilities are not mutually inconsistent.

After the wedding, Peter and Linda take a tram with their friends back to their small house on Farm Street, posing for photos along the way in the early summer sun. Peter has prepared all the food for the party, buying scallops from the fisherman next door—who tipsily tells the couple that he is enjoying their party more than his own daughter's wedding the week before because everyone is so happy and relaxed, sitting around tables in the small marquee out the back.

On Monday, Peter is back at work selling tickets at the train station during the day and cleaning a bank at night, where Linda comes to help out and keep him company. Soon he gets a better-paying job at a tyre company where the boss is a bully but, for the first time, Peter is finally able to start saving some money.

They look at a two-bedroom terrace on Benjamin Street in the suburb of Sunshine. As Linda makes small talk with the owner, Peter floats through the rooms, his mind reeling with ideas. Though the space is small and dim, he sees in it the home it will become: where walls and windows can be added and removed, how the furniture they can't afford yet will be arranged, the colour he will paint the walls, the shape of the garden he will landscape.

Peter will forget the name of the hospital where his first child was born and whether he was there for the birth, but he will carry inside him always, etched in miniature, the floor plan of this house which he bought, on vendor's terms, directly from the owner.

Turning up the music and propping the front door open, Peter and Linda build a front fence to the sound of Joe Cocker's 'Mad Dogs & Englishmen', taking turns to go inside and flip the records. They do the housework together and the gardening together and their friends come over in the evenings to visit. Linda's father comes over too, and helps Peter knock out the small front window and replace it with a larger one, and the freed light comes gushing in and over the bed where the couple wake excited about the new day, and curl up at night, whispering and laughing.

Peter starts renovating the rooms by himself, one at a time, using the skills he is gradually teaching himself by watching a neighbour renovate the house a few doors down. This is how he learns to build the exposed brick arches he is so proud of. He gets ambitious and installs an electric doorbell. Every time someone rings it, though, the lights flicker. 'I don't quite understand electricity,' he admits to Linda the first time this happens, and they dissolve into giggles.

She adores him, her tall blond husband who is so handsome and funny and gentle. She loves watching him fold eggs into batter and coax weeds out of the ground and twirl spiderwebs down from the mouldings, her Pete who teaches her so much and makes her feel so safe, her husband who is so unlike the under-fathered boys and drunken men she grew up twisting around like a void. She loves how he sees things so differently and what it will look like, this life they are building together on Benjamin Street in Sunshine.

She doesn't know that her whole family think he is gay and she wouldn't have believed it if anyone had told her. There's certainly nothing wrong in the bedroom, except for his frequent migraines. And the fearsome nightmares that make him thrash around, violently kicking her in his sleep. When he jolts awake, sweating, he tells her he is stressed by work: *the boss, that bastard, it's nothing, love, I'm fine, go back to sleep.*

But the dreams don't let up. So one Saturday afternoon when Peter is out with friends, Linda marches down to Olympic Tyres in Footscray, her thin lips set in a line. The door bangs shut behind her as she walks up to the dirty front desk and demands his pay, directly from the boss, informing him that her husband will not be coming back.

'Oh yes he will,' the man laughs, looking down at her.

'Wanna make a bet?' she replies, eyes narrowing. 'I'm pregnant and I'm getting kicked in the stomach of a night because of you!' She walks out proudly with the money she came for and goes home on the bus, looking forward to surprising Pete with the news that everything will be OK now. She can still work for another few months until the baby comes and he'll find another job soon, there's so many things he's good at. The house is still empty when she gets home so she waits up for him and dozes off, around midnight, on the couch.

When we talk about newlyweds in 1972, we talk about children—not just the babies conceived as soon as possible after, and frequently before, the weddings but about the couples themselves, who were often still teenagers. This was true of Peter and Linda, both of whom were just doing their best to follow the script.

Their son Simon, named for Peter's beloved younger brother, is born when Peter is twenty. And though he has been secretly seeing a man named Michael throughout Linda's pregnancy, he is truly delighted when the child is born. He is 'so fucking happy' in fact that he breaks things off with his boyfriend. Lighting a joint, Peter writes him a note saying, 'You need someone who doesn't use somebody up just because they are lonely. Please understand, I have a family now. I must go straight and just think of being a good father and husband. I want my marriage to last.' His second son, Nathan, is born nine months later.

'Irish twins,' he chuckles to the husbands of Linda's girlfriends when they stop by to visit the new baby. 'Every time I touch her something happens! We're like fuckin' rabbits.' The words feel strange in his mouth, like he's wearing, somehow, someone else's dentures. The words he can't say would feel much more natural: how much it has unsettled him; how their crying evokes within him the whiplash of his own father's rage; how he feels even less at home here than in the house in which he grew up; how he is scared; how he is not coping.

He isn't the one who hasn't slept through the night in two years because of pregnancy and nursing; it's not his hands that are cracked and bleeding from soaking dirty nappies in bleach and, unlike Linda, he goes to work, where he can finish a cup of hot tea. But still: Peter is, truly, not coping. He is constantly stoned. He cannot take a full breath. His eyes feel like dirty windows, he is so anxious that it is difficult to look outward. But, like his courtship and his marriage and his house and his kids and his shitty jobs, this unhappiness and increasing alienation from his wife appear to follow the script of normal life: the centre holds.

When Linda takes the children out, though, a peace suffuses their small house that has less to do with the absence of noise than with the space the silence clears for smaller sounds: the voice, for instance, that he practises softly in the shower behind the veil of streaming water. Not only pitch, but inflection, words, gestures. Or the refrain thrumming along his veins that signifies his only certainty and which says: you don't belong here.

Driving into the city, his mind wanders as the car is sucked down the dark roads and he forgets, for long stretches, that he is the one steering and accelerating. He speeds up despite his mounting conviction that he is about to be incinerated by something like lightning.

How Peter met Michael and how he found out about his first gay bar are two lost secrets of history. There is no community press, no community radio, no visible community at all. For the longest time he had no gay friends or acquaintances, it was just him and his good wife. Perhaps there was a stranger who approached after a meaningful look, maybe a friend of a friend. Rumours, jokes, a rough gem of information mined from the shit the guys at work give each other on their breaks.

Regardless of how he got the information, he is now in possession of an address and he is driving there. The Dover Hotel. The Dover Hotel. Folded inside him these last weeks, he now takes the name of his destination out and holds it open in his mind where it bestows upon his solitary and hesitant trip the legitimacy of purpose. No lightning smites him as he walks through the door of the pub and up a flight of stairs. There is just the smell of stale smoke and beer and, as if from far away, a barman asking whether it's his first time here.

'Yes,' Peter replies.

'Well, you're welcome to stay, mate, but things don't get going here till ten, ten-thirty,' the man says, turning to the sink behind him. It is 6 p.m. Peter thanks him and goes back down the stairs and out to the street to find a coffee lounge, where he sits nursing a coffee and pretending to read old newspapers until closing. Then he walks around the neighbourhood in large circles until it is late enough to return to the pub. But even though he's had a practice run now, taken these steps once before and knows where he's going, he still doesn't know where they lead or what to do once he gets there and sees, for the first time, two men together. The uncertainty plays across his face like the movie of his life for those who watch him as he hesitates at the top of the stairs. His heart gallops in his ears and voices churn around him. The carpet is soft under his feet, and the men move over it, too slowly it seems, walking from table to bar or standing in small groups or pairs. He wonders if he is dreaming and then warm voices say something kind to him and relief floods through him and he can finally take a full breath.

He walks into his new job as tall and as bright as the white letters across the roof of the five-storey brick factory that spell out DARLING. Peter takes great pride in his duties as a laboratory technician at the John Darling Flour Mill, which consist largely of examining the various properties of the flour as it is made into bread in the test kitchen. He checks how it rises, analyses the moisture levels and adjusts the colour so that it can be sold to clients like McDonald's and turned into idealised hamburger buns. He arrives on time each morning no matter how little he slept the night before.

It is early 1975. He's a regular at the Dover now and the more people he meets, the more he learns about other places to go. These nights out are not about sex but about socialising and relaxing and exploring a world he never knew existed and, there, himself. Now when he walks past the bins of soaking nappies and in through the door each evening his guts don't knot in dread because he isn't really there. When he steps around the food flung on the floor or smells the milk turning in bottles in the sink, or when cries momentarily shatter his sleep like a glass flung against a wall, he doesn't really notice because in his mind he is dancing at Annabel's with Joe.

Joe, part Persian, part Italian, he finds quite gorgeous. But Joe takes longer getting ready in the bathroom than he does, which is saying something now that Peter wears a little make-up. It's not really his cup of tea, this thing he has with Joe. But it feels more right than when Linda inquiringly rubs his back at night and, well, you do some things for companionship. Peter still wears his wedding ring but the radiant pride is gone from it now; that tiny manacle.

The pride is gone, too, from the house and the job and the kids, from the exposed brick arch and the funny old doorbell. It's harder again to take a full breath these days. It's harder to think and yet it seems like that's all he does, chase his thoughts around in circles, trapped inside his head. He gives up on the bathroom renovation he so enthusiastically started; the gouged socket where the bathtub used to be recriminating him every time he goes in there.

Peter is not interested in tits, so he's barely thought about it. But to the extent that he has, he just assumed that the showgirls' sizeable bosoms are part of their costumes: made of plastic and somehow connected up and into the thick, bedazzled chokers they wear around their necks when they dance up on stage. But then it dawns on him that some of the queens are actually living their lives as females, in real bodies that they weren't born with. Soon after this he overhears someone at a bar one night talking about taking female hormones and going through The Change.

It feels like a light switching on.

Finding a doctor is not easy. But he finally ends up at a small office in Carlton not far from the Dover Hotel. In response to Peter's request for hormones, the doctor explains that the thing he is asking about is a small part of a long process. He also explains that the hormones will be detrimental to Peter's health; they will shorten his life expectancy.

'Look, well, I could walk out of here after this and get hit by a truck and still not have done what I wanted to do,' Peter says.

'If you still feel the same way in a week's time, come back,' the doctor says.

Peter is back a week later, even more settled in his convictions; the doctor writes the prescription.

He gains so much weight that they tease him about it at work. They call him the Footballer, say he would make a good fullback, that he is built like a brick shithouse. He laughs along and says something about all the beer he's drinking, getting away from the missus down at the pub. Still. He grows his hair longer. Breasts bud beneath the collar of his shirt. At first, he is 'gigged silly by everyone' but then something changes. The odder he looks, the more protective they become of him. Even the rough guys who work out in the silo act kindly towards him. Maybe they admire his bravery, or feel sorry for him. Maybe they are simply making him feel as comfortable as he has always made them feel.

Each morning he takes out the stash he's hidden from Linda and dabs chalky powder from the plastic compact across his nose before applying a thin layer of creamy black mascara, his mouth held in a perfect O in the rear-view mirror. He thinks no one can tell, but they can tell. What he doesn't realise is that they no longer care. He is an excellent employee—efficient, independent, a gifted conciliator—and he not only gets along with everyone in the office and the lab, he has effortlessly endeared himself to his colleagues. He has impressed his managers, who have been paying to put him through a management course in the city. The boss tries to promote him to a role that would require increased client contact. Though his colleagues are quite accepting of him, Peter feels both acutely self-conscious and militantly committed to his make-up and his hormones. It is his strong conviction that he cannot continue to do what he needs to do and still bring the requisite dignity to the role he entered as a straight man. Despite the protests of his boss, and knowing that he is turning down a good career, Peter refuses the promotion.

He tries to get home after work to put in an appearance at dinner and occasionally he goes along to his in-laws' place for a family birthday, but for the most part now he acts as though he does not have a family. He goes out late at night without explanation. He is always high. He drops the names of places and people Linda has never heard of before. He vanishes on the weekends to go shopping with his club friends for cheap make-up and new clothes. He buys a blonde wig from a shop in the city and, though in retrospect he will describe it as a hideous plastic helmet, at the time he feels 'fucking gorgeous' wearing it into Annabel's and out on the dance floor. He is leonine, solar, ecstatic in those too-short hours before he has to hide it away in the backyard shed, to glow golden in the dark until next time.

Linda knows something is wrong. It tugs at the corners of her mouth as she tries, at the end of each long day with the babies, to conceal the sagging skin of her stomach under her one good blouse to look nice for her husband. One weekend her mother agrees to take the boys so the two of them can visit some friends, another married couple. Peter drunkenly proposes late Friday night that they swap partners. Linda reluctantly agrees because she thinks it will save their marriage. But after the weekend is over, after they've collected the boys and arrived back home, Peter announces that he doesn't love her anymore and that he is leaving her for the other woman.

She is shattered. Peter prepares to leave their home, a process that takes months, during which they still share a bed. She is viscous with sorrow over the death of her marriage, tortured by thoughts of this other woman and what she will tell the boys and the sight of the moving boxes in the bedroom. One night in bed, half-asleep, her foot absently grazes his. 'Don't touch me,' he snaps. 'I don't like women to touch me.'

Peter is upstairs at Annabel's, looking down at the dance floor. People are drunk and loose on pills. Sitting on Joe's lap, he feels good, anonymous, energised. They are talking closely, flirting and laughing. Holding hands on the way to the crowded bar, picking their way back across the room between sips of Scotch and Coke.

This is when he bumps into someone and absently mutters, ''Scuse', without turning his head. This is when Linda wedges herself in front of him, when he looks down at her small face and his own syllabus of errors.

He cannot explain to her that although he is at a gay club, holding hands with a man and wearing a wig and make-up, he is not homo-sexual. He can tell her only what he knows: that he is different. He doesn't have a word for what he feels, he doesn't know that such a word exists.

He also doesn't know his wife: it is clear now that he has grossly underestimated her, not just how much she notices but how much she genuinely loves him. She begs him to stay. She begs him to get psychiatric help for 'it', which at that time included shock treatment. He doesn't make his mistake of gross underestimation again. He really has to leave now. He begs Linda to let him take the boys. 'You can have more kids,' he pleads. Linda, incredulous, refuses.

'I was in fantasy land,' Sandra remembers. 'It wouldn't have worked because of what I had to do to survive. I had no confidence in myself, let alone bringing up a child, and what would it have done to a child in those days, to be brought up by this queer?'

Driving away from their house in his packed car, Peter is shaking under the staggering weight of everything he is leaving: his marriage, his children, his home, the majority of his possessions, and a letter for the lawyers which says: *To whom it may concern, I—Peter Collins— admit to being homosexual and wish you to grant my wife a divorce on the grounds of sexual incompatibility.*

He leaves Linda with two toddlers, a mortgage, no savings, no income, no car, no working bathroom and no way of contacting him. He leaves his need to please his parents; he leaves despite the fact that they will say they knew this would happen, despite the fact that it will provide conclusive proof of their longstanding conviction that he is unworthy of love. He leaves despite having no job and no home to go to. He leaves because, at nearly twenty-three, he is so old and so young. He leaves because of something that he still cannot name and because the only thing of which he is absolutely certain is that he isn't meant to be there, on Benjamin Street in Sunshine with his wife and children. He has never felt so alone in his life. He is shaking with the sorrow and terror of it, this driving away from and towards himself.

For years Linda will dream about Peter coming back to her. For his part, Peter will remember that Linda had long hair and dressed 'like a mod' in miniskirts and white platform shoes; he will say that she was 'quite a nice person, really'. But the other details of her personality, whether she had a good sense of humour, for instance, he will block out entirely. He will never really confront the exquisite hardship—financial, physical and emotional—that his leaving placed on Linda as sole parent of their children.

It is also true that he will be unable to celebrate Christmas for the next fifteen years; that the memory of Simon waving 'Bye bye Dada' at the front door will hurt his heart forever and that, despite knowing nothing at all about his sons for nearly forty years, when he turns sixty he will place a photo of those babies into a silver frame and carefully position it where he can see it each day upon waking.

Sandra remembers that she was barred not only from custody but also from access to her children because of her purported homosexuality: 'I were told I couldn't see them or they would catch what I had.' This is how she understands what she remembers of the divorce, but the *Family Law Act* did not automatically disqualify a homosexual parent from custody or access. Decisions were made on a case-by-case basis according to the welfare of the child, having regard to the parenting ability of each parent and to contemporary social standards.

The latter certainly did not bode well for the homosexual parent, but it did not inevitably bar him or her from custody or access. Linda remembers that, at the custody hearing, Peter was granted open access to the boys on one condition: 'He could come to the house any time he wanted to, but if he came in drag, he was not allowed to say who he was. It was too confusing.' Peter never visited the boys and he never showed up for the divorce hearing. When their divorce was finalised on 22 August 1977, Peter Collins, *also known as Stacey Phillips*, was listed on the papers at *address unknown*.

Sandra understood the impossible outcome of that custody hearing to mean that she was exempt from the legal and moral requirements of spousal maintenance and child support, forever. She told me once, in the context of settling her will so that her estate goes to fund scholarships at one of the wealthiest universities in the country, 'I just want it signed, sealed and delivered so that I know that my estate is going to be dealt with. Otherwise, it could go to my kids, it could go to my wife…'

When Linda remembers the end of her marriage, she is a little self-conscious but her tone is frank and never spiteful. Peter took the car 'but I got stuck paying for it', she tells me. 'In them days, the pension, I remember it distinctly, it was ninety-six dollars. My house payment was thirty-two fifty a week. That left me thirty-one dollars a fortnight and all I could manage to do with that was pay some bills. I was getting food vouchers every week. When [the welfare workers] saw the boys with what they had on their feet, they said, "Are those all the shoes they've got?" I said yes. With holes in them and everything.' Welfare would help at Christmas time, and so did Boys Town.

Peter still hadn't finished renovating the house. 'I was left without a bathroom. Nobody would help me do the bathroom. So, I had to bath the kids in the kitchen sink. I had to shower at the neighbours'. That was for three years I lived like that.

'My family wouldn't help until the house was signed over to me. I had to try to find him. Pete used to tell me about these people that he met, the nightclubs he went to and that he knew the spin-off group Play Girls from Les Girls. [One day, Play Girls were] on *New Faces* on Channel Nine. I phoned Channel Nine up and said, "Can I get a phone number for that act? I want to book them."'

Linda took the phone number to the police and told them she was trying to track down her husband, who wasn't paying child support. A detective matched the number to an address in the commission flats near the city. The woman who answered the door there told Linda where she could find Peter.

'I turned up. I had the boys with me and I had my sister with me. There was a girl there that looked like a guy, Pete was dressed as a woman and Simon was just staring at him, confused. I didn't tell Simon this person was his dad. I got him to sign the papers. I cried most of the way home.

'I was suicidal. I was at a psychiatrist and he put me on medication. I was going to overdose. I was going to kill myself and the boys. And I thought, "What if I die and they don't? Or what if they die and I survive?"

'I never said anything to anybody. I never saw any of our friends after we split. No one knew what to say to me. I wasn't close to my mother. But one morning at 8 a.m. she turned up at my doorstep. I said, "What are you doing here so early, Mum?" She said, "I just felt like you needed me." She saved me.

'I had to snap out of it. Over the years depression has come on and off. You survive for your kids.

'I was angry for a long time. I thought, if my boys end up like him, I'm going to find him and I'm going to kill him; that was how I felt in them days, but I got over that. I have never, ever criticised Pete to the boys. He was a good bloke. I did love him and for a long time I hoped he would come back. The only thing he did wrong was marry me, knowing the way he was. He said he did it because he wanted to be normal. It's honest. He wanted to be normal.'

There are two photos of Peter and Linda at Simon's christening. In the first, the couple stand stiffly in front of the brown wall of Our Lady of Perpetual Help with Bill and Ailsa between them, in a supremely awkward tableau. Little Simon, enfolded in white finery, is held by his grandmother Ailsa, who stares, unsmiling but not without something like pride, down the barrel of the camera. Bill, in a grey suit and tie, looks down at the baby, touching him stiffly as if in benediction or disbelief, the effect being less one of emotion than simply of a man unsure what to do with his hands. Next to Ailsa, Linda stands with her hands clasped in front of her, most likely already pregnant with Nathan. She looks radiant in her green dress, truly beautiful and proud. Peter, her opposite bookend, stands next to Bill at an angle to the camera; it should have made for a pleasing composition but the effect is jarring because none of the others have followed suit. Peter wears black pants, a knitted vest and a light purple shirt open at the collar. While the others are uniformly dark and plump and short, Peter is as golden and slim and tall as a sunflower. Looking at the camera with his eyebrows raised and his hands clasped behind him, he appears startled, as if he has interrupted someone else's family portrait. In the second photo, a priest in purple robes sprinkles water over Simon's head as Linda holds him over the font and Peter smiles—genuinely smiles—down on his son.

Sandra has kept these photos for forty-three years. She took them with her, along with her clothes, one towel, one set of sheets, one place setting, the punchbowl set received as a wedding gift and the car, when she left Benjamin Street. She carried them with her to the numerous houses she has inhabited in three states over the last four decades. She has lost along the way her parents, her siblings, one wife, one husband, her children, her stepchildren, numerous friends, two businesses, two houses, two cars and a big toe, but she has kept these photos close. The reason for their dearness, however, is less than clear.

'I don't know why I kept them, but I kept them...' she said, vague but not evasive, when I asked her about it. She has never displayed them or shown them to others. You can barely see her baby son's face. You can, however, see the faces of her parents and her ex-wife, none of whom she holds in particularly warm regard. So I wonder whether these photos are more in the nature of witness: I am the man, I suffered, I was there. I had a wife and baptised my son in our family's church. I tried.

Though her appearance and her names and her roles have changed drastically throughout her life, Sandra has walked through her days with the same heart and the same bones and this, I think, is what the photos are saying. Without a family to hold her memories—to reinforce her existence by remembering moments from the book of her life with joy or embarrassment or empathy or still-jagged resentment—she is the sole bearer of her entire history. If she doesn't attest to the early part of her life, the fact that it happened at all will vanish entirely. This is what it means to lose your mother, who carries within her irreplaceable memories of your personhood, and it is compounded exponentially by losing your entire family.

She gratefully accepted some of Ailsa's good crystal (offered by her brother Simon), after the mother who repeatedly rejected her passed away. 'I just loved crystal,' she said when I asked her why. For a moment I see the child who grew up admiring the rainbows trapped in that glassware. 'And there was probably something there as well, if you know what I mean...'

I do know what she means. It may be accurate to say that I feel it; that something inside me cracks crisply, as happens sometimes when boiling water is poured into glass. Just as Sandra keeps the good crystal, I keep a high school graduation ring, engraved 1973, six years before I was born. It is not in the spirit of fondness that a child who has been abandoned by her mother safeguards the physical traces she left behind. It is more in the way of self-confirmation: though I may be unlovable, to her, I am not so singularly grotesque as to have sprung fully formed from the ether. I am rooted just like others in the Order of Things and the Family of People.

The only time I have seen Sandra discomposed is when I ask whether she has ever attempted to find her sons using Facebook or Google. At this, she blushes so deeply that the whites of her eyes flare and her features wince slightly as though the muscles have cramped. For one heartbeat she says nothing. Just holds her head very still and looks at me through sea-blue irises under the high blonde bridges of her eyebrows. Great eyes, Sandra's. Huge, strangely healthy-looking. Luminous spheres moving in their sockets like the wet blue earth on its axis, taking in everything we never want to see here.

'It's not my right to go into their life,' she replies, too lightly. 'I'm quite happy with the status quo. I think, leave good enough alone. If they really wanted to search me out, they could.'

Could they? Her name has changed so many times.

'If they were looking for Sandra Vaughan, it would be very hard,' she concedes. 'They might even have grandchildren themselves. After all these years, it would be so complicated for them to tell their children. You think: Fuck, I don't know whether I want to be part of that mess.'

# Dorothy

As the heartwood of a tree sings to you of thousands of sunlit days and rainy hours—specific symphonies of soil and the seasons of weathering and revival that will grant you the structural strength to reach for your share of the light—the rotten core of Dorothy's house is a whispered scream that hurtles you backwards through decades of pitch darkness.

Dorothy's house is located around the corner from a cafe that makes its own raw almond milk and a boutique that sells a 280-dollar grey sweatshirt. Sandra and I and four of her cleaners arrived just before 9 a.m., and the first thing the cleaners did was take the front door off its hinges. This was because it would open only partially before it hit a solid, sloping mass comprising empty champagne bottles, newspapers, fast-food wrappers and small grocery bags of rubbish that reached a metre and a half up the walls and surged down the hallway like a great and frozen river.

The next thing the cleaners did was quickly don their face masks and thick rubber gloves, bend low at the waist and start scooping the rubbish into industrial-sized black plastic bags. This technique soon proved extremely inefficient. All the discrete items of rubbish had fused together over the years—partly as a result of drowning in and drying after the rain that poured unimpeded through holes in the roof; partly by being constantly compacted by Dorothy walking over it to fetch an item balanced on top (a pair of white sneakers, reading glasses, a magazine) or to settle on whatever softer part of it she used as a bed. So the cleaners used rakes to chip away at the mass, and a shovel was wielded like a pickaxe, and Joanne called out to Sandra at one point asking her to please pass the crowbar.

'See, people think "cleaning" and that you need a bucket of water and a cloth,' Sandra said as she went to fetch it. 'We need crowbars, spades, rakes, a sledgehammer…'

It was 2016 when I entered through the kitchen window, my fingers digging into both sides of the peeling white frame and my sneakers scrambling ridiculously for purchase against the crumbling bricks. It was 2016, and I could hear the drone of the talkback radio station Sandra had tuned in to on her portable radio. But when I lowered myself into the kitchen, my feet landing not on the floor but on a deep and shifting layer of cheap champagne bottles, it was 1977. Or so said the calendar on the wall and the His Master's Voice refrigerator and the brown newspapers folded neatly on the kitchen table amid huge piles of rubbish and rubble from the collapsing roof.

Outside, Sandra, arboreal in the morning light that fell across the overgrown garden, was picking her way over the broken beer bottles glinting in the grass. In a new pair of blindingly white canvas sneakers worn, as always, without socks, and a blue and white silk blouse fluttering in the breeze, Sandra should have been setting off from her Santorini hotel to buy souvenirs. Instead she leaned in through the kitchen window and took in that boneyard of empties with one hard look. 'The only thing that happened here after 1977 was the bottles,' she said.

This is the home of Dorothy Desmond, who slept here like a stillborn until yesterday, and of her mother before her. Dorothy, who has lived here for at least thirty-five years, probably longer, who is in her early seventies and who very recently came to the attention of the community organisation that contacted Sandra to clean her home. Dorothy, who is the subject of concern, definitely curiosity, also pity, maybe affection and possibly fear from neighbours who have known her for as long as she has lived in this house, but who have never once been inside. Dorothy, who, like her house and like Sandra here today working on her behalf, is at once too foreign and too familiar to be easily understood.

In the way that black is the presence of all colours, silence, for Sandra, is the presence of all noise. The things that silence says to her are so oppressive and terrifying that in order to fall asleep she requires, without exception, the aid of a sleeping pill and the noise of her television, which she sets each night to turn itself off, eventually, on a timer. To avoid waking up to a silent house, the first thing she does each morning before opening her eyes is reach for the wand of her remote and conjure the television back to life. This televisual drone and the murmurmurmur of talkback radio in her car, at a worksite, in her office (whether she is in it or not), the chiming of her wall of clocks on the quarter hour and the light conversation she can coax into existence with anyone, anywhere, constitute a precondition for life.

'I can't do quietness. I can't cope with quietness,' she has told me, admitting that her need for company is 'a bit of an Achilles heel'. But while she once surrounded herself with companions whom she supported in exchange for their company—synthetic friendships that poorly approximated the real thing—she now has a number of much healthier relationships.

Margaret and Sandra have been neighbours for four years. They are similar ages and are in frequent contact. Like Sandra, Margaret married and had children early; unlike Sandra she was left to raise an infant alone at the age of twenty-two when her husband died in an accident. A couple of years later, Margaret met John, who had come to Australia from Liverpool on a dare from the boys at the pub.

When I sit down with them, it is their forty-fourth wedding anniversary and they are still delighted by each other. Margaret and John have known great pain; they are fun and sweet and brave, they are wonderful company and they think the world of Sandra, whom they met when the units they all now live in were being built.

'She introduced herself and we just started talking,' Margaret says. 'She was just one of those people who you could click with straight away.

'She'd been quite sick, I believe, when she moved in. Well, as it happened, at the same time John had cancer. And he was going to the Alfred for chemotherapy and I found out that Sandra was in hospital. When he was having his chemo, I went up to the ward to visit Sandra, I hardly knew her then, and it sort of progressed from there.

'Going through the process of John having the cancer, she was absolutely amazing. She would ring me every day just to make sure I was OK and she was always trying to get me to come up and have a meal with her and make sure I was feeding myself properly 'cause I was running backwards and forwards to the hospital,' Margaret says. 'She's got *a lot* going on in her own life, but she finds the time for you. She's a very generous person with her time but also with her whole self. With everything.

'This may sound silly but when John was in hospital, I'd just got home exhausted, and she popped in. She said, "Ah, I've got something for you." In this little box she had a little green frog cake. And it seemed such a small thing but it was a big thing for me,' Margaret says, her voice shining still with the joy of it. 'And she would've probably had a really busy day doing all sorts of other things and trying to look after her own health, and then she stops on the way home and buys me this little frog cake.

'When you look over what she's been through, another person might say, "I can't deal with the human race anymore." But she's not like that,' Margaret says. 'Even with everything that she's gone through, she's come out the other side even bigger and stronger. She just seems to bounce back. I think you must just be born with it or something. It's in you just to be that strong.'

'And she's full of ideas all the time,' John adds. 'I honestly don't know where she gets the energy from.'

Both Margaret and John worry that Sandra is 'generous to a fault and people could take advantage', and people *did* take advantage of this quality, for decades. Now, though, it inspires care and admiration in the small, disparate, low-maintenance group of people she keeps around her.

Margaret describes how Sandra came out to her: 'We were just sitting there one afternoon, chatting away, and she says, "By the way, I'm not what I seem, you know." And I said, laughing, "What are you talking about?" That came out of the blue. And she goes, "Well, you know, I was a bloke once..." I went, "Oh, get out!" And then she told me a few things and we had a bit of a cry and a bit of a laugh. I asked how accepting people had been of her and she said that there'd been a bit of problems. Until she brought it up, it wasn't in your face, like "There's something different going on here." No, it wasn't like that at all. There's just this beautiful woman. I think she was incredibly brave to do what she did at that time. You're talking forty-odd years ago, and back then it would have been an incredibly hard thing to do. A lot of less stronger people wouldn't have got through it.

'Sometimes I feel like she's still struggling with it, even this far along. At times she does seem to be on guard. Like even going over to the shopping centre here in Frankston, she'll very rarely go there.

69

I do feel that she worries that people will notice. People have been really cruel, over the years, to her. I suppose she'd like to think that everyone would accept her as she is, she's a beautiful woman, but she worries that they'll pick it straight away. She told me that one person said to her, "Oh I told my friend and they said they'd picked it." Well, that hurt her. I just think that's horrible.'

Sandra has lived largely in stealth since the early 1980s. I didn't realise it at the time, but it was singular that halfway through our first interview she told me—a stranger still—that she had been assigned male at birth. I didn't know then why she chose to be that candid with me that early; maybe I was lucky enough to ask the right questions in the right way at the right time. But knowing her now, I suspect it had less to do with me personally and more to do with the fact that I crossed paths with her at the point in her life when she was, finally, bursting at the seams with her story, with the need to tell and be truly known.

Sandra is not close with any gay women or men and she has no trans friends: 'I don't associate with any sex changers at all.' This is because straight women are the people with whom she feels a genuine kinship. It is also because of something that an ex-boyfriend once said about the drag queens who used to form her social circle: 'If you really want to be a woman, you have to disassociate yourself from them.'

'That's why I don't have any gay, or any other sort, of friends. I don't choose to associate with it. I live a normal, everyday life, a normal everyday existence. I might look a bit strange to some people. I might look too tall, but everyone is different,' she once explained to me. Sandra's lack of friendships with other members of the LGBTQI community is not active; she would not turn away from someone on those grounds. But her frame of reference regarding that community is her drag days. Her aversion is not to gay people or trans people, but to the image of herself that she associates with that period of her life. She identifies her 'straight' friends with a healthier, happier, safer and more productive self. This forms part of the context when she tells me, 'I feel quite successful—I'm not financially successful—but I'm successful in my life. I'm not a prostitute or a drug addict. I have a healthy, normal lifestyle. I have fantastic neighbours who treat me like gold.'

There is also this. I once asked Sandra to write down memories and thoughts about her life whenever they struck her, so that we could discuss them later. On the back of her work calendar for 8 December 2014, among some notes about helping the nuns after school, she wrote, simply: *No old friends*. And also: *Can't connect to people on personal level*.

From what I have observed over time, this accurately describes her ability to form empathic, two-way, secure and lasting attachments. Her ability to make friends is matched only by her ability to lose them. One former friend, someone who had been particularly close to her, told me after their rupture that, although Sandra is fun and funny and 'would give you the shirt off her back', although this person—still—genuinely likes Sandra, 'rather than people leave her, Sandra pushes them away'. This is particularly true if you get too close, need her too much or, sometimes, if you cease to serve your purpose. And it is done, occasionally, in such a hurtful way that it obscures the true nature of the act, which is shield rather than sword, gaping need rather than grasping greed.

Besides the flamboyance of cheap champagne bottles, passage around Dorothy's kitchen is blocked by a haphazard mound of wine boxes that buries, entirely, one of two chairs at the kitchen table. But you can clearly see that the room is a time capsule: the newspaper reports that Evonne Goolagong is playing in the Open and that Jimmy Carter is gloomy about the American economy. A box of Arnott's

Uneeda biscuits is on the counter, cans of Guinness and bottles of Foster's bear their retro logos without irony. There is the bag from the McDonald's Southern Fried Chicken that was phased out in the mid-eighties. There is no water or electricity, the toilet is outside: a board with a hole in it. Sandra finds it, using a process of deduction, behind a thick veil of foliage.

Leigh is working in the kitchen, his heavy boots balancing on the shifting surface of bottles as he wobbles back and forth under spiderwebs, thick as dreadlocks, that dangle from the light above the kitchen table. We are surprised to find out, after he inquires, that we are the same age. He says I look younger; I think he looks older. For long stretches, there is just him and me, the crowded ghosts of Dorothy's life and their strange music, which is the clear clinking of glass on glass and abandoned cutlery and empty cans and the rustling of newspapers when wrestled up into a new plastic bag. Sandra coughs violently outside.

The scale of the squalor is striking but not as unusual as you might expect. It is similar to an apartment nearby that Sandra cleaned last year: same type of client (female, later sixties, office worker), same mountains of empty champagne bottles choking each room, same ammonia smell, same years without electricity. The neighbours at that job had complained because of the rats that started climbing up the building. It took six people, including Sandra, twelve hours to complete. It took eight people to move the three tonnes of rubbish out of the apartment. At the time, I asked Sandra what the woman looked like.

'She just looks like an old lady,' she replied.

'Is she unwell?' I asked.

'I think she's just lonely,' Sandra said.

I wobble up the glacier of glass and garbage out of the kitchen and grab the lintel of the doorframe for support before descending into the lounge room. From my vantage point atop this mountain,

I look down onto a gold-framed painting of gum trees hanging over the fireplace. There are two black and white TVs in one corner of the room and as I stare into the rubbish, two broken chairs emerge from the accumulated detritus like dolphins in a magic eye picture. In addition to the hundreds of empty bottles—champagne and beer and wine and gin—that reach up to the light fixture, there are also numerous empty packets and cartons of Marlboros. An ashtray over-flows on the mantelpiece; a few butts have burnt themselves out in the stuffing of a pillow. Against one wall a long, low display cabinet bares its rusted nails like fangs where the wood has rotted away. On its surface, amid the rubble from the caved-in roof, are cassette tapes of classical music and dirty pennies so worn the Queen's face has been erased. Behind its glass doors the good plates are still neatly stacked.

The women that Sandra is now closest to are, in the traditional sense, 'respectable' and 'normal' and they reflect those qualities back onto her through their friendship. They are very different from each other, but all are intelligent, strong and caring people in whom you can see a wicked sense of humour, a low tolerance for what they perceive to be bullshit and a mainstream, politically conservative worldview. Sandra herself is a 'long time Liberals supporter', a fact that initially startled me but which, on reflection, serves as a warning against the assumption that trans is an inherently radical position.

In other words, while it might not be considered consistent with her social interests or experiences, Sandra has the same right as anyone else to choose her place on the political spectrum for the reasons that make sense to her. Sandra's girlfriends are the women she genuinely likes and they are also, in various ways, the women whom she might very well have become had she simply been born female.

Katrina has known Sandra for nearly fifteen years. She stresses, as others do, Sandra's big heart and her thoughtfulness, and says how much she respects her 'because I don't know if many people would have survived that childhood'. She adds, 'Sandra is extremely private. When she is sick or sad or hurt, she doesn't want you around. It's almost as if she doesn't deserve goodness. I've seen her desperately sick, and she just shuts down. I remember when I took her to the doctor, and she was thinking more about me getting home and her being a burden. I could almost cry, because I just heard the little boy that nobody cared about. I left her at the hospital alone because it was too painful for her to have me there with her. Sometimes it feels as if her needs are so great, I'm talking about the lungs and the liver, and, I don't know, just everything.'

Unlike Sandra, whose position towards 'God-botherers' is variously annoyed, bemused or livid, Katrina is a church-going woman. 'I would hope that I would never judge her and just accept her for who she is,' Katrina tells me. 'I said to Sandra, "God sees you as a human being. He looks down on you and says, 'Wow, you are amazing, with all you have been through, you are still smiling, caring and sharing.'" I think we get our non-judgment from how we were brought up. It's none of our business what people do in their bedrooms.'

But as sensitive as Katrina is towards Sandra, there are moments when she exhibits an emotional astigmatism that serves to highlight the magnitude of Sandra's larger, lifelong battle for social acceptance.

'My husband thinks Sandra is lovely. When Sandra met him, she said to me, "He's the sort of man that I would like, but a man like him would never look at a person like me." Sandra is very sensible. She knows that people don't like poofters and transsexuals, and she gets it, because she doesn't either, that's why she doesn't hang around them. They are usually warped, weird, dirty and disgusting, and she doesn't want to be like that. She is working hard to support herself so that in her old age she can just have a nice, decent life, and I really hope that she has peace.'

'It's making me look like a fuckin' idiot,' Sandra seethes into her phone, pacing in front of Dorothy's house. 'I'm trying to keep my cool, 'cause you know how angry I get. We can't afford to be fucked around and I gotta get down to a double stabbing in Dromana soon. OK…So, how far away are you then?'

The bin company was supposed to deliver two skips by 9 a.m. It is now after eleven, so the cleaners have had to stack Dorothy's open garage full with bulging rubbish bags. More bags line the fence along the front of the house. Not only does this violate local council laws, it will waste time later in double-handling the bags to load the skips when they finally arrive. Sandra, who always ensures that she shows up to appointments early or, at the very least, punctually, is incandescent. Rule of Pankhurst: do not waste Sandra's time.

An older woman walks a small white dog towards the house. She is snow-haired, pink-scrubbed and wearing a sensible vest. As she passes, Sandra leans down to coo at the dog and the woman looks at her and the STC van and the mountain of black rubbish bags but she absolutely does not look inside the house, although the doorway is a few feet away from her sturdy white sneakers.

In a small voice, the woman asks after Dorothy by name, with quiet alarm. Sandra reassures her that Dorothy is being cared for. Telling Sandra how she has lived in the neighbourhood for forty-seven years, the woman recalls when Dorothy lived here with her parents and how Dorothy's mother died forty years ago. Moulding the dog's lead in her soft, white hands, the woman explains that Dorothy has no family now.

'She lives in her own world…' the woman says, her eyes drifting across the many rubbish bags, in search of somewhere familiar to

75

rest. Finding none, she walks on saying, mystified, 'But she's such an *intelligent* person...'

Dust billows out like smoke from the front doorway as Rodney and Jade chip into the solid glacial mass, calving large icebergs and smaller loaves that can be thrown into bags and carried away. Two hours have passed since they started and, through this back-breaking effort, they have cleared about a metre into the foyer, excavating, in the process, the ancient mosaic of the carpet, worn down to white thread except for a few patches where the deep reds and blues of the original design are just visible. Swaths of exposed brick run along the walls where the paint and plaster have crumbled away. Windows of blue sky appear through the missing slats in the ceiling and the holes in the roof.

Sandra walks back around the house and leans through the kitchen window to check Leigh's progress. Through nonstop labour, his morning's achievement has been to clear one small patch of kitchen floor—the linoleum is black and slightly moist, a clearing in the forest. He shows her where he just fell through the floor, also the other spots where the supporting boards have rotted away from the rains which poured through the roof, filtered through newspaper and bottles, pooled for a time and slowly seeped away. Sighing, Sandra zips one long, apricot-coloured nail across the screen of her phone and dials the job contact. 'I think there might be a bit of a problem if she wants to come back here because the floors are rotted through...'

Another neighbour stops out front. She has lived in the neighbourhood for thirty-five years and asks with concern after Dorothy. Sandra says lightly that she's just here today to help. 'I can't believe it,' the woman says, dazed. 'I was just speaking to her last night. She was sitting right outside here. She's clever, very clever. She travelled the world when she was younger, had a good job...' She starts wringing her hands in a way that makes the sunlight flare on her

Fitbit. 'You know when the gas went off?' she asks, referring to a two-week outage in 1998. 'It never came back on here.'

I think of the pot of bleached chicken bones on the gas stove in the kitchen, the holes in the roof, the razorwinds of eighteen winters. I think of how Dorothy passed dark time here surrounded by everything and nothing while the deluge of rubbish inexorably submerged her life like a village drowned. Though she remained inside her childhood home, changing nothing for forty years, that place was as far from her as the moon.

'We all live our own lives, you don't pry,' the neighbour says haltingly. From the footpath, I look up at the corroded gutters lining the roof; they have deteriorated so badly they look like lace. 'Sorry, my heart is hurting at the moment,' the woman says, palming her chest before walking on.

It's all still here. The tin mail organiser on the kitchen wall with neatly folded gas bills from 1971 (*$3.51, PAID*), the *Australian Women's Weekly* reporting how Jane Priest stole a kiss from Prince Charles, the polystyrene Big Mac containers, the neatly wrapped brown paper packages on the shelves in the fridge, the good dishes, the rubbish that hasn't been taken out for decades. But despite the food wrappers and the alcohol dregs and the pyramids of cigarette butts, you smell none of these things.

'Newspapers are broken down, furniture's broken down, everything's broken down,' Rodney mutters, hefting a bulging rubbish bag out the door. 'As soon as you start movin' it, it falls apart.'

An elderly Greek neighbour in an adorable pink cardigan wanders over eating an ice-cream, despite the early hour. Rule of Pankhurst: 'There's always a stickybeak.' She smiles at everyone and then her face folds down like an umbrella as she peers for the first time in thirty years into the house six metres from where she sleeps. 'What happened?' is all she can say.

Gripping my arm like a bird on a branch, she insists on leading me through her front garden and into her house, where she takes me on a tour. The layout is exactly the same as Dorothy's. Except the floors are mirror shiny and sunlight fills the rooms like music and there are photos, everywhere, of her children and their children. 'I see her, sometime, up there.' She motions towards the main road at the end of the street, shaking her head and looking bereft. 'I say, "Why don't you go home?"' Then she starts speaking only in Greek, which I do not understand.

# 6

*Transsexuals suffer the oppression of the homosexual, they suffer the oppression of women…They can't vote, most of them can't hope to leave the country to enter another country. Most of them can't get finance. All of them except for myself have been unable to carry on their previous profession. The only reason I could was because…I'd been fortunate, by some accident, to have fooled the Registrar of Nursing into thinking I was a Miss instead of a Mister when I registered…But I know doctors, I know psychologists, I know teachers, I know optometrists who have been struck off their registers and they have been refused entrance back into their professions just because they have had sex change surgery. So they suck cocks up in Victoria Street or take off their clothes four times a night in a strip club in King's Cross. Or they work as waitresses in hotels which is somewhat better, or perhaps worse, than sucking cocks.*

Vivian Sherman, 1975[1]

.

Once a week, on Saturday mornings, a group of sleek young men who call each other darl and queen and lovey climb the concrete stairs to someone's flat, fight over which record to play and who's taken whose spot on the sofa, roll swift joints from the communal bowl on the coffee table and then begin a ritual that starts with this: an assortment of metal files, tiny scissors, glue, solvent and bottles of red lacquer amid handfuls of plastic fingernails scattered on the table like runes waiting to be read. They smoke and snort speed and drink nice cups of tea or gin and do their nails.

First, the old polish or nail is soaked away. Then the natural nail is filed and an artificial one is glued down. When this dries, it too is filed and another artificial nail is glued halfway along its length. This makes the nail long but not long enough for the desired 'talon look' so the process is repeated until three artificial nails are glued securely in an ascending line, filed smooth to blend into each other. Lastly the long length is coated with layer upon layer upon layer of paint. The process cannot be rushed but once it is finished—hours later, just in time to run back to their own flats to get ready for the night—you cannot tell where the real nail ends and the fake nails begin. To the girls there is no question that they look better than the real thing.

The fifties and the sixties had been a time of great and stealthy preparation, unknown even to the preparers, in the boilerplate suburbs and the bone-dry country towns and the beachside villages bleaching in the sun; in the Catholic schools and the Anglican church halls, at the milk bar and the footy and the cricket. Every place where no one ever would have believed that the meek lads, the smart-mouthed, the mother-combed, the gangly young men loathed by their fathers, would break out to become Carlotta or Terri Tinsel or Danielle Lawrence or Debra Le Gae or Celestial Star the Girl with the 48-Inch Bust.[2]

Although unwelcome in his Footscray home, Peter had never

ventured far from it. The respite he found with the McMahons, his first flat, his share houses and his homes with Linda were all within a nine-kilometre radius of the street where he grew up. St Kilda was different. Not so much because it was more than double the distance from his old neighbourhood or because you crossed at least one river to get there, but because, for a boy from West Footscray, it was like entering another dimension.

Peter knows just enough people in the scene to meet more people. He rents a room in a share house in Balaclava and has an instant circle of friends to eat with and go out with and stay in with and learn from. There is Nicole, small and gorgeous, a full-time showgirl and Peter's best friend, whose attributes include: little hands, little feet, a deep voice, a dangerous mouth and a sister who is a fucking nut job. There is Carol, a bit of a lost soul, and also 'a gay guy-girl', whose particulars are now lost to history. Peter tries heroin and hates it; he tries speed and loves it. He spends hours at the dressing table built into the wall of his bedroom, reimagining himself and his surroundings. He hangs wallpaper for a feature wall. He disassembles his heavy wooden bed and lowers the mattress to the floor. His flatmates nickname him Joseph the Carpenter. He reassesses his nose. He ponders new names, practises new signatures.

At the time Peter thinks he looks fabulous but in the mirror of retrospect he stands there monstrous in his plastic wig and second-hand dress. Encouraged by some mates, he starts performing in the drag shows. He mimes the lyrics of the songs up on stage while wearing borrowed costumes and full make-up that he is gradually learning to apply by watching the queens work on their faces, like he watched his neighbour renovating a house.

It is an awkward period of adolescence that he will eventually recall cringing, and only with the help of royal remove: 'That was in the very early stages when we were a little bit ugly.'

The shows are where he hears a wig called 'a bonnet' and a john called 'a mug' and Bette Davis and 'J Crawf' referred to like everybody's close personal friends. The shows are where he becomes comfortable using female bathrooms, which are basically unisex anyway. The shows are where he learns to shape an eyebrow, to shade a jawline; where light should hit and shadow fall, what should shine and what should be matte, how to make lips and eyes bigger and noses and foreheads smaller, how to erase stubble and add lashes. How to transform himself from a timid, skinny dude from the western suburbs into a poised and elegant woman.

It takes longer, by far, to apply the make-up than it does to dance in the shows and although the same team dances in two or three shows each night at different venues around the neighbourhood, they have to completely change out of their hair, make-up and costumes just to cross the road. This is because if the cops catch men dressed as women on the street they will belt the shit out of them.

The cops beat Peter and his friends for looking too much like men, or too much like women, or because they are something in the middle, 'not ridgy-didge'. The cops beat them for the same reasons that the state has made it legal to arrest them and fine them and imprison them: their very presence is, to use the legislative terminology, riotous, indecent, offensive, insulting; grossly indecent; an outrage on decency. They are told that it is illegal to dress as a woman, illegal to wear women's underwear, illegal to loiter in a public place for homosexual purposes, whatever that means. The ones who are arrested are fined, or they are jailed in men's prisons, like Pentridge, where they are raped.

And so they erase themselves with tissues and cold cream, fold everything neatly into bags and put on their boy clothes, their actual costumes, for the short walk just across the way. If they can afford to avoid this 'constant off/on, off/on, off/on of gear' by sharing a taxi to the next job, they are allowed two minutes to walk from the car into the venue; any longer and they risk being beaten and arrested.

He does the sex work between shows at night and he does it during the day. He does it because the stage is 'pretty shitty money', and because sex and shows are his only choices. Though it is distasteful at best and, of course, dangerous, sex work is normalised in this world where the possibility of an adequately paid straight job (assuming you managed to receive the requisite education or work experience in the necessary domestic peace most often reserved for your cisgender peers) is virtually eliminated if you choose to live full-time in the sex you were not assigned at birth. Most of his friends do sex work on the side; if not, they're giving it away.

'I'm a bit of a capitalist in that respect,' he tells the girls when they go off with the punters who hang around backstage. 'I love a dollar, nothing for nothing.'

He won't remember any details about his first client apart from the fear and the adrenaline rush, but after that it becomes 'like water off a duck's back'. When Peter acknowledges that what he is doing is 'pretty risky', he is referring to the violence from the police and not the dangers posed by street prostitution. If the cops catch him soliciting they will arrest him or bash him senseless or both. So Peter and his friends rent a dark basement apartment in a beautiful old building on Grey Street where they can take clients. It's always safer to work inside—and you *never* take them back to your own house.

In this way, although it's a long way from his lab at the flour mill, he starts earning again. He buys furniture and clothes and costumes and make-up. As 'the main supporter' of the share house, he buys food and booze and drugs for everyone. He thinks nothing of spending fifty bucks at Clare's Cakes on lemon tarts and vanilla slices, inviting people over for afternoon tea and then sweeping all the leftovers directly into the bin because he is no longer that boy who grew up scrounging for food.

'It's always Grand Central at my place,' he complains proudly. He knows that he drops money like this to make himself feel better; his generosity is 'a lonely thing'; a plea. He takes money for contact and he spends money for contact. But unlike the different service he offers to the faceless mugs who nod at him on the street, these bright things who pop over for a bite or a drink provide him with the friendship he needs to keep moving.

It is 'action stations all the time', there is always a party to go to. Peter lives now in an intensely social environment, a swirl of people—gay, lesbian, straight; queens and the moles that orbit them like lesser planets—all roiling together amid the audiences of hens' nights and bucks' nights and office workers out from the suburbs for a good time. Their shows have names like Les Girls and Play Girls and Belle Boys and Street Boys and Pokeys and Between the Sexes. His friends are guys and girls, 'sex changers' and not. They have the nicknames Gorilla Grip and Croc and PT, which stands for Painfully Thin.

They include those he will forget forever and those he will remember with forgiveness, like his boyfriend Frankie the Italian Stallion, 'who'd root anything that moved, except the missus at home payin' the bills'. Frankie takes Peter's money but it's nice to have someone to come home to, and for this, Peter forgives him everything, even when Frankie writes off his beautiful orange Monaro. When Nicole asks Peter why he lets Frankie stay, he smiles. 'You pay for what you want,' he says. 'Everything in life has a price, you just have to decide whether you're going to pay for it there and then or not.'

On the coffee table in every house is a bowl of mandies, a bowl of weed and a bowl of speed, all graciously offered like mints for visitors to help themselves. No one carries drugs, because of the police harassment they already attract by walking down the street in their own skin. For prescription drugs, there's a doctor in St Kilda and another in North Melbourne who'll give you pretty much any-thing. The girls go back and forth between the two. Peter never hears a quibble about who had how much, never hears anyone ask to be paid back. Life is communal for safety and for fun but also because, for many, this is now their only family. This also explains why, when Jullianne Deen closes the show with her number 'You'll Never Walk Alone', slowly wiping off her make-up as she changes back into her boy clothes, 'there isn't a dry eye in the house'.

Peter looks at the shoes: three pairs, standing there like ghosts waiting for a train. The man who used to own them is dead, folded carefully like his work shirts and his pants and his vests into a couple of large rubbish bags that wait by the closed bedroom door.[3]

'This is really it for good,' Peter says to himself over and over, the thought like a shard of sea glass, wave-churned, smooth, but still with a sharp edge here and there. He's already spent a week feeling like he's been flayed alive, his cheeks bleeding, hardly able to speak. His subsequent visits three times a week for both waxing and electrolysis were far less painful and because he is so blond he never gets 'the bluebeard regrowth look'.

He is still taking hormone pills from his doctor in Carlton but, after hearing some of the girls talk about hormone injections, he visited their doctor near the corner of Chapel Street. He has not shared with that doctor the fact that he is also taking hormones in pill form; he believes that doubling the hormones in this way will make them work better and faster. He willingly assumes the risks, and will never express regret: 'Yes, it probably shortened my life, what it done to my liver and kidneys. But it also gave me the life I wanted.'

Now, this whole morning, he has been clearing out his small closet and few drawers, methodically but with intense emotion that encompasses both sadness and joy. This is a process he is going through alone, and though it is seismic, no one else is aware it is happening. He wonders every few minutes whether he is doing the right thing or if this is going to be an expensive and embarrassing mistake. He can't say for sure what is driving him or where he is going or that it will be OK when he gets there; he just feels that this is the way he has to go.

Peter keeps folding and bagging, folding and bagging, and when the last item is done, she gathers up the bags and leaves the house in a long kaftan dress, locking the door behind her. As she walks out that day Stacey Anne Vaughan, sometimes known as Amanda Celeste Claire, shares many things, of course, with Peter Collins but the most important is that she will never fear what is ahead of her, only what is behind her.


Stacey has the best tits you've ever seen. Renee Scott, one of the Pokeys Dreamgirls, was meant to be the first to get the tit job with the incision under the arm, to keep the scarring out of sight. But Renee either got sick or chickened out, so Stacey became the first to get it done. Like most of the other girls, she went to the fancy surgeon on The Avenue in Windsor. Unlike most of the other girls, her breasts are now enormous, and with the double doses of hormones she has also put on weight. She returns to the surgeon to have her nose smoothed to a more delicate slope and then to have her eyes lifted. Her beauty, her plump softness, the ease with which she moves through the world as Stacey all mean that passing is never a problem. She is proud of the incredulity she regularly encounters. People say, 'You're not a drag!'

'But I *am* a drag,' she replies, smiling.

One day she is speeding to get her hair done when she is pulled over on the highway.

'Nooo,' the police officer says, patronising, looking down at the card she hands him through the window. 'Not your *husband's* licence. *Your* licence.'

'That *is* my licence,' she says.

He stands there for a long moment. He walks back to his car. Then he returns, puts one hand on the roof and bends down to peer in through her window. 'I don't know what to do,' he says quietly. 'Just go. I'll wait here for five minutes, and you can go.'

She rolls into her costume fittings with Jullianne Deen the Costume Queen, who calls everyone queenie or sweetpea and whom the girls call Mother. Here she spends hours gossiping and laughing, being fitted for the looks she will be wearing in the next show. On stage she is festooned, resplendent in Mother's creations. As Celestial Star, she has hair the colour of a Coke can and transcendentally long legs, and she gets introduced on stage as the Girl with the *Big Personality* on account of her forty-eight-inch bust. The girls call her Celestial Monster in mockery of this abundant bosom.

She loves the music, exults in the movement and the lights and the audience and their applause, which she feeds off as validation that she looks 'OK'. And she feels wonderful, energised, out-of-control-alive as though she is both starring in and watching herself in a movie playing on fast forward. As everyone says, 'mandies make you randy', a fact of which she is acutely aware each time she wakes up naked under a sinkful of vomit in the bathroom of an empty bar, not knowing when she passed out but feeling like she had another pretty good night.

She lives in Balaclava. Strathmore. Brunswick. Kensington. East St Kilda. Northcote. Carnegie. Caulfield. North Melbourne. Cheltenham. Everywhere.

Also nowhere, for an extended period of time. There are always a couple of people living with her and off her. Though they might do an occasional drag show, none of them works or contributes towards rent or household expenses.

When Nicole points this out, Stacey waves her concern away. 'I'm always a bit of a suck to have people around and look after people. But that is the nature of me: I always provide, for some reason, I don't know why. I always provide,' she sighs.

Stacey shoots up speed with a little glass syringe that glints like jewellery and drives across the city between the house she is renting in Brunswick and the shows she's dancing in and the brothels she's working at. She makes good money in the twenty-buck fuck shops, those dark terrace houses along Nicholson Street in Fitzroy. The trick is to get the guys in, get them excited and get them out as quickly as possible. The more she can do fast like that, the more money she makes. She returns home to cook up a storm in the middle of the night; practises dance routines in the mirror; knocks down the back wall, planning on turning it into an atrium, airy and light, but then it all just seems too hard so she simply moves. The wind blows in through the broken bricks and over the old couch where she nodded off so many times just as the sun was rising; it chases itself around the empty rooms, stirring the rain and leaves and animal droppings that collect, eventually, on the floor.

She is Celestial Star and she is Stacey Anne but she is also the person to whom the letter is addressed which appears one day at her house like a haunting. It is mystifying to her how Linda found her address. All Stacey knows is that Linda must have found out that she was 'making some money' and decided that she 'wanted a piece of the action'. So she changes her name and moves to another house. Stacey Phillips. Stacey Anne Vaughan. Celestial Star. Amanda Celeste Claire. Sandra Anne Vaughan. While these name changes are a normal and integral part of the process of finding who she is as a woman, they also make it easy to disappear altogether.

Her first and continuing reaction to her ex-wife is one of indignant flight. This does not change over time. 'Linda already had the house, had everything, all I left with was just the car and clothes that I had and that was it. Everything else was for her.' I ask Sandra whether she had left Linda with any savings (no) and how she thinks

88

Linda would have managed to support their children and make the repayments on the house (don't know). When I ask these questions, Sandra genuinely seems to be considering them for the first time and uninterested in pursuing them further. We have floated across the line and here we stay, becalmed, past her outer limits. The mediaeval horizon where you simply sailed off the edge of the earth or were swallowed whole by the monstrous beasts that swam there.

Two scenes of a homecoming. First: a charity dinner dance. She does not remember where the dance was or what it was for or how she ended up there, only that she 'didn't dream for one minute' that she would see her little brother Simon there. He is now in his late teens, thin and serious and darkly handsome. He too has been kicked out of home by Bill. Suddenly, despite all her pride and all her confidence, she finds her face burning and her heart racing as she smiles at him and, above the sheer volume of everything that is not said between them, tells him she is happy to see him. She is genuinely so happy to see him.

'Well,' Simon says in his quiet voice as he looks at her shyly. 'You're the only Collins boy who's ever done what he really wants to do.' And then he puts his arms around her and he hugs her.

Months later, when she runs into him again, this time on the street, she is struck (even though she is speeding off her face) by the fact that he looks 'like a hobo'.

'What the fuck are you doing here?' she asks him, astounded.

He tells her that his wife left him for his friend. That she took everything from their house one day while he was at work, including his Stones records. Sandra brings him back home with her and he stays there until he gets on his feet. Later, he enlists in the army where he will spend twenty-one years working as an engineer. They will always, each in their own way, adore each other.

Second: It is 1979. Sandra finds out that her father died six months ago. She calls her mother's sister. 'Aunty Bessie, this is...you know... who it is...Peter,' Sandra says.

'Oh, hello dear! Your mother would be so pleased,' Aunty Bessie says, sounding happy to hear from her.

'Well, I don't know about that, because so much has happened...'

'Oh no, she misses you terribly,' Bessie soothes. 'She'd love to hear from you. You know, she's working at Fosseys in Footscray. She finishes every Saturday at noon and she's home by twelve-thirty. Give her a call then, darl, she'd love to see you.'

Sandra works at a brothel on Saturdays so she arranges to take a day off. She stays in on Friday night to do her nails and gets up early on Saturday to wash and set her hair. And then she waits by the phone until twelve-thirty when she can, finally, call home.

'Hello?' Ailsa's voice comes clear through the line.

'Mum?' Sandra says. 'It's...me here.'

'Huh. You,' Ailsa says and, for a long moment, she holds her silence before her like a switchblade. 'You *fuckin' killed* your father. I *never* wanna fuckin' speak to you again.'

The sound of her mother swearing shocks her more, momentarily, than the words themselves or the spitting contempt in them.

'You can get fucked!' Sandra screams into the phone. She hangs up and slumps into a chair like a bag of ice. And it is as though she is still sitting there thirty-six years later when she tells me what was said at 12:31 that afternoon in 1979, her voice still thinned out by the hurt of it. 'Had my hair done in anticipation of I was gonna see my mother...And...'cause...you know, I'd look after her when she was getting bashed, I climbed in the house through the window to go look after her when he was bashing her and then she'd make up with him and then I'd get bashed for looking after her! You know, so...it was a fuckin' rocky road...'

That was the last time Sandra spoke with her mother, Ailsa

Maggie Collins, who would die fourteen years later, on 2 November 1993, three days after which a requiem mass was offered at Our Lady of Perpetual Succour for the repose of her soul.

They dance in shows at the Prince of Wales and the Night Moves Disco and Bojangles, which they call Bowie's or Bongland. They party at Annabel's and Mandate and Spangles, the Whiskey A Go Go and the Key Club and the Savoy and the Dover Hotel and the Union Hotel and Maisy's Hotel and, if they're up that way and out of options, that cheap and nasty place in North Melbourne run by the gay guy with tragic shows full of people only starting out in the scene (a biting assessment which shows not only how far Sandra's settled into her skin now, but also how far the city has come).

Sandra missed the early days, in the late sixties, when one of the few chances to socialise in safety was at the private camp dances, organised by Jan Hillier, that migrated around Melbourne. It was all very furtive: couples would spring apart and grab the nearest person of the opposite sex if a cop showed up to check the liquor licence.

So despite the constant threat of police violence, normalised by a society in which homosexuality is officially a mental illness and a crime, the fact that Sandra and her friends now have commercial venues to visit should not be taken for granted. When Hillier and her partner, 'drag impresario' Doug Lucas, first approached the Prince of Wales in 1977 about establishing the regular gay night that would become Pokeys, the hotel manager doubted that a drag show could fill the pub's entire first floor. So they were given only one room, with the consequence, so the story goes, that on opening night hundreds of customers were turned away.

By the late seventies, progress in open socialising reflected and encouraged changing attitudes; it was possible now to think in terms of an actual gay 'community'.[4] The degree to which that community reflected and promoted the rights and needs of *all* its members—transgender men and women in particular—is open to question. However, it was better than what had gone before.

When I ask Sandra whether she was involved with any of the activist groups in the seventies, like Gay Liberation or Society Five, her answer is both surprising and not.

'No,' she says, batting away the question. 'I was never political. I never drew attention to myself.' And her statement is not untrue because she was Celestial Star the Girl with the *Big Personality* twirling topless on stage night after night. It is untrue because in exercising her right to be who she was and to not make it the focus of her life any more than, say, the fact that she was adopted or from the western suburbs, she was in this, yes, quiet way of insisting on living her own life, powerfully political.

When Sandra and I visit Doug Lucas, they work out that they have not seen each other since around the year I was born. It must be quite a trip to come face to face with someone you haven't seen for thirty-six years, but Sandra is zero awkward on first greeting Doug and during the initial small talk, and the deeper dive that follows. Although, as Doug puts it, she 'just disappeared' one day from the scene, leaving him to always wonder what happened to 'Stacey', she slots enthusiastically back in, asking after old friends, paging through his photo albums, laughing when he wistfully recalls what a good-looking man she was, hopping up to make tea because Doug has put on enough weight now that it's taxing for him. Sitting side-saddle at his kitchen table, Doug fills Sandra in on where all the girls are now. Sandra hears the names of people and places forgotten for over three decades and when this happens her eyes squint and then open joyfully, the skin snaps back a little, it is 1978 and she is young again.

Explaining her disappearance she says, 'I think probably the best bit of advice I got was from Rick, who I was going out with—we brought up his daughter and put her through school—and he said to me, "Whenever you're around your gay friends, you act gay. If you want to be a woman, hang around real women." And that's what I did. I disassociated myself, really, from everybody.'

'I find that a bit sad,' Doug says, tapping his long, unpainted, almond-shaped nails on the tabletop in contemplation. 'Because the thing is, they're part of your life and you shouldn't have to cut that part out. He probably looked at it like: "That's a journey you go through." But it's not so much the destination sometimes, it's the actual trip that's more important.'

Doug is right. It is sad. Because this is the old guard who walked through fire together: warriors in silken feathers and bright war paint. They are the only ones who truly understand what it felt like to walk into 'unexplored territory', to be at once home and 'in a foreign country'. They are the only ones who are stabbed in the guts, still, by the term 'queer'; who always stumble over the word 'trans-gender' because, to them, there are only guys and girls, really, and regardless of whether you've had The Change or just put on a frock for the night, they will call you a girl and mean it. Sandra's wholesale loss of these ties was the loss of a chance for true connection and support.

But Doug is also wrong about these losses. In the same way that he, who insisted at various times on running male-only bars, clearly prefers the company of men or queens, Sandra prefers the company of straight women. That's who she feels most herself with. The fact that her drag days were a period of adolescent experimentation from which she felt the need to move on must be understood in the context of her entire life. So while Peter and Stacey and Celestial Star have not disappeared exactly, they exist now only to the extent that the sun and the motion of the earth exist in the wind. As she told me once: 'I'm just Sandra. I've lived so long like this that I don't refer to the other side. The other side is foreign to me.'

Doug rings Jullianne Deen the Costume Queen, with whom he is still close, and excitedly informs her that Stacey is here. Sandra smiles at Jullianne's audible delight. Jullianne tells her that she is still designing and, though she experienced difficulties with her eyes, has had the loving support of 'the man of her life', her partner of twenty-five years. Sandra mentions that she, too, had a long-term partner, was married for fifteen years, though it went a little pear-shaped towards the end because he wanted to own her, ha, good luck.

And here it is, in Jullianne's happy voice bouncing down the line and in the slight angularity when Sandra brandishes her second marriage and when Doug invites us into his dark bedroom, fires up the computer and shows us hundreds of photos of his past glory: the costumes and the applause and the parties could give you nothing that you weren't willing to give yourself.

So though they sit watching the screen with the same wistful smile that makes their wet eyes wrinkle at the corners, though they have both gained weight and lost elasticity, though they remember with great fondness the same names and laugh the same delightfully wicked laugh, though they sit there, side by side, the distance between Sandra and Doug is the distance between planets.

The thing she has with Maria is different.

When the girls ask her what that thing is, she explains that, no, she's really not interested in women per se. 'It's just probably more her soul that I like.' Maria is good to her, 'like a gentleman'—despite the fact that she is significantly smaller and younger than Sandra, still in her teens. Part Aboriginal, part Italian, Maria Gloria Paten is 'quite boyish looking but in a beautiful way'. She wears a uniform consisting of a black T-shirt, a men's business shirt with the sleeves rolled up and baggy khaki trousers. She is eighteen years old and lives at home with her mother and her sister and brother, both of whom are young enough when Sandra moves in that she refers to them as 'the kids'. The mother welcomes her daughter's tall, blonde girlfriend into their home. For the first time in a long time, Sandra starts thinking about the future.

The tide is out and they are posing for a photo together on the dunes. Sandra stands lower down the slope and steers Maria slightly in front to reduce their height difference. They look towards the camera, squinting in the harsh light against a grey page of sky. In red pants and a baggy old blouse, Sandra wears, for once, no make-up.

'You know how the big op is coming up,' she says after they break away from their friends to walk down the beach. Maria nods, walking with her hands jammed deep in both pockets and her shoulders hunched up, eyes gazing down at her sneakers kicking through the sand.

'Yeah, so,' Sandra continues, 'this is the last chance I'll have to have a child, or, like, a family, so I was thinking, maybe…' She stops and looks down at her girlfriend, who is looking, now, out across the water, her thin eyebrows pinching together while the wind animates her short dark hair. Maria reaches for Sandra's hand and they smile at each other and start to giggle

They go about executing their plan with great practicality, despite the circumstances of their lives rendering it fairly unrealistic. They decide that Maria will be admitted to the hospital under Sandra's name so that Sandra can later 'be known as the mother'. They contemplate names, browse baby shops. When they find out that Maria is pregnant, they are delighted. 'That was our aim,' Sandra explains, looking back. 'But we didn't realise what the consequences would be, didn't think about the complications. Could I have worked? Could I have done prostitution? Life has a funny way of working itself out, because it probably would've been quite tumultuous for the child.'

.

Phillip John Keen, whom the newspaper will describe as 'an expert in certain aspects of the martial arts', lived in West Footscray one kilometre from Sandra's childhood home. He was on the door at the Night Moves disco the night Maria went to see Sandra perform in the show. He was in charge. And Maria comes in, all swagger, to watch her red-haired girlfriend with the amazing tits. Maybe Keen has it in for her. Maybe he has it in for dykes. Maybe he's jealous of her. Maybe he's jealous of the girlfriend. Maybe he's repulsed that he's jealous of either of them. Maybe he hates Maria's dark skin and beautiful face. Maybe he hates that she is not afraid of him. Maybe he just wants to feel the force of bone on muscle.

The great Celestial Star has a few minutes before she goes backstage to get ready. Once made up she'll go straight on stage; the make-up has its own momentum and it's best not to dissipate that energy, but right after she performs they'll go home, to Maria's mother's place. Maria can't stay up as late as she used to and they don't need to be out to have fun anymore. It is a time of becoming for both of them; Maria is three months pregnant with their child and Sandra is pregnant, in a way, with herself, about to start the process for the bottom surgery that will complete her transition. Maria leans back in her chair, looks over towards the stage and pops her sneakers up on the table as Sandra lights the cigarette poised between her long nails.

'Feet off the fucking table,' Keen barks as he walks by, hitching up his pants. Both women glance up with mild surprise at the bouncer. They hadn't noticed him approaching.

'Fuck him, he can come back and ask me nicely,' Maria says. Sandra chuckles as she stands up, blows Maria a kiss and walks through the crowded club to the stage door. Just before she disappears backstage, she looks back. She sees that Keen has returned to their table, sees him throw Maria's feet down. Maria stands, furious now, and glares up into Keen's face. He pushes her roughly towards the front door of the club and out. As Sandra jostles her way back over, Maria reappears and lands one great shove into Keen's chest. This is when he throws her on the ground and jumps on her stomach, landing on her with his knee. Then, after a long moment, Keen— panting, triumphant—grabs Maria under her armpits and drags her outside.

Though her pulse quickens, Sandra is sure it'll be all right. Because Maria is Maria. Because it has to be.

But Maria doesn't get up. Though Sandra kneels by her side and shakes her shoulder and says, 'Come on, love, let's go home,' her head just jiggles softly. Maria is still not getting up when someone shouts to call an ambulance, or when the cops suddenly materialise because they're always around the neighbourhood anyway. Maria is still not getting up when Sandra starts wailing and is escorted gently by one of the cops into the back of a divvy van, which is the only peaceful place the man can think of.

But then, like a prayer fulfilled, ambulance sirens confirm that Maria has finally come to; is about to be taken off to be made better again. Only now can Sandra take a shuddering gulp of air, unfold herself from the car and look around. This is when the reporter with his notebook curled in his fist comes racing across the street and hawks her hope out of mid-air as he shouts at the cop standing next to the car, 'What's the dead chick's name?'

That's how the world ends. Though she stands there, taking up space on the pavement in her red wig and tight dress, she is suddenly gone; nobody to no one.

Sandra does not need a physics lesson to understand that time dilates; life taught her early that some seconds are cruelly quick and others are torturously slow. She is floating away, unmoored from the grounding mass of the earth and suddenly, somehow, it is morning and she is scared to go back home after giving her statement. She is scared of showing other people her pain, and her grief is too large to hide, so she stays away from her friends and Maria's family. She is scared, too, that they will blame her for not protecting Maria. She is scared that it will come out that Maria's girlfriend is actually a drag queen in the club where she was killed and, also, that Maria was pregnant with their baby. She is scared of the way Maria's family will look at her when they find out that their daughter's girlfriend, who has been eating with them and laughing with them these many months, was an imposter all along. With each realisation, she falls further down a hole so black it inhales light until she is trapped in each too-slow second with no way of escaping and nowhere to run to if she could.

A tall, gaunt figure with broken nails and dirty hair, she hunches into the front door with her key one last time, when she knows Maria's mother will be out cleaning houses and the kids will be at school. Glowing with shame, she gathers up her few things, wounded by the couch and the cracked bathroom tile, by the view from the window and the hum of the fridge—by how completely unchanged it all is and the fact that the last time she stood there, she was a different person. Someone with a home, loved by the woman in the warm body beside her with a second chance at family floating inside it.

She crashes wherever she can. The cops are cracking down again. She cannot make money by pro-ing down Acland Street or Robe Street or Fitzroy Street or any of those streets. So she goes to a brothel on the Nepean Highway. When the freeway expansion goes through years later, this house will be demolished, taking with it the small, dark rooms where she knelt or lay face down: bound, bleeding, white-pale; quivering like something slapped down on a butcher's counter.

This is unregulated submissive BDSM work, work Maria never would have allowed her to do, work that is 'like a mind fuck': the bottom of the food chain. This is where, like Maria, she just lies there, internally wounded, and does not get up.

But she is not Maria and something continues to beat inside her. She supplements what she makes there with quick money from the cheap brothels in Fitzroy. Through this long Melbourne winter, she is focused on doing the work she has to do, not just to survive but to flourish. On the first anniversary of Maria's death, she will be complete.

Eventually she will remember Maria with warmth and sadness, though when she calls her 'Marie' it will be unclear whether this is affectionate or forgetful. But today she is putting a small suitcase into the boot of a taxi and directing the driver from East St Kilda into the city, telling him the quickest way to get to the hospital on Lonsdale Street. The car slows to a crawl in traffic and she turns away from the cold glass, through which the finer details of cigarette butts, drink cans and chewing gum make her think that perhaps nothing ever really gets thrown away.

Then they accelerate, and her elbow bumps hard up against the pane, that line separating here from there, invisible, almost, and she looks impatiently up ahead. She is inches behind the driver. She is listening to his radio station. She is inhaling the air he exhales. She is trying not to watch his flesh spill out like flood tide from under his T-shirt and around the buckle of his seatbelt. And then they are stopping in front of the hospital and she is handing him banknotes warm from her pocket that are now warm in his hand.

She is slamming the door shut behind her and forgetting to say goodbye because she is now walking into her future, and that is a thought she pulls up and over herself like a blanket.

# Driver

I wouldn't call this a home but it is where a bus driver lived until earlier this week. Sandra says he bled out through the nose, something to do with alcohol poisoning or an infection, she's not sure. But it's a small house and a small job, requiring only her and one other cleaner, Trent, who is tall and thin and quick to offer a gummy grin from under his baseball cap as he drags the cleaning equipment in from the van. As they gather the driver's scant personal possessions and prepare the house for the next tenants, the way he died takes up less of their energy than the way he lived.

Gordon shared his small front lawn, with one large tree and some pink flowers just starting to bloom, with the unit next door. The shadowed front porch, caked with so much bird shit it looks like someone spilled a can of white paint, was his alone. A broken armchair slumps there, its seat slit down the middle. The front door is battered, streaked with dirt, and it opens into the living room with the blue couch where he died.

The walls are bare. There are brown bloodstains on the couch and on the carpet, which is a sea of hand-rolled cigarette butts flecked with eggshells and dried dog shit. Though there are a few pieces of furniture (two armchairs pushed up against the wall, an end table) and some bits and pieces (a dictionary, a plastic watering can resting on the couch, an incense burner on the radiator), the room is arranged so that there is really just the couch and an enormous TV resting on a low shelf coated with white–grey dust, pristine like new snow.

The house is cold from the air blowing in through the open screen door, diluting but also diffusing the intimate and awful smell of death. I trail Sandra as she follows the bloodstains from the couch into the small kitchen and up to the sink where a waterlogged, bloody singlet lies in a heap. She wonders aloud whether he took it off to staunch the bleeding; then, accepting the uncertainty, she starts appraising the bench. Lemon halves turned mahogany, the black fingers of bananas flecked white with mould. The drawer she yanks out contains, instead of cutlery, unused paint brushes and thick white paper.

The pantry is full of instant noodles, canned soup. Empty dog-food and water bowls lie on the floor next to the miniature fridge. She peers down at the coins and papers scattered on top and, seeing an identification card, notes in passing that she and Gordon were born in the same year. 'Mouse shit,' she says, tracking a glossy nail along the top of the small table pushed up against the front window.

I wonder, not for the first time, who will do this work for Sandra when she passes. She is open about her plans: 'I've left any money that I've got to the university to educate someone who can't afford to be educated in the medical side of things. My body goes to the university to be used as a guinea pig, you know, for trials or whatever. I do not want a funeral. I just want to be here one day and gone the next. Enjoy me while I'm here, but not when I'm gone. Really, to me it's false bullshit when we all say, "Oh, such a lovely person." Oh, crap! I was a bitch at times, I was this, I was that, sometimes I was nice; get over it. Everyone who dies is perfect.'

She shapes the various medications scattered across the table into a small pile for collection. Then she strides down the short hall into the bedroom, leaving Trent to clean the living room.

As the boss, Sandra is, variously, mother hen ('This guy had bled out quite badly and Lizzie sorta buckled under and cried. So I called her mum and said, "Give her a ring, she's feeling a bit stressed."'); bad cop ('Look. I'm three times your age. I need glasses to read and I can spot a cobbie at a thousand paces. And you've told me you've *done* the cobwebs? I don't think so.'); and hanging judge ('A new broom sweeps clean!'). Though she naturally inhabits the role of commander-in-chief, Sandra's disdain for administrative detail as well as her 'disease to please' have not always sat comfortably with the exigencies of managing staff.

From a human-resources perspective it can be said, historically, of the STC cleaning staff that there has been persistent tardiness, absenteeism and inefficiencies in the use of company property. There is a Himalayan attrition rate among the employees. Some are transient, others have made the error of mistaking Sandra's equitable manner for weakness. This has resulted specifically in a few incendiary dismissals, and generally in the decision to move the STC offices from a room in her small house to commercial premises in an effort to become 'more corporate and more disciplined'.

Integral to this shift in messaging was the hiring of Melissa as office coordinator. Though Sandra is dreadful at delegating, she knows she cannot expand her business without it. Further, assuming it is indeed more effective to be feared than loved, Melissa keeps Sandra at a certain remove from the employees who might otherwise take advantage of her good nature.

On the surface, trauma cleaning as a career may have a darkly attractive quirkiness, but in fact it is dirty, disturbing, back-breaking physical labour of transcendentally exhausting proportions. Take, for example, a story baby-faced Dylan once told me while carrying bags of rubbish from a hoarder's house to an enormous skip (thirty cubic metres, weight capacity of eight tonnes) Sandra had placed in the driveway.

'Up in the country,' he said—happy that day because it was his last before moving back home to New Zealand—'this boy broke up with his girlfriend and made a homemade shotgun and shot himself in his garage. It was forty-eight degrees outside, it'd been baking in the garage for, like, four days and it was like fifty-eight or sixty degrees inside. We were supposed to be wearing those white suits but it was that hot and I was like nah, boxers and a singlet. Eleven and a half hours to clean. He had his gun safe left open so we had to clean it out completely. His tool box was open, we had to clean every single tool, and—'

'—the roof,' Lizzie interjected, walking by with a heavy black bag in each hand.

'Yeah, the roof, we ended up just pulling half the roof off. Using scrapers and just pulling it out,' Dylan remembered.

The STC cleaners I observe at work are fairly upbeat on the job, both under and away from Sandra's hawk-eyed supervision. They tell me—with the euphemistic sloganeering of army recruitment—that they like the fact that 'every day is different' and are stimulated by the 'challenge'. But the reality is that at this level it is not work you choose as a vocation, nor is it work you stick with if you have better options to support yourself or your family.

I have observed among the various cohorts of STC cleaners: anger problems, reading problems, housing problems, Olympic smoking and a couple of people missing large tracts of teeth. Some of these workers have to budget so closely they can't afford to send an extra text message. Sandra confirms that her cleaners 'come from the School of Hard Knocks' and she prefers it this way. They're more compassionate on the jobs that are the bread and butter of a business in which every client 'has a problem of some sort'.

In 2015, after twenty years of running her business from home, Sandra moved the STC Services corporate headquarters to an office building in downtown Frankston. She took over one small office suite initially and then the one adjacent, knocking down a wall to expand. The resulting offices have no exterior windows, the ceiling is pitted, the heating doesn't work and the easiest entry is through a bleak carpark at the rear, but Sandra has renovated the space with her magic touch.

'I must say that I've got a very creative mind,' she told me once. 'I can see through things, or past things, or imagine things. I always had this thing that I want more out of life. I still have the belief that you're as powerful as your mind. An idea could come and if you think you could go with it, you take the gamble and go with it.' Sandra's happiest times are when she is embarking on one of these new projects—a new business venture, a new lease; a new car, beauty treatment, renovation. At these times she is buoyant with enthusiasm, seeing only infinite positive prospects in the embryo endeavour, which she then progresses obsessively and at grand prix velocity.

This could be no one else's office: it radiates the charisma of Pankhurst. Her corporate motto—*Excellence is no accident*—'hits your face as soon as you walk in'; it is painted in white curling script directly onto a cherry-red feature wall and decoratively framed in white. There are red feature walls throughout, with black and white accents: the STC 'corporate colours'. Symmetrical rows of ornate white frames showcase the professional and charitable achievements of employees past and present. There are mirrored tables with fanned brochures and flower arrangements and scented candles and when you walk from room to room, you do so on a freshly laid taupe carpet.

Sandra's personal office is off to one side of 'the boardroom'—an open space with a glass table that seats six. Next to her desk is a pristine glass sideboard set with flower vases and framed photos of

Lana and the new dog, a rescue called Moët Chandon. Also a bottle of Scotch and a set of glasses, should anyone require a fortifying drink. Though she operates largely out of her car and from job sites, the radio on her desk is always on, ready for her return.

Walking through the boardroom, you arrive at the training room where today Melissa is standing in front of a table laden with cleaning products, leading new STC recruits through their first training session in an authoritative and slightly nasal monotone. She has written the agenda on the whiteboard behind her:

- Time management— Working together
- Cloth's—washing + drying, colour order
- Caddies
- Uniform—what is right uniform?, footwear, tattoos
- Sick days—How much notice is needed
- Mobile phones
- Disciplinary action
- Turning up for work on time

The audience, five men and five women divided informally but rigorously by gender, as at a high school dance, sit on cherry-red chairs. Anglo–Australian to a person, they wear work boots or sneakers and, like Melissa, sunglasses propped up on top of their heads. The men range in age from mid-thirties to late fifties, and though some have more facial hair and others have fewer teeth, they look like brothers in the sense that they are all the same type of man: white, reserved, sun-leathered, too thin. The women range in age as well, although more towards the younger end of the spectrum. On the floor are various plastic caddies—yellow or red according to whether they are intended to service kitchen or bathroom—filled with cleaning products.

A 'mental health nurse by trade', Melissa was the underpaid coordinator of the cleaning business downstairs until she defected upstairs to the greener pastures of STC. When she speaks to the room it is with the voice—strained but resolved—of someone with an unshakeable work ethic who is not comfortable with public speaking. You can hear the words of Sandra, who has instructed her to crack the whip.

'Time. Why are we having problems with time? One at a time, put your hand up,' Melissa asks.

'Lack of communication,' someone offers.

'What else?' Melissa asks.

'Organisation,' someone else calls out.

'Spot on,' Melissa says. 'That is the only reason we are having problems. The only way you are going to meet timeframes is to work together as a team. At the moment I'm hearing a lot of feedback. This person is not doing this and this person is struggling doing this, but you know what? I don't want to hear it. It's about teamwork, guys. If you can't do it, we might as well close the door now. It's harsh, but do you understand where I'm coming from?'

'Yes,' a morose chorus.

Though her voice thins out sometimes, self-conscious, Melissa's style of Socratic questioning appears to be having an effect.

She pauses, her mouth set in a straight line. 'Some jobs, you may come up against a tricky situation. If you feel it's going to take an hour longer, don't ring us when you're due to walk out the door. Call us when you do your walk-through. Are there any other questions on the timeframes? If youse've got questions, now's the time for youse to fire them at me.'

One employee raises his hand. 'Just that sort of job that we did, that putrid job, where it was squidging right out the back door. That was hard because we had the client changing her mind all through it...'

'In situations like that, the chances are that the client has been billed with extra,' Melissa answers before moving on. 'Does anyone know what a rectification is?' Silence. 'A rectification is when I get a phone call, and the client goes, "Look, everything else with the clean was great, bar this particular area." Now, we offer a hundred per cent satisfaction guaranteed. If the client is not happy, we go back and we fix it. Now if we go back and we fix it, you still get paid for it, but who does it cost?'

'The company, I suppose,' one of the men answers.

'As of today, that is not what happens,' Melissa says.

'We've got to go back and fix it for free,' someone says.

'Yes,' Melissa confirms, slowly looking around the room. 'Those who don't know me, I can be really cutthroat. Really cutthroat.' She raises her eyebrows and nods solemnly. Moving on. The cloths. There ensues a discussion about how they should be kept (sixty per bag inside of which lies another bag, differentiated by colour, for the 'dirties'), folded ('nicely'), stacked ('Neat and presented. If I go out to a job and they are not like that? By jeez, look out!') and washed. The last topic opens up a lively debate. The cleaners have been encouraged to take their cloths home and launder them to bring to their next job.

'We live in a boarding house,' one of the men says. 'And our friends are jacking up about putting these things through the washing machine, which I did not blame them at all...'

'I don't blame them, either, especially if it's somethin' real dirty,' another agrees.

'I've been going to the laundromat,' says another.

'So, whose responsibility should it be for the cloths?' Melissa breaks in.

'Yours,' says one of the men.

'Really?' Melissa asks, blinking at him.

'Yes,' he replies. 'To make sure we've got clean cloths to work with. If we have to go to the laundromat in our own time and wash 'em...'

'Well, if you are washing them in your own time, at home and what not, fill it in your timesheet,' Melissa tells him. 'Now what happens when they come to my place? I put them in the washing machine. I put them in the tumble dryer. And while I'm sitting watching *Home and Away*, looking after my kids, I start folding cloths and get 'em ready for the next day. Now I do that in my time. Why do I do it in my time?'

'Because you can,' one of the men replies.

'Well, no, I've got kids. I have three children,' Melissa says evenly, staring back at him. 'It's because I want to see the company grow, OK? I'm more than happy to take them to my place, literally to boost the company. So if you don't want to wash them and put them in the dryer, drop them off at my place. Create more work and drop them off at my place, OK?'

'I can't afford to pay for them no more,' one of the men says.

'Let's work on my place at the moment,' Melissa says. 'I'll speak to Sandra and come up with another scenario, even if we have to get a washing machine and dryer and put it somewhere.'

Silence.

'We do care,' she says, looking around. 'I think you all know that Sandra takes care of you as best she can.' And then, referring to her old boss: 'You can always go downstairs and work for that mongrel.' She walks back to the whiteboard.

- ~~Cloth's.~~

'Sick days: obviously because you are employed on a casual basis, you don't get paid for it, OK. However, if you are going to call in sick, I don't care if you text at one o'clock in the morning, but please try not to text us at six-fifteen. Sandra has always got her phone next to her because she is on comms with the trauma,' she says, referring to the government unit that coordinates responses to homicides around the clock.

Next item: 'Mobile phones. I know some of you have pre-paids and it's hard, but when you get your text of a night to say what time you've got to start work, just send a reply, "Received" or a thumbs-up,' she says. 'There must be at least one person on every job who has a phone. If I need to get hold of you, I need to get hold of you. With the work that you do, we want to check to see that nothing has happened. So that covers that. Now the big one. Caddies.'

She reaches towards a red plastic caddy on the table behind her. 'The caddies have come back atrocious and it's not good enough. Nozzles should be faced out and closed off.' She peers into the caddy and plucks out a spray bottle. 'No!' she says triumphantly, finding the nozzle open. 'Why do we close nozzles off?' she asks the room.

'So they don't leak,' someone replies.

Melissa nods. 'Everything we do makes sense. What do we need in the caddies? Let me tell you what we need in the caddies...' She then whips through the core cleaning products, many of which bear the fey names of cartoon ponies.

'Glitz. What is Glitz?' Melissa asks.

'It's got to be multipurpose, wouldn't it?' Leigh replies.

Melissa nods in confirmation. 'It's awesome stuff. Just don't get it in your eyes because it burns. What's it for?'

'To remove the mould around showers, build-ups underneath the shower screens,' someone calls out.

Nodding her approval, Melissa selects a bottle of bubblegum-pink liquid. 'Speed. What is Speed?' she asks.

'Mainly for grease, mainly for kitchens, tiles and oven tops,' another responds.

'Would you call it an all-purpose?' Melissa tests.

'No, not really,' he replies.

'It *is* a multipurpose, all right? In every kitchen caddy we must have Speed.' Melissa then plucks a small yellow bottle with a green lid from the caddy. 'I love this stuff. It's my favourite chemical in a caddy. Jiff. It's incredible, there are millions of uses. You can use it on walls, it's great for making the property smell nice.' She briefly holds up another bottle. 'You've got your Exit Mould, unfortunately overrated.' She returns to the Jiff, cradling it in one hand while patting its green lid with the other, her square acrylics catching the light. 'I want you to go back to basics, all right? I used this in a squalor clean the other week. My God, the joint smelled amazing. Correct usage of Jiff?' Without waiting for an answer, she grabs a plastic bucket from one of the caddies and elaborately squirts the bottle into it. 'That's it! To a full bucket of water—or three quarters.'

Then she stops and calls for questions.

'We've gone through a spate of really bad cockroaches,' Rodney starts. 'It doesn't matter how hard you clean, you're going to end up with cockroaches straight back into the mop buckets and everything. I've tried bombing them beforehand, I've sprayed and the cockroaches just stay.'

'The thing with cockroaches, and when we do bedbugs...' another employee joins in.

Raising her voice to be heard and directing her answer to Rodney, Melissa answers, 'Yes, the same as when we get fly faeces. Look, it'll sound rude but once we do a job, and the client gives us the OK, it's no longer your problem.'

'Yes,' Rodney replies, 'but when you get thousands of them, though...it's getting to the point where you cannot work comfortably...There are nests above your head and they're fallin' on you...'

'We might look at getting it sprayed before you go in,' Melissa replies, gathering up some plastic implements from the caddy. 'Squeegees for the shower, spatula, there's to be two scourers per caddy...'

With its bare walls and empty shelves, Gordon's house has less personality than a cheap motel room. There are no sheets on the double bed, cratered in the middle from the weight of its owner. Stuffing spills out from a duvet with no cover; its fabric, like the pillows nearby, is a strange, urinous colour.

'Was this white or tan?' I ask.

'They don't make that shade of tan,' Sandra says archly as she pulls out a drawer in one of the bedside tables. It is lined with a single crisp sheet of newspaper dated 6 November 1995, on which rests one bar of yellow soap, an empty velvet jewellery purse and an Estée Lauder Pleasures fragrance sample. A headline on the newspaper identifies Yitzhak Rabin's assassin. Used towels and wrinkled clothes and books are strewn over the bed. *Isis Magic: Cultivating a Relationship with the Goddess of 10,000 Names, Kabbala, Enochian Magick*. There's an empty chocolate-milk carton on the floor.

Under the bedroom window, on a sideboard covered in dust, stands a small Egyptian-style statue of a woman with the head of a bird. The broken wings of a similar statue lie nearby on the carpet. The body is nowhere to be seen but the feet stand on the sideboard, tiny and absurd, like a poor man's Ozymandias. The drawers in the sideboard are empty except for the bottom drawer, where Sandra finds a collection of cards: tarot cards, cards with Hebrew text, cards with saints and religious scenes, cards with prayers. One depicts the Angelus, another St Peter. One has a prayer for motorists.

The open shelves built into the wall across from the bed are bare, save for some carefully rolled bath towels and a large Esky. Similarly the closet is sparsely and randomly populated with shirts, two suitcases and a barbeque in a box. On the otherwise empty upper shelf is a squat pile of books: *Painting Birds, Wildlife Painting*, a field guide to birds of the region. Sandra finds a plastic bag stuffed with birthday cards. Christmas cards from Gordon's mother. Father's Day cards, one for every year going back at least a decade, from Gordon's son.

Of course everyone is somebody to someone. But it is hard to reconcile the accumulated mouse shit and cigarette butts with the son and father so steadfastly honoured in these many cards with their painstaking rainbow-coloured letters. As the years they inscribed in the top left corner ticked by, did his family actually know this man? Or were they—through his choice or theirs, through circumstances too large to circumvent—merely close strangers, like the passengers he picked up?

Trent calls out to Sandra from the living room. Smiling, he hands her a roll of five hundred dollars in cash that he found stashed under a couch pillow. Sandra thanks him without ceremony and places the money with the other personal effects she will turn over to the landlord.

It doesn't feel like anyone died here because it doesn't feel like anyone lived here. It is hard to talk about the presence and distribution of 'vibes' in these small rooms without sounding like someone I am not. But something I have learnt in my time with Sandra is that, yes, spaces—like people—have voices.

I stand here, and listen to what Gordon's house is saying in its vocabulary of ash and crumbs. It is that the true form of this house is not its apparent form. The lawn and the bathroom and the laundry room do not exist. The kitchen table and chairs do not exist. The bedside tables, sideboard, closet, washing machine: none of these exist. In this house, there is really only a triangle consisting of couch, pantry and bed. This internal geometry delineates the physical space essential for rest and sustenance, and oblivion through sleep or smoke or food or alcohol or undifferentiated visual traffic on TV. That space, however, was not sufficiently important to warrant the traditional separation of purposes: the carpet is a toilet and an ashtray and a trash can. The couch is a grave.

I flip through Gordon's field guide and his wildlife painting books, wondering about the secret history of the pristine brushes and paper lying in his kitchen drawer. Gordon is no firebird. He neither burns brightly nor rises up from the ashes coating his carpets.

I cannot get a clear sense of him. But I do know that for a time a man lived here who sought something in spells and in symbols. I know that Sandra is here instead of someone closer to him and that—because he was both a son and a parent—this would probably make him both sad and happy. I hear the silence between these walls that weighed on him before he died and while the life dripped out of him and after it was gone. It must take years to master the ability to paint a bird in flight, the angle of wing in air, the rise of muscle under feather. But you could practise for a lifetime and never capture the stillness it leaves behind.

# 8

In June 1980, Sandra strode through the grand complex of the Queen Victoria Hospital, her palms electric with excitement. In those days, the Queen Vic was on the north side of Lonsdale Street. It had been, since the late 1960s, Monash University's teaching hospital for obstetrics, gynaecology and paediatrics.

The plastic surgery department initially comprised a senior plastic surgeon, Lena McEwan, and a young assistant plastic surgeon, Simon Ceber. At first, the clinic's work consisted mainly of correcting cleft lips and other congenital abnormalities, including hand and genital abnormalities. In 1976, however, the surgeons were approached by Professor William Walters about a patient requiring a type of surgery not routinely performed in Australia. After corresponding with Professor Shan Ratnam in Singapore (who had, at that time, five years of experience in sex reassignment surgery) and reading the literature he suggested, the two surgeons 'decided to go ahead and do one'. The surgery was successful.

'So that's how I got into it,' explains Dr Ceber. 'Having done one, Walters had another one within a few months. Word got around that we were providing this service.'

It wasn't that this surgery had never been performed before in Australia—there had been 'eight or nine cases' in Melbourne. Rather, it had been performed extremely rarely and somewhat covertly. There was word that a small group in Sydney was performing operations, that a surgeon at St Vincent's Hospital had been treating transsexual patients for a number of years, and rumour had it that over at the Royal Melbourne Hospital there was a surgeon who would operate on a Sunday morning in a locked theatre and transfer the patient to Mont Park mental hospital for clandestine post-operative care. In other words, these surgeons were as brave as their patients. By 1977, an interdisciplinary committee had been formally established at the Queen Vic to supervise the assessment and management of patients seeking sex reassignment surgery. By 1982, they had successfully treated about eighty-five patients.

Though she has no recollection of him, Dr Ceber—Sandra's surgeon—is a meticulous and soft-spoken man whose grey-bearded face rests in a reserved smile. He carries within him almost the entire history of this branch of medicine: it barely existed when the weight of performing it for a significant portion of the Australian population was placed on his shoulders. 'Initially I was just part of the team. It was exciting, challenging surgery because it was different. Later, there was no one else doing it. If I stopped, the whole clinic failed. So, that kept me going for thirty years.'

Was there anything that united the patients he treated over his career? 'An obsessionalism about wanting to get their surgery,' he says. 'I think that's what impressed me the most. The older ones, with professions and kids and wives, sacrificed a lot. Yet to them it was worthwhile. Transsexualism is not a choice.'

When I ask him how this work was perceived by the broader community of surgeons at the time, he hesitates for a beat before saying, 'It was looked down on. They looked at you as if you were doing something terribly immoral.'

There were successes; but mostly Sandra remembers that they came back from Cairo like the walking dead: maimed, burnt, scarred, 'drug fucked'. Even with the flights and the hotels, going overseas for the operation was cheaper: 'You'd just whore it for a week or two and you could go to Cairo.' And the process at the clinic there was shorter and simpler—no waiting period, unlike Melbourne, where the doctors wanted you to live full-time in your gender identity for two years before surgery. But she had seen women who expected to come home exalting in their new bodies returning instead with stories of being burnt by faulty lighting or cut open in outdoor sheds. Sandra worked and saved unrelentingly for the right to walk into—or, more accurately, out of—the elegant building on Lonsdale Street: to have her surgery and recover in safety.

When she first inquired about the procedure she was told unequivocally that even the most straightforward cases take a minimum of two years to complete. She wanted it done yesterday but she still played the game, showing up early to her first appointment with the psychiatrist, smiling and overdressed. She had already had the feminising rhinoplasty and an eye lift; was not in possession of any obviously male facial features that could cause 'incongruencies' after her surgery, making it more difficult to integrate socially as a woman. She had breasts and soft hips, and moved with casual grace in her own skin.

'I know this operation is a new sorta thing,' she had told the psychiatrist as she settled onto his couch, casually crossing her legs and placing her handbag by her ankle, 'and not many have been done. I reckon that's about right, when you think about it, 'cause it should be saved for those who are *absolutely certain* that they need it. Well, doctor, what would you like to know?'

Eleven months later she was on the operating table.

Though the sex work she does and the drugs she takes and her overriding need for constant company frequently mean that she is not in control of herself or her environment, she is excellent at acting otherwise to conceal any vulnerability. So she does not cry in public and, while she might comment in the same tone as one comments on traffic that she is experiencing pain or discomfort, and though of course, she feels pain deeply, she never actually shows it or makes any practical adjustments to accommodate it. She is supposed to stay in her hospital bed for a week following her surgery, but after a few days she gets restless.

'Cuppa tea? Cuppa coffee? What would you like, darl?' she asks, leaning down and smiling into the faces of the other patients. Seeing that the nurses are run off their feet, she figures she may as well help with breakfast. Later that morning, bored, she asks one of the nurses if she might be able to go for a little walk? Thinking that she means to stay on the ward, the woman gives Sandra a brief nod of approval. She does not see Sandra put on lipstick or hitch her catheter up underneath the belt of her good kaftan dress; no one is at the front desk when Sandra walks into the lift.

Crossing the road towards the religious shops selling rosaries and bibles, Sandra is feeling slightly woozy but grateful for the fresh air when she catches a glimpse of a woman, tall and slim and blonde, reflected in the mirrored wall between two shops. She automatically appraises the stranger for a moment, enviously thinking, 'She looks lovely,' before realising that she is looking at her own reflection. 'It is fucking ME!' she says to herself, marvelling, incredulous.

She will forget the details of her surgery, boiling it down to its vaguely constituent steps. 'First they remove everything and then insert it all and they had bolts inside you to realign your stomach, which was pretty painful. Then you go back and have the bolts taken out.' She will, within the next three years, forget the year of this surgery. She will forget the names of her doctors and where she recovered and how long it took. But this moment—when she knows, not simply that she has done the right thing, but that she has been righted—will live forever, undiminished. There is harmony, correction, congruency; physically and mentally everything is finally in its place. This is the first time she sees herself, truly, as a woman and she will forever describe it as the happiest time in her life. Exuberant, she goes shopping to celebrate.

She buys chocolates and flowers for the nurses, new clothes to wear home and new records to play when she gets there. Checking her watch, she decides to head back to the hospital so she retraces her steps through the city. She grows impatient waiting for the lift, takes the stairs instead and enters the ward with her shopping bags, singing out her return to the nurses at the front station. They immediately go ballistic. She is suddenly surrounded by people and doctors come running, as though it was the emergency room, to check whether she is bleeding, whether she's ripped her stitches. She is ordered to stay in her bed and lectured about how she has recklessly risked everything that has just been done for her. But she feels fantastic. 'It was me. It was fucking me!' she thinks from her bed, replaying that moment in the mirror over and over and over.

It takes a while before it hits: a pain she is at first unwilling and then unable to describe. It gets worse and worse until eventually all she can manage is a whispered '*Pain...pain...*' The nurse on duty gets a doctor. He's heard about this one, and takes his time sauntering over. Due to her earlier robust display and the fact that she is a transgender sex worker, he thinks she is trying to scam extra drugs. And despite the fact that the pain is so intense that she cannot speak properly, her anger raises her momentarily aloft. 'You think I'm here...for *drugs*? If I...want drugs, I can buy drugs on the fucking... street. How *dare*...you...think I'm going through this for...' But the doctor only closes his notes and walks away.

Time stops under the weight of this stabbing pain radiating from her guts. There is only the endless dark beyond the high windows and the insectile buzz of the fluorescent lights boring into her temple. At some point in the night, she crawls out of bed and over to the nearest window where she claws at the pane. If she had the strength to lift it open she would throw herself out; hurl this body where the bad is devouring the good out onto a bed of air and nothingness. This is where a nurse finds her, sobbing, resting her burning cheek against the cool glass. The nurse has her carried back to bed, examines her chart and orders an enema that resolves the problem entirely.

When Sandra is discharged, finally, she says to this nurse, 'I don't know how I can ever thank you.'

'Just don't show up here in three months,' the woman replies with a tight nod, referring to the high rate of suicide attempts among Sandra's peers. Sandra dutifully keeps her two-month follow-up appointment with Dr Ceber. But she never returns after that, despite the need for at least a year of aftercare.

She lives on her small savings while she recovers, growing bored and increasingly nervous about her seeming stasis and financial insecurity. She rolls joints and drinks tea and re-reads the same magazines while the rain beats down on the roof. Unable to use her body, at least for a while, she obsesses about finding new ways of making income.

'I just need the rent paid. It's like a cooperative, really, but I hold the reins. I only take ten dollars from every job, no matter what it is. What you do is your concern,' she tells the new girl briskly. Then she stands up from the couch with some trouble and slowly shows her through the small house on Buckley Street in Footscray, where she has just taken over the lease. 'Clean towels from here, dirty towels go there. If you're between clients, hanging out in the girls' room, just give a knock after a half hour's up. That's how we let each other know.' Through the front window, she sees the cops pull up outside and excuses herself for a moment to let them in. They stand in the front hall for a few minutes where she jokes with them, has them laughing, slips them their cash, sees them off. Everything has run smoothly here, apart from that night when she lost her cool with one of the girls who was carrying on like a fucking banshee about something or other. Sandra picked up a bottle and threw it at her. 'Just missed the TV by a bee's dick! Would've smashed the TV to fucking pieces,' she explained to the heads that popped out of the rooms at the sound of glass shattering against the wall.

She opens a small bric-a-brac shop in North Melbourne with her friend Robyn. The rent is only twenty dollars a week and she loves scouring estate sales and garage sales, loves tweaking the displays in the window, loves the process of turning nothing into something. But as soon as her body feels ready, she grabs the chance to make some real money. By October 1980, four months after her surgery, she passes the brothel on to one of the girls, hands the shop over to Robyn and heads for Kalgoorlie.

Sandra does not remember how she heard about Hay Street and the money to be made out west. But Kalgoorlie, six hundred lonely kilometres inland of Perth—itself one of the most isolated cities in the world—has been a frontier gold-mining town since 1893. Its brothels have long been part of popular lore, and it is also likely that Sandra would have encountered women in the Melbourne brothels where she had worked, going to or returning from their 'tour of duty' in the goldfields.

In 1980, Kalgoorlie was still the Wild West. Still very much that frontier town of miners and prostitutes, people arriving for the gold, working long hours on short-term contracts and divided by gender, with the attendant drinking and fighting and fucking. Whether you drove or took the train or flew in direct from 'the eastern states' (a phrase which still carries an air of cultural divide if not outright suspicion) your overriding impression on arrival would have been one of dust and tin, of heat, impermanence and remoteness.

While prostitution itself was not illegal in Western Australia, most prostitution-related activities, such as soliciting or brothel-keeping, were. But for nearly one hundred years the Kalgoorlie police pursued an unwritten but immutable practice of selective policing known as the Containment Policy, which 'grant[ed] criminal immunity to a limited number of brothels, in order to "contain" the activity and enforce unofficial restrictions on the businesses and the work force'.[5]

The tin brothels of Hay Street became a major tourist attraction for both paying customers and voyeuristic visitors. By concentrating prostitution in one place, Containment had made Hay Street—and Kalgoorlie—infamous. Sandra, when she arrived, was not aware of the policy, but she came to know its terms intimately. They structured her life for a year and a half.

When she first gets there, she goes straight to the police station to register. Name, address, age, marital status. Photograph. They tell her the rules: prostitutes must reside on brothel premises and submit to weekly medical examinations; they are prohibited from visiting the town's pubs, cinemas and swimming pool. They warn her that if she breaks these rules, she will be out on the next plane or train. Then the madam of her new house, whom she spoke to before leaving Melbourne, takes her on a tour of the town. Sitting in the hot car, Sandra listens while the madam explains the hours, curfew, job prices, payment protocol and the requirement to keep her doctor's book up to date; also the house rules, which culminate in the admonition that should she fuck a black man, she will be thrown out.

Sandra's house, like all the brothels on Hay Street, is a low-slung corrugated-iron shed. There are individual bedrooms for the girls, all in a row, and a communal lounge room and dining area. Each bedroom has two doors: one opens back into the house and the other opens onto a long outdoor corridor running across the front of the house. Directly across the corridor from each of these front-facing doors is a second, open doorway which looks out onto Hay Street. She is expected to have her tea and be sitting in this doorway by 6 p.m. each day. There, under the lights, is where she will solicit clients while being gawked at by the tourists and townspeople who drive slowly past.

Taking her suitcase out of the car, Sandra asks the madam about the thick wire over the windows and light bulbs. The madam explains that the miners are paid fortnightly: every second week, there is no money in the town.

'They want it but they can't pay for it, so they get drunk and come up and raise a riot,' she explains. 'If something like that happens, you just lock the doors, love, and they can't get in.'

She assigns Sandra to the first room. Number one. The room number corresponds to a number on the row of mailboxes lining the common area. In her mailbox Sandra will deposit, after a brief discussion with each client, the up-front payment. The madam will collect the night's earnings from her mailbox each morning, tally it up, take half and return the remainder to Sandra. But sometimes Sandra will be groggily cleaning up her room and a hundred-dollar bill will unfurl from beneath an overflowing ashtray like a creature disturbed under a log. Another hundred might be shaken out from, say, the folds of her sheets as she strips her bed or plucked from between the empty bottles covering her bedside table like a stand of trees. These are the bills that maybe she doesn't place in her mailbox.

The doctor, officially the obstetrician to the town's married women, also visits Hay Street every week. In each brothel, the madams set aside a room for examinations. There he swabs for the common local sexually transmitted infections. Once a month, he takes blood to test for syphilis and hepatitis B and C. While many of the women are hepatitis B positive, and there is 'a bit of chlamydia, a bit of gonorrhoea', the overall rates are not high in the early 1980s, despite the fact that 'practically no one used condoms'.

Many of the women get in to get out. These women work in Hay Street for four to six weeks straight before leaving Kalgoorlie with enough money to pay for their housing or education, or a trip or a car. Some madams make employees who stay longer take a week off every three months so they don't burn out. Some women take a few days off when they are menstruating; others just insert a sea sponge and keep working. Like them, Sandra is there to make money. She becomes one of the top earners. She makes a lot of money. 'A *lot*.'

She glistens in the doorway like something edible, narrows her eyes against the glare of late sun. She lives in the time before. When she has showered, long and hot despite the heat, while airing out her room. When she has washed her sheets, hung them to dry too fast in the stabbing sun and smoothed them back on her bed. When she has nested the pillows back in their places, given them one quick karate chop to make them sit just so. Cracked a joint. Chatted with the other girls. Regaled them in a whisper about how—despite the fact that her mailbox had been particularly full that morning, to the delight of the madam—she discovered yet another hundred dollars on the sink in her bathroom.

'Huh!' she marvels theatrically. 'So I go to myself, "Fuck, what'd I do last night? If nothing else, I'm a good slut."' When they have chuckled and drunk from the bottles she buys for the house. When she has set her hair. Glued a nail. And finally, when she has angled a folding chair just so in the doorway, to enjoy the gentle warmth before it fades to a feeling barely remembered.

She shares with the other girls what she's been taught. To put a towel down on the bed. To slide across the bed, melting into 'the goddess look'. To say, 'Put your arm around me and kiss me.' To heat a glob of Vaseline in one hand while the customer is thus distracted, then to throw a leg up near your head and reach that hand around the outside of the thigh and underneath, placing the lubricated fist in front of your crotch. 'I have this thing that I don't actually have sex with them,' she says. 'If you get the position of your arm right, and warm up the Vaseline right, they'll *fuck your hand*! I'll say, "Just kiss me a bit more," (not that I want to, but to distract them) and they'll get off like a rocket. Bang bang bang. Straight onto a blanket, you do the actress bit and then off you go. So I never really have sex. It's quite ingenious really. That's how I make my money.' To assist her in this, she pops a lot of pills. This she also shares with the girls: 'Mandies make you randy, make you root like a fucking viper and be making a lot of money.'

But she also makes her money by looking like she has already made it. Each small room comes furnished with a double bed, a locking wardrobe, a dressing table with mirror, a bedside table and a washstand where the women wash the client while inspecting them for signs of infection before getting started. During her free time, Sandra cruises the secondhand shops in town and buys furniture. In her tiny room she sets up a wall unit and a free-standing bar stocked with liquor; she brings in a lamp, a rug, coordinated bedding, soft music. There, in that tin shack on the edge of a great desert, she transfigures an oasis into being.

She steps back to check that the wine-red curtain is hanging straight and one of the younger girls stops in the hallway to gaze in.

'It looks like a luxury to come into my room,' Sandra explains. 'I always make out like I'm very wealthy and well to do because it creates an illusion around me.' What she does not say, because she has not realised it yet, is that the more she makes, the more she spends because the more miserable she is, really. Furniture, gifts, clothes, accessories, booze, drugs. She came here with the specific intention to make money and she is unrelenting about it, but unlike some of the other women who get in to get out, she is one of the girls who parties. It drains her savings, but on the other hand she remembers those pilled-out nights as 'fun times, to say the least'. It is not quite a house, this long, low shack with its tin walls radiating heat in the summer sun. But it is home for a time.

No one is sure how the rumour starts, but word gets around that there is a drag queen working on Hay Street. Drunk, laughing, enraged, the men have resolved to hunt him down—a preoccupation that survives when the alcohol wears off and renews itself in the pubs where they gather, reeking of cigarettes and beer and fried food and sweat. They are saying that the bloke is in the first room of the first house. The fearful vigilance Sandra carries just beneath her skin like shrapnel twists inside her now. She is tall, huge-breasted, she has large hands. But so does the Swedish girl in the room a few doors down who is taller, bustier, larger.

'You know what we'll do?' She smiles, this beautiful woman Sandra will always be grateful to, but whose name she will forget. 'We'll swap rooms.'

From the girl's sparsely furnished room nearby, Sandra strains to hear what's being said as the men walk up the veranda and through the door of room number one.

'Gentlemen?' the woman greets them.

'We reckon you're a bloke,' the spokesman says menacingly.

Later the woman will tell Sandra how she responded. How she opened her robe so that she was perfectly naked. How she leaned back on her elbows and splayed her legs. 'Do I look like a bloke?' she asks evenly. 'Do I fuck like a bloke?' She addresses this question directly at one of the men.

'No,' comes the muttered reply.

'Well. You best get word round town that you're dreamin',' she says lightly.

Down the hall, in the room that feels like a cage, Sandra's heart is racing as the men clear out. If someone told her then that eighteen years later this town would elect a transgender former prostitute and brothel madam as a local council member she would have died laughing.

She flies back to Melbourne and the memory of Maria to testify against Phillip John Keen. Back also to the doctor who refills her prescriptions for hormones and for drugs. Back back back.

There were two reports in the *Age* on the coronial inquest into Maria's death. The first, 28 February 1980, described evidence that '[a] bouncer at a disco jumped on the stomach of a pregnant girl before she died...Maria Gloria Paten gave an awful scream and moaned before the bouncer dragged her outside'. The coronial court was also told that 'Miss Paten was dressed as a male at the time' and heard evidence from Miss Amanda Celeste Claire 'who described herself as a trans-sexual and Miss Paten's lover'.

One month later, the 'pregnant girl' had become 'a 19-year-old woman' who incidentally happened to be 'three months pregnant at the time'. This article shows how, in committing Mr Keen for trial on a charge of manslaughter, the Coroner laid a good deal of blame on the small shoulders of the victim: 'Mr Griffiths said Miss Paten had provoked Keen...but that his actions in refusing to re-admit her to the disco on June 26 last year had "overstepped the mark".' The Coroner said: 'I have no doubt that the deceased provoked Mr Keen into doing what he in fact did, that is when she was on the floor, he jumped on her, landing knee first on her stomach area.'

It would be twenty-five years before the Victorian legislature recognised this language for what it was and repealed the defence of provocation on the grounds that it predominantly operated to excuse male violence towards women.

Sandra gives her evidence, reliving that night on the stand, and afterwards she drinks alone and takes her pills and sleeps with the television on in a shitty motel at the edge of the city. Then she catches a plane back west where she sits still for five hours straight, grey as a dead tooth.

Sandra remembers how Keen responded to the suggestion that his attack on Maria was racially motivated by offering his Asian fiancée as proof that he wasn't a racist. But she has forgotten whether he was found guilty of the crime. She thinks he went to jail; can't say for sure. The court file on the matter contains only the charges and various adjournment orders. I wonder whether Sandra's uncertainty is proof that, in the end, retribution is irrelevant. Or whether it just shows how good she is at escaping.

She leaves the first brothel to go work for another Hay Street madam who made her a good offer. One day she wanders into the shared kitchen and opens a cupboard. Sorts through its contents, throws out expired packages and cans, arranges others according to size and shape. Inspired, she moves on to the fridge. Then the pots, the pans, the cutlery. She goes shopping for food. From her own pocket, she starts cooking meals for the house.

'You've got a flair for this,' the madam comments appreciatively. 'You make *a home* for them.' Looking to retire and move to the suburbs of Perth, the madam asks Sandra if she would be interested in taking over the business. Sandra is flattered by the show of confidence but declines.

'I sorta really don't want to make a life career out of this, you know,' she replies. 'It isn't really what I want to do long term.' And by the time Sandra leaves Kalgoorlie, they are—perhaps strangely—very good friends.

Sandra left Kalgoorlie but where did she go? In the fathomless cosmos of her twenties and thirties, dates and places float completely free of each other. The name of the Swedish girl is lost. The names of the madams are lost. The names of the brothels, the precise length of time in Kalgoorlie, all lost. I scrap draft after draft of my timeline and even when I am assisted in my task by Sandra's recollection, the narrative remains a tangled necklace. Events link into one another only so far before they halt, abruptly, at some great knot where they loop over each other so tightly that some seem to disappear altogether. Still, I pinch at it and pick at it, seeking slack, until, sometimes, it loosens and a line—a dented, mangled line—spreads out.

It is most likely that sometime in 1982 Sandra took what she had managed to save and bought a ticket to Sydney, perhaps on a tip from the madam or one of the other girls. There, she worked for a few months at a brothel in Lidcombe because that is where she met Rick, a client who kept coming back just to visit her and, soon, to take her out. Rick, who looked like Clint Eastwood and whom she called Clit Eastwood. Rick, for whom she went to sleep wearing make-up and for whom she woke up early to reapply it. Rick, who told her he would've married her if it weren't for this 'mental problem' he had with 'the whole gender thing'. Rick, who was never faithful to her and who lived off her like a gut worm for years and called her 'Frank' behind her back.

But Rick keeps coming back and for that she is willing to pretend it doesn't hurt so much. She is excellent at patting this pain down, blending it into the landscape the way she contours her foundation. They make plans to move to Melbourne together.

Despite all her hard work, her savings are drained by the money she spends on drink and drugs, on partying, on the people around her and on Rick. When she moves back to Melbourne she returns with nothing, to nothing; she discovers that Robyn has ripped her off, selling the furniture she left in her care as well as everything in their secondhand shop. Sandra never even knew she was a junkie. She has to start over again, sleep on floors again, work long shifts again at the brothels to save enough to make things comfortable for Rick when, eventually, he joins her.

The line between who she once was and who she is now is concrete, but it is also porous. She gets dressed up one evening and drives back to Barkly Street, Footscray with a friend to play bingo, have a few drinks. Does she return to her old neighbourhood that night out of pride? As a claim of right? Perhaps it is a test, a personal challenge. Or it could just be hard loneliness, that type of desperation that makes one accept the stab wound of familiarity as a substitute for true connection.

Her friend Kat, chain-smoking rollies held between thumb and index finger, reminds her of Maria; dresses and acts like Maria. Adrenaline shooting down her arms, Sandra steers past the darkened Sims grocery store where she still expects to see her mother walking out with flour and sugar, past the post office and the barber shop and the floors she used to sweep while the men smoked and laughed at her for being such a little poof. She parks and gets out of the drivers seat, hoping and dreading that she will see a familiar face. But even if she does run into someone, she will be protected by her make-up and her hair, her clothes, and her body. Like the time her cousin walked into the brothel. Looked right at her before he chose another girl. Didn't even recognise her.

'You'll never guess who's here,' Colleen hisses urgently into the phone near the bar.

'Can't hear you!' Linda yells, standing in her kitchen. Between the noise of her brothers drinking at the table and the kids playing footy inside and the roar of the pub behind her sister on the other end of the line, it is impossible to hear what Colleen is saying. 'Hush, will you? It's Colleen,' she yells at the boys.

'Peter's here!' Colleen says, louder now. 'Dressed like a woman again! But I recognised him! The bingo down near Barkly Street!'

Linda herds both boys outside to play. Closing the back door, she explains hurriedly to her brothers as she runs into the bedroom to change her clothes, 'Pete's down at the pub near Barkly Street. I'm going, you've gotta go home.' The large men exchange looks. They slowly finish their ciggies, drawing down to the filters. They leave their beer cans on the table and shuffle outside to jump on their motorbikes. Too pregnant now, at eight months, to catch a ride, Linda jogs over to borrow the neighbour's car.

She scans the crowd for the blondest head. Walks over and stands at the end of the table and sees, almost, like words erased from a blackboard, her Pete chatting with 'a girl that looked like a guy'. Sandra looks up with a polite smile that shatters into shards. 'Linda!' she says too brightly over her heart beating so hummingbird fast it feels still. She turns and strains to explain casually to Kat, 'Just going to catch up with an old friend, love.'

They sit on the steps for close to an hour as people push by to get to the toilets. Linda explains about her new man, how he is good to her and to the kids, though he doesn't live with them. How Ailsa stopped speaking to her once she got pregnant. About the boys, how big they are now, how they're doing at school, the way they remind her so much of their father. Maintaining eye contact, like a bird seeking land, she tells it all to Pete, but Pete is not there.

'Hmmm,' Sandra says. And also, 'Really?' And then, oddly, 'I don't like men anymore.'

Linda nods at the words, too perplexed at first to feel a sting. Wonders whether that means he's a lesbian now. Sandra stands suddenly and says that it's been nice, really. Bingo is long over, and the pub is closing up. Sandra finds Kat's familiar face; they join the people wandering out into the night. Absently stroking her stomach, Linda starts to ask for a phone number, but then she sees her brother out on the footpath, scanning everyone streaming out: hunting. His anger is a dark gift to her but she doesn't want it, not now.

And then it happens quickly. Linda's brother pulls his fist back. Linda throws herself between them. Sandra reflexively raises her long, thin arms high in the air and stands there, eucalyptic, in the shadow cast by the street lamp. Then she pivots and runs down the street, her stomach lurching. He pursues her. 'Look at that man chasing that woman,' people shout on the footpath. Heads whip around in alarm.

'Hoy!' Kat barks and takes off after them.

Linda, with her huge belly, follows for as long as she can before she has to stop, puffing, under that great weight.

'It's funny, I know. It's funny now,' Linda tells me, though everything in her eyes and her face and her yellowing photo albums spread out before us says otherwise.

# Janice

It unsettles me whenever I think about it, my too-late realisation that Janice was actually talking; so still was her jaw, with its under-bite thrusting teeth up into the air like fence palings. But when everyone held still, you could feel it more than hear it, like the ocean in a shell, the low voice that barely murmured over her lips before being swallowed back down to the darkness from which it came.

'Youknowwhatmyproblemis? I'mtooslow. WhydoItakesolong?' Janice was saying, smiling ruefully at Sandra while depositing a rubbish bag at the bottom of her front steps. Then she dashed back inside her house, locking the door behind her.

Sandra and her crew of cleaners have been waiting outside Janice's house for half an hour because, although Janice agreed to a 9 a.m. start when Sandra came last week to do the quote, she is now reluc-tant. Speaking to Sandra from the darkness behind her screen door, Janice politely asked for an extra half-hour during which—Sandra would see!—she'd do the work herself because this really wasn't necessary after all.

Sandra agreed to this request as a tactical measure and because the industrial-sized skip she'd ordered for Janice's houseful of rubbish was still delayed in traffic. Two birds, one stone. She handed Janice a few jumbo black plastic rubbish bags and pulled a face mask out of the pocket of her purple parka. 'Wear this over your mouth and nose, dear, you'll feel better for it,' she advised. Janice grabbed the mask and shut the front door.

Sandra is perched gingerly on the low bricks lining an empty flowerbed, under the perfect blue sky. She checks her watch and her emails and banters with her employees, most of whom are standing in a circle nearby and smoking hard. Every few minutes Janice emerges, slightly bent over and gripping a bulging rubbish bag which she hefts onto the tiny patch of dirt and weeds outside her front door. She comments too brightly on how well and fast she's working, before disappearing back through her door.

In her garage there is a mountain of bulging rubbish bags, but this striking amount of rubbish is sufficiently concealed that, were you to stand in the driveway and face Janice's house, there would appear on first glance to be nothing unusual. Then your keener senses would register the discord between the gorgeous morning light and the blind yanked down so hard over the single front window that its excess length has puddled up at the bottom. And, were you to approach that window, you would see the black mould creeping up the glass and the condensation dripping down like tears.

Exactly at 9:30 a.m., Sandra calls out to the cleaners to get suited up. Lizzie—calm, obese, hair slicked back into a bun—saunters over to the back of the truck where she scoops up a wad of flat plastic packages, each of which contains one extra large, disposable white bodysuit. After distributing them, Lizzie hands everyone a disposable respirator mask and a pair of gloves. Soon the cleaners are ready but the door remains locked. They stand in the hot sun and smoke some more, the top halves of their bodysuits peeled down around their waists. They chat lightly, giggling and giving each other vast amounts of shit. Sandra, of course, does not get suited up.

9:50 a.m. Sandra's bracelets jangle loudly as she answers a call from the driver telling her that her skip is nearly there. She asks Lizzie to please get a silver canister from the truck.

'And be very careful with it, darl,' Sandra says distractedly, typing on her phone, nails clicking on the screen with each poke. 'It's five hundred dollars for a litre.'

'What is it?' Lizzie asks, scrunching up her face.

'Clove oil. For the mould.' Sandra puts her phone down and palms non-existent wrinkles out of her immaculately pressed skinny jeans. 'You add a quarter of a teaspoon to a litre of water.'

'Why's it so expensive?' Lizzie asks.

'Dunno. Gotta get the oil out of cloves. Must've needed a shitload of cloves.'

The truck hauling the skip now pulls up, as does a second truck with a trailer of furniture that Sandra selected from her personal collection to install in Janice's house once she finishes the clean today: a side table, an armchair, a couch. 'To give her a new start,' Sandra explains, walking over to ensure that they survived the journey unscathed. I ask how she knew that Janice would need these pieces.

'I just figured that because there'd been a flood of faecal matter here, everything's gonna have to go,' she answers dryly. One day in 2010 Janice's only toilet broke and started to overflow. She couldn't fix this herself and she didn't call anyone for help.

10:15 a.m. Sandra strides up to the front door and raps on it briskly, saying in a warm but firm voice that it's time to get started. No response.

'Come on love, time to get a wriggle on,' Sandra calls out brightly.

Silence.

'Janice'—stronger voice—'you asked for extra time, I gave you extra time. Now it's time for you to let me in.'

Janice emerges clutching a full rubbish bag. She starts negotiating again. Could Sandra come back next week, maybe? That would be best, really. Janice vacillates between meekness and stubbornness. She is dressed like a librarian in a forties movie. She has the polite formality of a bygone era, which accounts also for her lipstick and long dress and the pantyhose she wears, despite the heat, with a dried liquid stain running down the front like a tear. This formality, together with her habit of hunching like a squirrel over a nut, gives the impression that she is much older than she is.

'We'll do it together, OK?' Sandra says gently.

Janice looks up at Sandra. With a dirty hand, she smooths back her closely cropped hair. Then, looking at her hands, she says, 'My nails are shocking.'

'You'll be able to have your children over,' Sandra says encouragingly, harking back to a discussion they had last week when she came to do the quote.

'And I won't be stressed,' Janice agrees, suddenly, with relief. Her affect changes entirely. She makes and maintains steady eye contact with Sandra. 'Why do I do this? Why?' she asks.

'Because you've had to let go of so much in your life,' Sandra answers.

'There was a trauma here. There was a death here,' Janice says quickly.

Sandra recalls how Janice previously mentioned that she would like to burn sage inside to clear the bad energy. 'We've done that before, we could do that here if you like,' Sandra offers.

Janice chortles 'I was half-joking,' she says dismissively and then her smile instantly slides away and her eyes widen. 'But, do you think we should? With the sage? Do you think it's a good idea?'

'We can do it if you want, love. Let's decide later, shall we?' Sandra says, reaching for the doorknob. Lizzie calls after Sandra to make sure she puts on her mask; the black mould is particularly dangerous for her lungs. Annoyed, Sandra stops and puts on her mask. Then she steps through the front door and flicks the light on.

'See that?' she whispers, staring matter-of-factly down at her finger. 'That's faeces on the light switch.' She pops her head out the front door and looks around for Phil, her senior cleaner. He materialises and she hands him her car keys with her other hand, asking him to get the large bottle of hand sanitiser she keeps there.

It is night inside Janice's house and, while it is true that the toilet overflowed several years ago and that both the shower and bathtub drains have been clogged with wet clothes for some time, it is not true that the house was ever fully submerged under water. But that is precisely the image conveyed by these sepia-stained walls and the strangely moist furniture and the accumulation of rubbish and random items strewn everywhere: floodwaters rushing in and under the door, inexorably rising, filling drawers and cupboards and fabrics and lungs and then, gradually, muddily, receding.

Vaguely aquatic, the indoor environment also brings to mind images of fire, which are no less vivid for being paradoxical. The black mould spotting the browned walls and powdering the rug looks like soot; it is as though some naughty sprite stole ashes from the hearth and smeared them along the walls, liberally dusted them over the furniture and, in a final act of vandalism, dumped the excess in the corners. When Sandra insists on opening the blind over the large front window, the mould crowding the edges of the dirty glass makes the vista of blue sky and neighbouring houses appear burnt at the edges, like an old tintype. Flood and fire. These rooms are small but within them there is pain of biblical proportions.

Sandra picks up a flaccid rubbish bag and her eyes do a quick sweep of the living room leading into the kitchen. The extent of the damage here won't become apparent for hours. This is because it is difficult to see anything under the layers of lesser dirt and rubbish that cover the bones of the house like skin and fur. Ungloved, Sandra starts stuffing mounds of newspapers and old magazines and crushed bottles and empty tins of catfood into the bag. She makes little progress before Janice snatches it out of her hands.

'I'd like to finish it myself,' Janice insists. 'I'd like to check the bag to see if there's anything in it.'

'Janice, it's obviously rubbish,' Sandra says calmly.

'Yeah, but you never know,' Janice says, her head deep in the bag as she roots around in the newspapers. 'Sometimes good things get mixed up in the rubbish...'

Having heard this assertion thousands of times over the course of her career, Sandra recognises it for what it is: the mark of the 'true hoarder, textbook hoarder'.

'It's all rubbish, Janice.' Sandra is firmer now.

Phil comes back in with hand sanitiser. Wearing a black polo T-shirt with the STC label on the pocket, Phil is a small, energetic man with a shiny bald head whose pluck and perpetual good cheer remind me of a robin. Phil wears shorts regardless of the weather and is, like Sandra, effortlessly excellent at the type of sweet small talk that puts strangers at ease. Joining Sandra, he wordlessly grabs a rubbish bag from the box by the door and starts filling it with empty bottles and the old tea bags, wrung like necks, that are strewn across the floor.

'Yeah. But I want to do something myself!' Janice insists and suddenly rips the bag out of Phil's hands. 'I can bloody well do it! Mind your Ps and Qs!' she shouts at him with the prim rage of someone deeply uncomfortable with expressing anger. And then, like a wave breaking and receding, she is instantly apologetic. 'I know you're only doing your job...'

Phil stands still, looking towards Sandra for his cue. Sandra's staff are instructed that their interaction with clients should be limited to what is absolutely necessary; they are to be respectful and as close to invisible as possible. Now Sandra has had enough. 'This is for your own good, Janice.' She raises her voice like an angry mother.

Shocked, Janice calms instantly. 'I'm sorry to be angry with you,' she says to Phil, who is entirely unaffected by her outburst and still calmly awaiting Sandra's instructions. Then she starts again, saying loudly: 'I don't like this bloke here!' Phil appears benign to me but Janice clearly sees someone altogether different, and not this man whose voicemail message implores you to 'Have a chipper day!'

An engineer once told me that the way glass shatters hints at the cause. Janice is not saying that she doesn't like '*this* bloke here', in the personal sense of hating Phil. She is saying 'this *bloke* here': I believe she is having a traumatic reaction triggered by the presence of a man in her house. I quietly suggest this to Sandra and, to my surprise, she is surprised by it. But she actions it anyway, promptly reassigning Phil outside.

'I'm sorry,' Janice says, calmer now. 'He didn't say a word but I got upset. He looks like someone else. I don't want to have a melt-down. I just wanted to do it myself.'

'That is physically impossible,' Sandra says looking towards the big couch that takes up much of the living room, and the side table, barely visible under accumulated detritus, next to it.

'My children should be here,' Janice says.

'They should,' Sandra agrees. 'Please call them if it'll make you feel more supported. Here, use my phone. What's the number?'

Janice doesn't want to say in case Phil hears.

'So type it in yourself.' Sandra hands her phone to Janice, who takes it and dials the number with her blackened fingers. Speaking with her son makes Janice calmer. She hands Sandra the phone and, after speaking with him as well, Sandra slides the phone, its screen filthy, into her back pocket. The son will be here in an hour.

Lizzie and Cheryl quietly start cleaning, bending low and coaxing armfuls of empty bottles and cans into black bags. Soon a different stratum of filth, closer to the carpet, is exposed. This one comprises small scraps of paper—magazines and newspapers and junk mail—some of which contain sufficient text that they can be dated like pottery shards (2012, 2009, 2008), indicating how long human life has existed here like this. Moving on from their first pass at the living room, the cleaners go into the kitchen. As they fill more bags, more of the floor there becomes visible too; rust circles on the linoleum betray how long empty cans have been left there. The cleaners continue into the bathroom and bedroom that lie in the darkness beyond the kitchen.

In the living room, Sandra painstakingly checks each item with Janice before dropping it into a rubbish bag. She is working on clearing a small space of floor where the living room leads into the kitchen. When the last magazines and newspapers are lifted away, one page of an old *TV Week* remains plastered onto the wall like papier-mache.

Aside from the large couch and a side table, there are two TVs in Janice's living room. The first sits in a wooden entertainment unit covered in sooty black mould, thick dust and spiderwebs. The second sits askew on a chair directly in front of the first and is currently showing a woman demonstrating how to make a green smoothie. Though this is the sum of the furniture in the relatively large living area, the space feels claustrophobically small due to the piles of undifferentiated household paraphernalia and rubbish which populate the couch and which are spread around the room in diverticulitic pockets.

There is the box that a space heater came in and the box that a water filter came in and the box that one of the TVs came in and the box that its antenna came in and the boxes that the DVD player and the fan and each of Janice's last three kettles came in. There is a nest of spent tea bags behind the first TV and a stash of empty water bottles and cat-food boxes behind the second one. Among the items strewn across the floor are: a jar of fresh cream, a packet of sliced white bread, a puddle of flannel pyjamas; flies, moths, spiders.

There is no room to sit comfortably on the couch but this is where Janice sleeps, under a thin blanket, in a space so tiny it does not take up one full cushion. The couch floats in a galaxy of gossip magazines, clothing, empty cat-food tins, loose change, personal care products and boxes of dry biscuits. On the couch there is also a plaster angel statue, a pair of sunglasses, a box of tissues, an unplugged telephone, a shoeshine brush and a tub of cream cheese. Small spiders scurry for new cover whenever one of these items is disturbed.

As a person, Janice is of course more than her house; but it is also true that her house is an indicator of what it feels like to be Janice. And what it feels like to be Janice is to be asphyxiating, slowly and helplessly, under the crushing and ever-multiplying weight of the past and the present. I picture her here on this couch, curled into herself like a fern at 4 a.m. And though it must feel like a catacomb in that dark hour, and though every hour behind these blinds has been dark, the house is spinning with movement: mould is travelling up and down the walls, food is rotting, cans are rusting, water is dripping, insects are being born and they are living and dying, Janice's hair is growing, her heart is beating, she is breathing. Which is to say that this, too, is life. Like the creatures that swim in the perfect blackness of the ocean floor, the ecosystem here would be unrecognisable to most people but this, too, is our world. The Order of Things includes those who are excluded.

There is a drumbeat of light thuds from the bathroom where Lizzie is throwing numerous empty shampoo bottles into her rubbish bag. As Sandra makes her way around the living room, Janice talks about how it wasn't like this when she first moved here. 'It was quite nice,' she says.

'That poor man,' she says, referring to Phil, who is now working outside loading bags of rubbish into the trailer. 'I should've done all this last weekend.'

'Love, you should've done it years ago!' Sandra says warmly, as if this was all a matter of a simple chore put off too long. The normalising effect buoys Janice as though the tide has just come in. Lizzie passes through on her way from the bathroom to the trailer, two swollen rubbish bags in each hand.

'Have you ever seen as bad at that?' Janice asks her with a high, nervous laugh.

'Yes, actually, I have,' Lizzie replies sweetly, and also truthfully—despite the fact that she has just spent a significant amount of time clearing a hallway full of grey shopping bags containing the human faeces she is now carrying.

Sandra motions towards the dark bathroom where wet clothes are splayed on the floor and floating in the bathtub amid centipedes. 'Those clothes have gotta go, darl,' she says resignedly.

'No,' Janice says.

'They've been in sewage, love. Stay focused,' Sandra coaches.

Janice grabs a bag out of Sandra's hands.

'This is obviously rubbish,' Sandra sighs.

'I know that,' Janice says and emits a high giggle.

'Then why are you going through it?' Sandra asks calmly, pointing to an empty food tin that Janice has extricated from the bag.

'I'm worried that something good may be mixed in with something bad. I mean, you know, there's not a million dollars here, I suppose…My folks don't know about this. They'd faint on the spot! Is that bad?' Janice asks, looking up at Sandra with wide eyes. 'Should I spray around some Glen-20?'

'Go ahead,' Sandra says.

The mould creeps up the walls. It rests in ashy black piles on and under everything. It streaks Janice's top and her face and her hands, which she thrusts, again and again, into the rubbish bags, desperately clawing out each item, sorting through everything for something valuable to save because she believes, if not in the absolute value of every item under her roof, in the possibility at least that something infinitely precious may be left forgotten in the curl of a cat-food can or in the folds of an old newspaper, which to discard irretrievably would be to experience a small death.

'Nothing good there?' she calls out to Lizzie and Cheryl, working in the kitchen.

'No, nothing,' comes the answer, amid the clank of cutlery and dishes.

'Oh,' Janice says softly.

'You've got to relax a bit,' Sandra soothes. 'You're being too hard on yourself.'

In a dream I sometimes have, I am frantically trying to save as much as I can from my childhood home before I am forced to leave forever because of some disaster. In this dream, from which I awake with my jaw clenched like a fist, I grab whatever I can reach, take whatever I can carry. Always my childhood books and our family photo albums, but sometimes also the silver candlesticks, the things on my father's desk, the paintings on the walls. Maybe it comes from the speed with which my family changed shape one day, maybe it comes from moving, maybe it comes from my grandmother's hinted horror of losing everything in the Holocaust, but I cannot part with the dented pot that I remember my mother putting on the stove each week. Or the sofa my father bought with his first pay cheque, which was never comfortable when I was growing up and is not comfortable now. I cannot part with the lipstick I found softly rolling in an empty drawer months after my mother left. Or a shopping list on an envelope in her handwriting. In a world that changes so quickly, and where everyone eventually leaves, our stuff is the one thing we can trust. It testifies, through the mute medium of Things, that we were part of something greater than ourselves.

Janice's house is more than a question of homey clutter, of tiny shelves and the things we place there. But pain is a sacred puzzle, where any piece, however misshapen, fits seamlessly. In the context of facing her fears alone, Janice's fortress of shit makes sense.

Janice starts sorting through the piles on her couch, tossing things into the rubbish bag that Sandra is holding open for her. She holds up a photo from her teens; in it she is young and beautiful, sitting in the sun with friends. Then she holds up a frame but the photo inside looks like black scribbles on brown cardboard.

'This got wet,' Janice says woodenly, before explaining that it was an old family photo. She then picks up a nail buffer; scrutinises it for a while. 'This is just a nail buffer. I don't really have nails anyway,' she says, placing it in the bag. And then, speaking to herself, sharp and low, 'Why do you do this? You know what rubbish is.'

'Because you see yourself as rubbish,' Sandra says. 'Time to start seeing the good in life. You deserve it.' The angel statue suddenly slips off the couch and bounces on the carpet; a wing snaps off.

'Is that a bad omen?' Janice asks, looking up at Sandra frantically.

'You know what it's saying?' Sandra answers with a smile. 'I'm broken, but I'm not dead.'

Though Sandra's older sister Barbara and her youngest brother Christopher are alive, she hasn't had contact with them in decades and so it is more accurate to say that her only remaining family consists of Kerrie, her brother Simon's widow, who lives in Queensland. Kerrie has known Sandra for thirty-three years. Their relationship is amiable and, while not intimate, it is a significant one in Sandra's life in that it is the only one that she has consistently maintained from the period following her sex reassignment surgery through her last years as a sex worker, through the time Sandra 'was heavy on drugs, alcohol and things like that', through her various relationships, businesses and health issues. Sandra describes her relationship with her brother and her sister-in-law as fond, but not particularly close: 'there was an admiration but also a distance'.

Kerrie and Simon met in 1982 and were together for twenty-six years. Very early on, and without fuss, Simon explained to Kerrie that he had 'one brother, one sister, and a brother-sister'. Despite the five-year age gap and Simon's signature quietness, the two siblings were similar in significant ways. Both were beaten by Bill as children and kicked out of home by seventeen. Kerrie describes Simon's ability to handle painful memories or events as 'making it water off a duck's back. He left it behind. He didn't carry things with him to make him a nasty person'. The corollary of this particular type of forward-focus, shared by Sandra, was that 'if you crossed him, he did not care about you anymore. He would just wipe you out of his life'.

Sandra loved Simon early and long. She named her first child after him. In turn, Simon 'loved his sister. He was very accepting of her and her decision. He never, ever turned his back on her'. On trips back to Melbourne, he and Kerrie would always visit Sandra. But they did not tell Ailsa. Back at Birchill Street, Sandra was verboten. 'I did try to talk to Ailsa, one time, about it,' Kerrie told me. 'I said, "Ailsa, sometimes people are just born with the wrong genes, and they can't help how they feel." But they were a generation that did not accept that sort of stuff. She would never forgive her.'

Once, Sandra asked Kerrie to see if Ailsa would speak with her on the phone. 'Ailsa said, "No, I don't want him ringing here. I don't want him to come here." Sandra never got the opportunity to make peace with it and that's why I think her sister was very wrong about the funeral.' Kerrie is referring to the fact that when Ailsa died, Sandra tried to attend her mother's funeral. 'Her sister went off her scone, so Simon, for the peace of it, just said to Sandra,

"Barbara doesn't want you there, she is carrying on a treat." He didn't care if Sandra came and sat in the back of the church. But she didn't come.'

One of Sandra's prized possessions is a guest book in which her past houseguests have left notes and in which, in 2001, Simon wrote: *Certainly worth the trip for your fabulous cooking and company. After the obligatory crap—just remember that you are much loved, and that Kerrie and I think of you often. No matter what, always your brother, Simon.*

Simon, that little boy whose older brother Peter bought him a chemistry set with his first pay cheque, was awarded an Order of Australia for his army service in the field of engineering ten years before he died suddenly in Papua New Guinea, where he had been doing consulting work. Besides having photos from Simon's award ceremony around her house, Sandra will speak proudly of her little brother's achievements and show photos of him on her phone whenever it is near-relevant in conversation.

No one is quite sure what became of Barbara after she 'married some Asian gentleman' but Christopher is an executive at one of Australia's top private companies. In Kerrie's opinion, 'Sandra has sort of reached a point in her life where she is, I wouldn't say "happy", I would say "content with herself" and how her life has panned out.'

All four siblings came from the same small house in West Footscray but if the metrics could be standardised, Sandra may be seen to have come the furthest. 'Sandra has achieved quite a bit in coming from nothing and she has done it all on her own. She is an amazing woman, she really is, an absolutely amazing woman.'

Sandra guides Janice outside for a rest. Overdressed for the day's heat as though bundled against the memory of cold, Janice sips a little water and stands sweating in the sun. She cannot remain outside for more than a few seconds before she is compelled to run back inside and check that the cleaners haven't thrown out anything of value. You can see the compulsion overtaking her, strangling her like a vine. At first she makes little excuses each time she darts back inside: she forgot her phone, her keys, she just needs to check on something, needs to check one last thing, oops, forgot one little thing, just one moment, be right back. But then, despite assuring Sandra that now she'll really have a good rest out here, Janice gives in to the pressure mounting up inside her and dashes back in to claw through the rubbish bags. I can see it and I can feel it: intrusive thoughts are circling Janice like sharks, they are snapping at her, giving her less and less time between assaults, before dragging her under. Janice is drowning, she is being eaten alive.

Seeing this, Sandra reminds her about the goal they are working towards. 'Come on darl, remember the vision we discussed? You and your kids and a cup of tea on the couch?' This is a Pankhurst trademark: encouraging her clients to think in terms of small, achievable goals. Where a client is even moderately receptive, Sandra will use this language repeatedly, returning to it like a refrain over the course of her day or days spent working with them. And it is based on a practice she follows herself.

I once asked Sandra whether, given what she deals with each day, she was a pessimist or an optimist. She replied without hesitating: 'I'm an optimist, yep, I'm an optimist. Always look on the bright side of life. You can achieve whatever you want and do whatever you want as long as you apply yourself and have a positive outlook.'

Janice unfurls for a moment, but the peace passes quickly as a new worry comes slicing down. 'You're not throwing anything out?' she calls out to the cleaners through the screen door.

'No,' comes the answer, and she is released to try to make small talk with Sandra for the few seconds of her respite. But almost immediately she wonders aloud where a small box with some photos went, and when she cannot find it, starts frantically pulling rubbish bags out of the trailer.

One of Janice's kids arrives and hurries up the driveway. 'I'm here, Mum,' he says and starts rubbing Janice's back. Janice, still bent over the rubbish bags, immediately enlists him in the search for the photos.

Sandra calls the son over and tells him that his mother should drink some fluids because she's been working hard all morning and that, while he's welcome to go inside of course, if he does, he'll need to wear a mask because of the mould. The young man nods like Sandra has just read him the instruction manual for a device he has never seen before. He takes a mask, disappears inside for a few minutes and when he emerges it is obvious that he is struggling to inhabit the role of his parent's parent that has just been thrust upon him completely and irrevocably. Shell-shocked, he says in a low voice to Sandra that he hadn't realised how bad the house had got. It didn't look like this, with all the mould, last time he was here.

'When was that, darl?' Sandra asks.

'Five years ago,' he answers. 'She won't let us inside anymore.'

Lizzie emerges with the box Janice thought had been thrown out. The son, embarrassed, starts tying up the rubbish bags they've disturbed. 'Just go comfort your mum, love,' Sandra says.

Phil and Leigh are instructed by Sandra to go inside and remove the couch so that it can be replaced with the one waiting in the second trailer. The men shift the couch away from the wall, revealing a thick pile of dirt and ashy mould studded with rubbish and lost items so diverse I wonder about the circumstances that brought them here: three shoes, a Disney clock, a full bottle of mouthwash, empty packets and boxes, a bottle of vitamins, air fresheners, spiders.

'I couldn't get behind the couch, obviously,' Janice says wanly, staring down at the mess. And then she drops to the floor and starts hunting feverishly through the pile. As the men push the old couch out the door, Sandra turns and—despite not wearing a mask herself and the particular vulnerability of her lungs—shouts angrily at Leigh to put his mask on. 'You get a mould spore on your lungs and that's it!'

Phil pulls Sandra aside. He tells her what he noticed when he was crouching down to lift the couch; the walls have 'gone soft' from the mould. Sandra checks to confirm this; they are spongy. Her face falls as she realises the implications.

'There's more to do here than what a clean's gonna fix,' she sighs quietly.

The house needs to be immediately shut down for health and safety reasons. Everyone out. Stepping over the random mosaic of rubbish that is still thick on the ground and spilling into the holes in the walls, the cleaners and Janice and her son and Sandra file out one by one, defeated, leaving the house to its mossy darkness and small forest noises as the door closes behind them with a dry thud.

Everyone gathers around the old couch in the middle of the driveway. Janice huddles close to Sandra like a rabbit sheltering under a tree. Sandra daintily spreads a white bodysuit over the arm of the couch and sits down. She takes out her phone and starts tapping, perfect nails flying across the filthy screen. Janice sits with her son's arm around her shoulders. She will go back to his house tonight.

'You're right,' she says, 'stuff doesn't replace what you've lost. You can't put a price on what I've lost.' Her lips are set in a line and she stares ahead. 'Did we get my hairbrush?' she asks suddenly. Sandra replies that it's in her purse. 'OK. Should I go get the tea bags and the milk I bought yesterday?'

'Leave it, love, the mould gets in everything,' Sandra advises.

'I feel like I'm in another world,' Janice says, unblinking.

Sandra sails smoothly on. Speaking calmly, she remains insistently chatty, leading Janice by example: everything is all right.

'I like your perfume,' Janice says to Sandra.

'Chanel, love,' she answers while motioning to Phil to lock the door before going into a soothing commentary on how different fragrances smell different on different people, throughout which Janice murmurs in agreement.

The furniture that Sandra brought lies untouched in the trailer out front. She would have given Janice 'a new start' had conditions allowed. She would have removed all the rubbish and contaminated furnishings from the house and disinfected the floors, walls and ceilings. From her own stores, she would have installed for Janice new furniture and sheets and towels, perhaps not matching (as is always Sandra's strong preference) but clean, and folded with military precision. She would have organised Janice's closets and cupboards, fanned out a few of the most recent gossip magazines on Janice's coffee table and fluffed the new pillows on the couch. 'I have a bit of a thing for lifestyle programs on housing, designing, and all that,' Sandra once told me. 'I utilise a lot of that in how I present houses for people, especially with hoarding. I have a firm belief that we change the concept of the house from what it was, so that they have in their mind that things are different now. It helps with their processes of dealing with the change and then it's a constant reminder that they're not following the same patterns and things need to be different.'

A change in domestic topography is, sometimes, enough to set the interior life of a client on an improved course. Not so much (and here I differ with Sandra) due to the power exerted by one's environment—although that, of course, has significant influence—but rather because of the fact that someone cared enough for them to actually do this. This transfer of lamps and microwaves, of sofas and pillowcases, is not a panacea for deep-seated illness or dysfunction, but it is good for the heart.

And it goes both ways. By making a home for her clients, Sandra has made a home for herself. Despite having experienced worse blows than many of her clients, she is the one who comes in to make order out of their chaos. The undeniable boost this gives her is not a simple question of schadenfreude or, at the other end of the spectrum, altruism. It is the product of meaningful work: the sense of purpose we create by cultivating our gifts and sharing them with the world.[6] And yet, it is often not enough to imbue those clients with the type of wellbeing that Sandra enjoys. It would have taken more than a new sofa to give Janice what she needs.

What happens to Janice next is out of Sandra's hands. She will relocate, which will not stem the flow of rubbish that will follow her like a polluted river if she is allowed the great swathes of solitude she insists upon.

Soon the couch will be lifted into the skip and everyone will pack up and disperse and Sandra's brief hours of helping Janice will be over. But for now she is here, looking Janice in the eyes and chatting casually to her in the sun, actively eliciting her responses, calling on her opinions, calling her out from wherever it is she longs to be left: if just for these moments, calling her back.

# 10

If anything was going to make her regret reporting it to the cops it was this little man arguing before the court that the whole case was a joke because, as you could clearly see, the victim was no trembling flower, she was a big burly bloke who would have fought him off if it had happened the way she—*or is it he? Apologies, your Honour, I'm confused, I think we all are, what was it again?*—claims it did.

Sandra returns exhausted from her first day of giving evidence. Rick is lying on the couch watching TV.

'How'd it go?' he asks without looking up.

'Shithouse,' she replies, fixing them both a drink. And then she says more to herself, in a defeated tone he hasn't heard from her before, 'What am I gonna do?'

He peels himself away from the screen. 'Look, just tell 'em to check out the photographic evidence,' he says.

'They have all that already,' she replies in a monotone.

'Nah, you know, the photos that the cops took. The ones of the door, you know, where he tore it all off in one piece.'

She tilts her head to one side, waiting.

'Just tell 'em. "It was solid wood, mate. If he did that to the door, what do you reckon he done to me?'" And then he turns back to the TV.

For once, he has earnt his keep. The next day she makes Rick's point in court. The defence requests a brief recess. When court reconvenes, a guilty plea is entered.

'This guy come bangin' on the door.' That's where she'll start the story when she tells it thirty years later, her voice absolutely steady: with bone and muscle and flesh on wood and how she knew he was strong from the volume of it. A fist like a horse's hoof.

The Dream Palace is just another brothel, a small house down a poorly lit street in an industrial suburban neighbourhood 'away from everywhere', where she has worked for about three months. It is a Saturday night, mid–May, and the day has gone just like any other Saturday. She started around 10:30 a.m., intending to work a double shift, finishing when they close at 4 a.m. Sunday. By 8 p.m., she has seen six or seven clients. It is just her and Jenny, the other girl working that night. Lucifer, the madam's large black guard dog, is asleep out the back.

She is between jobs, wearing a full leotard and stockings, sipping tea with Jenny in the lounge room and trying to ignore that banging on the front door. Though her sobs have turned into infrequent sniffs, Jenny is still distraught from her last client, a huge man who choked her. Hearing Jenny scream, Sandra enlisted her client to throw the man out, and he left, carrying his shoes in his hand. But now here he is again, pounding on the door.

'It'll be right, hon,' Sandra says absently to Jenny, huddled at the end of the sofa with her hands wrapped around a teacup. Any type of violence causes Sandra to panic, so the whole thing's thrown her off a bit, but she's sure if they ignore him he'll get bored and piss off like all the other drunk fuckheads. 'God, we get all sorts in this job, hey?' she says lightly, looking up briefly from the joint she's rolling.

Celestial Star

Maria Gloria Paten and Sandra, then known as Amanda Celeste Claire

Late 1970s–early 1980s

At a brothel on Hay Street, Kalgoorlie in the 1980s

Sandra and Rick

She is about to lick the paper closed when there is an almighty crash, which is the sound of wood ripping as the front door splinters open. And they both scream, she and Jenny, these women who do not scare easily, and suddenly the man at the door is in the lounge room, so large that he blocks out the light. He grabs Sandra and then Jenny by their hair and at first the pain doesn't register over the fear as he drags them like rubbish bags down the hallway, growling, 'If you do what you're told, you won't get hurt.'

The improbable name of this man is Mel David Brooks. On this night, he is on bail for previous charges of burglary and aggravated rape. Brooks pauses near the front door where he makes both women kneel low to the ground. He forces them to remove all their clothing. He unzips his fly and removes his flaccid penis. He forces it, again and again, into the mouth of each woman. After a while, he decides that he wants to turn the porch light off. Though she is terrified, Sandra tries to preserve the possibility that a client might come along and inadvertently scare Brooks away. 'You can't turn the light off—it's on a timer,' she tells him. So he steps onto the porch and looks around for the fuse box. Jenny stands up and he barks, 'Get back down on your knees!' Then he turns the power off at the main switch and the house disappears into darkness.

He returns to the hallway, stopping to prop the front door up from where it dangles on one hinge and shove it closed again. The nearest occupied house, another brothel, is at the end of the long street. There is no one to hear Lucifer barking. Sandra is shaking, silently crying. Jenny tries to talk Brooks down. She tells him, 'Whatever you want, we'll try to do it.' He shoves his penis back into her mouth and then into Sandra's, where he ejaculates. Her stomach lurches. 'Keep it in your mouth,' he warns. She is going to vomit. She grabs the towel that Jenny has been wearing and furtively spits into it. The dog is circling them, mouthing at their arms, wagging his tail; now he thinks it is all a great game.

'Get into the bedroom!' Brooks shouts at both women. He pulls up the blind so that he can look out over the front yard. He forces Sandra to kneel, and repeatedly and painfully forces his finger into her anus. 'Lick my arse!' Brooks says as he turns around and bends over slightly. She can see clearly how dirty he is and, revolted, grabs the towel to wipe him. He warns, 'Do it properly. Pull the cheeks apart.' She tries not to vomit.

Jenny is kneeling in front of him. Suddenly he says to Sandra, 'Now you get in front.' The women switch places. She is too scared to notice what Jenny is doing, too scared to disobey him although she thinks he will kill them both anyway. The doorbell rings.

'I'll go and answer the door, put him in another room,' Jenny tells Brooks.

'No, tell him we're closed,' Sandra says, thinking maybe the man can go and get help.

'If you do anything foolish I'll kill her,' Brooks warns Jenny as she leaves the room.

Casually answering the door with the shit-stained towel wrapped around her, Jenny gets rid of the caller and returns to the room, where Brooks is demanding money.

Sandra tells him the madam has already collected it. He asks where her car is.

'We got dropped here, don't have cars,' Sandra says, thinking of her car parked out back and the keys in her purse.

Brooks nods. 'Get dressed, both of you. We're going for a walk.'

Sandra reaches for her leotard but he allows them only to wear towels. He grabs their hair again and walks them out of the house and across the road into the deserted parkland. They walk for some time, deep into the park, until they come to a cyclone-wire fence and cannot go any further and become just shapes moving on the dark grass; a lion tearing into its prey in the moonlight.

'Spread your towels on the ground,' Brooks commands, releasing their hair. He makes both women alternately kiss him on the mouth and suck his penis. Nauseated from the violence and the pain and the terror and the smell of his beastbreath and his dirty skin, Sandra feels even sicker as he repeatedly shoves his fingers into her vagina. She knows from the way he is talking and behaving that her life is in danger.

'Get in the sixty-nine,' he tells them. Sandra starts crying again. 'Don't worry,' Jenny whispers to her. 'It'll be all right.' Sandra flinches as he shoves his finger again into her anus. 'Lick harder! You're not doing it properly,' he shouts at the back of her head, which is now between Jenny's legs. Shaking, she tries to do what he says. She doesn't know how much time passes as he rearranges them, again and again, like dolls.

She looks up for a moment and sees that he has just ejaculated. She does not hesitate. She punches him in the balls, as hard as she can.

Brooks goes to hit her but she ducks, grabbing his testicles and squeezing them hard with both hands. He just looks down at her. He doesn't even flinch. Both women start yelling for help but the sound sinks into the night like ink on paper. Brooks darts again at Sandra but this time she fights back. They are struggling now, grappling in the half-dark. He digs his nails into the skin around her right eye. She looks around wildly, sees that Jenny is gone. Barefoot and naked, Sandra struggles to stand up. She throws Brooks off her and when he stumbles, she starts to run.

She runs through shrubs and long grass and gravel and then out onto road; she runs back to the brothel and through the open door and down the black hallway and into the lounge room where, shaking, she feels around the sofa for the phone. Peering into it, she rings triple zero. She hears a thousand noises outside that are all Brooks coming to kill her as she frantically answers the operator's questions. He tells her that the police are on their way. She hangs up, freezes, listens hard. Hearing nothing, she dials the madam.

'Fucking get someone here, get someone here,' she whispers when the woman answers. Hanging up, she feels in the dark towards where she left her purse. Looking, now, down the long hallway through the open door she sees Brooks loping up to the house. She runs down the hallway, towards the room they call the Dungeon, near the back of the house. Before she gets there, the lights suddenly come back on and she freezes for a second as though zapped. Turning, she sees him at the end of the hallway, hulking, enormous, framed by the gaping hole where the front door used to stand and staring right at her. 'There you are,' he says.

She races into the Dungeon, throws her purse deep under the bed and grabs a towel to cover herself with and a studded leather strap with a wooden handle; runs out the back door and crouches on the gravel behind her car, looking out for his feet. Lucifer starts barking at her, giving away her location. She hits him with the strap to try to silence him. Then she hears a car pull up outside.

She sprints around the side of the house to safety, whipping her head around wildly to check whether Brooks is onto her. She makes it out the front but it isn't the police; it's just another client. She calls out and pounds on the passenger door, but he drives off.

She bolts down the middle of the road, past the factories, towards the other brothel. She is torn and bruised and bleeding, holding her towel up with one hand and fighting for the breath that her terror and her asthma are stealing from her.

Panting, she runs up to the door of the other brothel and starts banging on it and ringing the doorbell. Through the window, she sees the women silhouetted against the yellow light inside. They can hear her pleading to be let in but they do not open the door. She starts begging, 'Please let me in, pleaseletmein, please…'

A police car pulls up.

'You the one that called us?' one of the two officers shouts through the car window.

'Yesyesyes…'

'Get inside now!' he orders, pointing towards the door.

'They won't let me in,' she cries.

'Fuckin' let her inside!' he roars at the women in the window, who only now open the door.

By 3:00 a.m. Sandra has identified Mel David Brooks from photo-graphs shown to her at the police station. By 6:10 a.m. she has given a ten-page sworn statement to the police.

*My full name is Amanda Celeste Claire. I am thirty-one years old.* That's where she starts her evidence, ageing herself by gratefully accepting the benefit of her upcoming birthday, still weeks away. The next day Brooks, a thirty-one-year-old machine operator from New Zealand, is located, arrested and charged.

To understand how remarkable it is that Sandra pursued a case against Brooks, you must reflect on a number of things.

The first is her relationship to the police as a transgender woman in the early eighties. At the time of her rape Sandra had witnessed and experienced years of institutionalised police violence towards transgender people. Despite this, she called on the service of the police and explicitly told them, in her statement: 'I had better mention that I had a complete sex change at the Queen Victoria Hospital. Since then, I have lived as a normal female and have all the functions of a female.'

Then there is her relationship to the police as a sex worker. She was aware of the culture of corruption involving some uniformed police and detectives. When she was the manager of the brothel in Footscray she had paid bribes directly to the police to be allowed to operate. She had knowledge of thousands of dollars in bribes paid to a consorting squad detective by Geoffrey Lamb, the owner of one of the brothels she worked in. Just up the road from Dream Palace, members of the Caulfield police had been the subject of credible allegations that they attended an illegal brothel where they drank and had sex with the workers for free; one such gathering allegedly ended in shots being fired and a sex worker being raped.

In these circumstances, to call on the police for help shows how desperately Sandra feared for her life. But to then proceed with her statement, thereby prolonging her contact with the police, was, in the particular policing environment of the early eighties, to insist with notable courage upon equal justice.

There is also the consideration that she participated in prosecuting her attacker at a time when the equal protection of the law was not afforded to sex workers. Her case was processed three years after Victoria's highest court held that the rape of a prostitute was less serious than the rape of a 'chaste woman'. Years before this position was expressly disavowed—and despite being well aware of these prejudices from a cultural, if not a legal, position—Sandra nevertheless insisted on showing up at the County Court and giving evidence at the trial of her rapist.

As countless other rape survivors have found, choosing to make and proceed with a statement means choosing to relive the violence of the rape again and again. Now, there are at least some protections designed to safeguard the mental health and wellbeing of survivors who walk this path. Such measures were unheard of at this time. In addition, Sandra chose to expose herself to this process knowing that she would have to withstand the additional disrespect and embarrassment of having her gender publicly scrutinised, questioned and misunderstood. This was the strange and hateful cost of the basic respect that she insisted upon for herself.

The last remarkable thing about Sandra's response to her rape was the result. She provided sufficient evidence for her rapist to be apprehended, charged, tried, found guilty and sentenced: six years, with the possibility of parole after four. It was a breathtakingly short sentence given the context of his offending, the prolonged duration of the assault, the infliction of additional violence and humiliation, and his record of similar sexual offending.

But it was relatively heavy when you consider that, between 2010 and 2015, the median prison sentence for a rape conviction was five years and that thirty years ago public attitudes held that raping a prostitute was only slightly more possible than raping your wife. So, yes: Sandra was not only spectacularly courageous, she was also remarkably successful.

# Shane

What can I tell you about Shane? I can tell you that it is both true and untrue that his street was like any other street, that his block of flats was like any other block of flats, that the grass in the communal lawn that spread out before his front door like a dirty blanket was as green and as brown as any other grass. It is true because it all looked unremarkable and it is also untrue because hanging over everything was the smell of living death and the sort of too-loud silence that makes small creatures run for higher ground. I can tell you that the first impression one gets from looking at Shane is of bluntness. He appears both dopey and physically edgeless; there is something in his short limbs and rounded nose and stubby fingers and the open O of his goldfish mouth that suggests he has been dulled somehow—perhaps by using himself as a hammer against the anvil of the world.

Shane is a convicted sex offender. And his eyes on this morning are charged: they are prowling, measuring, calculating. It would be wrong, therefore, to regard Shane as obtuse; his symmetry is still fearful. And while I do not think he is the type of hunter who would expertly stalk you by playing the wind, I believe he would not hesitate to act if you happened to wander off from the pack.

Shane is not allowed to be alone with Sandra, who has come today to clean the wet and dry squalor in his small flat, nor is he allowed to be alone with any other female. Although vaguely intrigued by this, Sandra is not bothered by it in the slightest. She has come with four of her cleaners: Lizzie, Cheryl, Phil and Jarrod, who is six foot five and weighs at least 120 kilograms. But Jarrod is not the reason Sandra is unruffled. Though Sandra has not been told anything about the nature of Shane's offending, and though she is a survivor of rape herself, it is in her nature to be entirely practical. 'Regardless of what his convictions may be, it's really just another job,' she tells me. This position is not ideological or altruistic. It is bound up with the fact that Sandra is driven to do each job excellently, regardless of conditions.

Sandra raps smartly at the front door. Shane stumbles out like a bear from a cave onto the cracked concrete of his small front porch and stands squinting in the morning light.

'I need to have my breakfast, hey.' A gravelly voice and the clumsy cunning of a toddler. 'Can I get a few extra minutes?'

Sandra responds lightly that she'll return in ten minutes. 'He probably had a few pieces to put away,' she muses. 'Probably planted them in with his clothes in the closet.'

I ask her what she thinks he is hiding.

'My mind boggles,' she says, uninterested, checking her phone under a dove grey sky.

Formerly known as Crossfire, Multi-Task is a cleaning product that Sandra uses to strip surfaces of food or nicotine stains. To it she adds a hospital-grade disinfectant called SanSol when she needs to address the additional presence of human off-gases and/or bodily fluids which may carry 'HIV or bacterial infection'. This is the admixture that Phil is currently using to mop the ceiling of Shane's bedroom.

Lizzie and Cheryl, spared the job of cleaning the carpets because Sandra has determined that they are beyond saving, will use the Multi-Task/SanSol cocktail to clean the brown stains off the door and floor of his bathroom. No one is suited up today. 'We use the suits on extreme cases,' Sandra explains. 'This is a regular, run-of-the-mill job.'

Sandra's knowledge about the process and instruments of very specific, diverse, urgent, complex and large-scale cleaning jobs is encyclopaedic. She indulges me when I hit her with hypotheticals about various types of jobs.

'Death, no blood?' I ask.

'Death no blood I wouldn't be called in for unless there were body fluids,' she corrects me.

'OK, say it's been a couple of days and there is a smell,' I say.

'That is decomposition and that is heavy,' Sandra sighs. 'Decomposition: the first thing I think of is what has to be thrown out. What surfaces are there? Is it carpet or is it on lino? Because if it's carpet, nine out of ten if it's a decomposition, we'll have to take the carpet out. That also guides me into whether we need a vehicle to be able to transfer the goods, because the prescribed goods handling course is quite specific,' she explains rapidly.

'Or it could be the mattress,' she continues. 'We buy huge bags that seal the mattress because the odour can be quite offensive. The first thought would be to get any soiled matter out of the property, because once the cause has gone, you can start eliminating the odour. You go through the sterilisation of cleaning everything. Everything in the house then has to be wiped down. If the body has been there for quite some time, then gases and everything would've impregnated the walls, the fabrics, all that sorta stuff. So, I would wash the walls down and the ceilings down, and then we would put the odour-control machines in to affect the fabrics and all that. You have to disconnect the smoke alarms because they will

162

go off. You would open up wardrobes, cupboards and things like that because the smell would have gone into the clothes and everything there.'

'Does that all have to be thrown out?' I ask.

'No, we'll fumigate it with the odour control,' she replies. 'It just sprays into the room. It's almost impossible to breathe and it's supposed to be natural.' She rolls her eyes. 'Ho hum, but you go with it. You let it fog up the house. You leave the house locked up for twenty-four hours, and then it should be hunky dory. In extreme cases, we have to put machinery on that'll go for three days and three nights. You could have to remove flooring or whatever, if it's soaked into the timber flooring.'

I ask whether she has had to do that.

'We have, on one occasion only,' she replies. 'It was dripping down into the apartment downstairs, so we had two apartments to clean. The guy downstairs had noticed this steady drip coming into his lounge room and the smell was in his place downstairs, so it was pretty bad.'

'What would you do if there was a death *with* blood?' I ask.

'First you would know by the colour how deeply it has gone into the carpet,' she explains. 'If it's light, you can usually get that out of the carpet without it affecting the underlay. We would spray solution over all the carpets to see whether there are droplets of blood, it illuminates the blood. This tells us where we've got to work and what we've got to work on. When we're taught these skills, they say that if there's an armchair that's contaminated, you cut out the contaminated piece. To me, that's a no-no. I would just take the whole piece of furniture away, because if you were the family coming back and having to deal with that chair, it's going to be forever in your mind: that is where Dad died, if you know what I mean. Whereas, to me, you've got to be very particular about how you set the house up. It's got to be as close to being back to normal as possible, but

163

there might be some things missing. To me, you do not mark X as the spot.'

Sandra tells me that male suicides are generally bigger jobs than females. 'Men are dirty killers whereas the women are very tidy in the way they do it,' Sandra says.

'Like cooking,' I offer.

'Yeah,' Sandra agrees. She goes quiet for a moment. 'By the same token there was one guy who blew his head off, and he put plastic up in the bathroom, just so it'd keep it quite clean. It all went way over, but the thought was there.'

Sandra is certified by the Institute of Inspection Cleaning and Restoration Certification in carpet cleaning and by the National Institute of Decontamination Specialists as a crime and trauma biorecovery technician. Aside from a vast amount of technical skill that needs constant updating, I ask Sandra what else the work requires. 'Compassion,' she replies solemnly. 'Great compassion, great dignity and a good sense of humour 'cause you're gonna need it. And a really good sense of not being able to take the smell in, 'cause they stink. Putrid.'

The team has been inside Shane's flat for about twenty minutes when an unpleasantness arises in the form of Shane, convinced that Jarrod has been 'staring him down', inviting Jarrod to fight. It is extreme-ly unlikely that Jarrod was, in fact, staring him down. Though he is tall and solid, Jarrod is shy and softly spoken and calls everyone 'bro'. In addition, Sandra is closely supervising everyone and Shane's flat is tiny. Nevertheless, Sandra calmly and swiftly reassigns Jarrod to clean the bedroom with Phil. When Shane saunters in there a few minutes later, Jarrod greets him with a simple 'Hi, boss' and all is well; the power balance has been restored. Phil, in his usual black shorts despite the winter air blessedly blowing in through the open front door, asks Shane if his folks are well. Shane replies, 'Yeah,

yeah,' as though they're all just catching up at a barbeque.

Dried brown fluid drips down the yellowed walls of the bedroom. The blinds are drawn. There is a bed, a chest of drawers and a coffee table which has been pushed up against the wall. In keeping with Shane's practice of leaving items where they fall, the brown-stained carpet is strewn with dirty clothes, plastic bags, numerous leads and wires, toilet paper rolls and broken appliances. There is no cover on the pillow or the quilt or the yellowed mattress which lies sagging and slashed at one side, grey stuffing prolapsing from the wound. This could be the result of its age and quality, the many moves to which it has probably been subjected or an inelegant effort by Shane to conceal valuable and/or illicit property in its belly. On the floor are magazines (*Sexpress*) and books (*How to Increase Energy, Reduce Stress and Improve Hearing in 90 Days*). There are three televisions in the bedroom; two are enormous and they rest, side by side, on the top of the chest of drawers, screens turned towards the wall. The third television is tiny and it sits on the coffee table next to an unplugged blender base caked with dried brown liquid. The glass of the coffee table is black with dirt and mostly concealed under random shoes, wires, broken appliances, a bong, papers and books. A digital alarm clock flashes the wrong time. A dirty brown towel is crumpled on the floor like road kill. Shane wanders off into the kitchen and Sandra quietly instructs everyone to avoid all eye contact with him because, she has been advised, he will misread it.

'I'm just making sure that everyone's paired off in different rooms to get things done, making sure that they're safe at all times,' she whispers to me. 'I really don't have to worry about the staff because the staff are perfect in handling anyone who's mentally ill or drug and alcohol affected or whatever. And this is just another one of those jobs, really, you know.'

Her phone rings. The caller requests a reduction in the price she quoted recently for a job. 'As you know, rubbish is very expensive to get rid of,' Sandra replies matter-of-factly, 'especially when it's covered in urine and faeces.'

Ending the call she peeks into the bathroom, appraising the progress made by Lizzie and Cheryl. Though nothing can be done about the holes punched into the door, they've sprayed off the brown streaks. All of the thick brown stains are now gone, too, from the floor and the toilet and the sink and the bathtub. Standing on the white floor with her creamy pink lipstick and her crisp purple parka and her blonde hair catching the light that filters in through the frosted window, Sandra is a Monet haystack; golden, many-hued, familiar, rising up from the linoleum landscape to catch and comfort the eye. Satisfied for now, she strides out towards the kitchen.

The sound of his fridge does not please Shane. There is something about the pitch that upsets him, and so he unplugged it some time ago, allowing the contents to rot. Flies buzz out of the fridge when the door is opened, and it must now be emptied, disinfected and taped open to air out the smell. Cheryl addresses this while Lizzie tackles the various plates scattered around the flat from weeks of one-man dinners, abandoned with their piles of discarded bones and solidified grease puddles. These plates are balanced at odd angles on the kitchen bench and on top of the items crowding the bench; each bears a fork and knife, crossed like the diner is just taking a breather. All the kitchen surfaces are streaked brown with dirt. Brown fluid drips down the front of the cupboards and the oven. The stovetop is tiny, but on it rest two huge stainless steel cooking pots, and on one of the pots a frying pan is balanced, black with burnt food. Flies cover everything. Rat shit is sprinkled like seeds inside the oven.

Despite the state of his house generally and his kitchen specifically, Shane is meticulous about the type and quality of the food he eats. The numerous health food products in his kitchen include: organic coconut oil, puffed millet, a fifteen-dollar bag of grain-free muesli, camu powder, fasting tea, maca powder and a large variety of vitamins, supplements and protein powders. Sandra is bending down to pick up orange peels strewn across the lounge-room carpet.

'I don't drink milk,' Shane announces to her. 'I'm going off meat, I'm going more pure. More pure lifestyle. And no prostitutes. Just kidding.' Sandra remains focused on the orange peels.

Shane has been strolling around the small rooms, watching the cleaners at work. He now goes and parks himself in the front doorway where the female cleaners have to brush past him when they take bags of his rubbish outside to the trailer behind the STC van. When he exits the living room, Sandra looks down at the enormous barbell plonked in the middle of the floor and wonders, quietly, if the purpose of this equipment is 'to keep his strength up for what he likes to do in his "playtime"'. Shane also goes to the gym often and takes daily walks. 'Maybe he's on the lookout,' she says grimly. 'You can only surmise…'

Sandra starts picking up larger pieces of rubbish that are inter-mixed with Shane's possessions in random heaps on the furniture and floor. Shane re-enters the room now and stands too close to her with his arms dangling down by his sides.

'I've been under a lot of stress lately,' he says without moving. 'You might think that it's disgusting in here but I've been under a lot of stress. That's why I can't clean.'

'What's that, darl?' Sandra asks him, standing up from where she has been squatting to scoop rubbish into a plastic bag.

'I've been under a lot of stress lately,' Shane repeats louder. He then coughs up into her face.

Blinking down at him, Sandra points to a TV on a low, dirty coffee table. She suggests transferring it to the bookshelf. 'This way, you would use the table for your coffee,' she says.

Shane smiles. 'But I don't drink coffee.'

Sandra turns and places her hand on a small wicker bookshelf, piled with slightly soiled magazines and books (*The Lazy Way to*

*Success: How to Do Nothing and Accomplish Everything, Chicken Soup for the Soul, T'ai Chi Chi Kung: 15 Ways to a Happier You*). A porn magazine is balanced on top of the books; a woman smiles out from the cover, a yellow star shielding her vagina.

'Is there anything here you want to keep?' Sandra asks pleasantly.

'All of it,' he replies. So she starts tidying the books and Shane wanders off again, arms at his sides. It is possible to see, just, the shape of the boy that he was.

'Regardless of what the situation is with him, I see past that. I see, really, just mental illness. Just another day at the shop,' she sighs. She finishes up an hour later and walks down the street to say a quick hello to another client she helped a few weeks ago.

## 12

It's not the first time she's had crippling pain that she pushes into a tight little marble and drops down through the grates of her mind, somewhere deep below. It's also not the first time she has had to instantly change everything. But that doesn't make it easier.

After the rape she is unable to work at all. Then, when she recovers physically, she finds that she is unable to do the sex work that has constituted her income for the last decade. She has Rick, and Rick has work, but that doesn't mean much; Rick's money is Rick's money and her money is Rick's money. In addition to food, shelter and transport, her needs include the drugs and alcohol she requires to deaden her mind enough to live and to sleep, the ability to supplement Rick's lifestyle so that he hangs around, and the cosmetics and hormones which are not merely aesthetic but vital to her dignity. She has few savings, no one to ask for help; no safety net.

Heavily made up and fizzing with self-doubt, she goes out each morning to apply for work. She picks up some hours behind the counter at Shield's Drycleaners, her 'very first straight job' as a woman. The money is abysmal compared with what she is used to earning and it is anaesthetically boring, but it is a stepping stone.

Soon she looks elsewhere and when she gets a call in response to her application to Black Cabs, she wilts with relief; it's her 'very first break'.

Sandra works the radio at the taxi company. She doesn't mind the nightshift—she's worked nights for a decade—and she tolerates the awful salary, but the restrictions on what she can say to the drivers over the radio are unbearable. 'Mac one, mac two, fucking rah rah rah,' she jokes quietly in a robot voice to the other girls, after the first time she is disciplined by management. She is only supposed to pass on information about pick-ups and traffic, using a formal and impersonal tone.

Instead, she knows all the drivers' names, tells them jokes, discusses the day's news with them, flirts, gives them shit, gives them nicknames, asks about their wives. The drivers like it because she keeps them awake, keeps them entertained and, in these days before mobile phones, keeps them safe. She calls the police a few times for drivers in trouble, and they send her flowers which she displays on her small desk. 'The drivers love me, but you've gotta conform all the time,' she protests as she packs up her things on the day she is fired. 'Not everything fits into a box, though.'

To be honest, she's not too cut up about it. The experience has built up her confidence about holding down a straight job. Which is good—she'll need to find another one pretty soon, because Rick's not going to be any bloody help.

She moves into a smaller flat to save money. Spends long days driving around the city, filling out job applications with a smile on her face. Weeks pass and she hears nothing back. She starts taking the bus to save petrol money. Then she starts walking, to save bus fare. She returns home in the early evening, her feet beating with fatigue, to sit alone at the table and stare at, and then through, the job classifieds. Waits for the phone to ring or for Rick to come home, maybe. The power bill is overdue, the rent is overdue. Her throat feels too tight, her chest too small; she starts yawning frequently just to feel like she's getting enough air. She is aware, every second, that she could solve everything on the street or at any of the brothels where she still has connections, but that work is simply no longer possible for her. So she turns up the radio and drinks in the dark and when she starts thinking about ways to kill herself, she gets up and she walks. She spends whole nights pacing around her coffee table like a lion in a cage, this tall woman in a tiny flat too full of old furniture.

Hungover, she yanks the local paper out of the mailbox and flips automatically to the back pages as she climbs the concrete stairs back to her flat. Something inside her stands to attention. *Funeral conductor/arranger.* She spends the day doing her hair and putting together her outfit and only has three drinks that night. She gets up early the next morning to do her make-up and go down to the WD Rose & Son Funeral Home to apply in person.

There, in the soft breeze of the air-conditioning, her desperation is masked under her charm and small talk and knowing nods and cute one-liners; she pushes down the hunger inside her and gives only the impression of sweet proficiency. She shakes hands and smiles goodbye and then returns to the sarcophagus of her flat to wait with a hope that sinks and dies slowly over the next two weeks. So when the telegram finally arrives, it soars in as if it were the Annunciation itself: congratulations on becoming one of the first female funeral conductors in the state.

The funeral home will give her self-confidence, a legitimate and ample salary, friends, a husband, a lover and the contacts she will use to start over, a decade later, when everything falls apart again.

They dress like bruises, the old women clutching felted balls of moist tissue; the old dears with their interchangeable hats and griefs and

171

polyester-clad elbows. Sandra crosses her legs under her desk, quickly yanks her skirt back down to her knees, taps a silver pen on a blank pad of paper, and begins: 'As your funeral conductor, I make every member of the funeral party become involved in it so that they become *very emotional.*'

Perplexed, the women on the other side of her desk remain silent.

'A funeral should be like a play. You get it up to a crescendo,' she explains, drawing a hill in the air. 'You get everyone's emotions there,' she pokes the top of the hill with a long red nail, 'they bubble over, then they boil down, and they get on with their life. Otherwise they're up and down trying to deal with it for years. So, it's just like conducting a play and getting everyone involved in the scenario.'

The women nod, then smile.

'I'll ask everyone to take a flower as they walk in and then they can go put it on the coffin. They become involved like that,' she says, pouring out two glasses of water, urging the women to take them. She explains the running order and asks a few questions about music and flower preferences. 'I think Pachelbel instead of Bach—more soothing, don't you think?' she says. 'But if you have a song that was special to him, you just let me know and I'll work it right in.'

Rising now, her bangles crash as she readjusts her shoulder pads and holds out her hand to help the widow up. 'I know you'll do a wonderful job, dear,' the old woman says. Her daughter nods as Sandra herds them gently towards the reception area.

Despite the implications of the name, an undertaker's skill does not reside principally in the physical business of putting a body in the ground—although competence in that regard is non-negotiable— but rather in the satisfaction with which the living remember the experience. In the words of Mr Eric G. Walters, manager of the Milne Funeral Group and for the past few months Sandra's big boss: 'We should all feel proud of our association with an industry which holds an essential place in the lofty pattern of human loyalty, dignity and high ideals.' No one has ever spoken to Sandra like this before. Of course she comes alive in this house of death.

The funeral homes of Joseph Allison, Drayton & Garson, WD Rose & Son and Graham O. Crawley were united under the Milne Funeral Group umbrella through the corporate colours of magenta and light grey, a penchant for 'coloured flood-lighting' and a morbid strain of the sense of humour best characterised as Office Ecstatic.

The cover of the 1987 newsletter in Sandra's hands informs employees:

- Joseph Allison's convincingly beat Drayton & Garson's in the inaugural table-tennis tournament
- More than 500 attend memorial service for still births at Fawkner Cemetery
- Odd spot—five wives and two stepdaughters do not know each other!!
- Eric's World, Keith's Book Reviews, Birthdays, Grave Humour and more...

And there she is, one of the featured employees in the section called 'Around the Branches: New Faces and Old', elegantly resting her chin on the back of her right hand, smiling slightly, lips closed and looking into the camera with a steady gaze under a hairstyle that would have sat comfortably on the head of Princess Di. She lingers on the page while finishing her lunch, licks the crumbs from her fingers with gusto and then carefully tucks the newsletter in her bag to show Rick.

Standing in her kitchen that evening, she reads aloud from the page, even though she knows it by heart now: *Sandra's previous work experience included supervising Black Cab Taxi schedules and supervising tourists in holiday resorts.* She looks up to check that he's listening. *Her energy and enthusiasm have quickly endeared her to the team. Her interests*

*lie in all musical forms, dress and house designing and interior decorating.*
*Sandra has two teenage children.*

Though her previous work experience 'supervising tourists in holiday resorts' is a euphemism worthy of veneration and the 'two teenage children' are in fact Rick's kids and not her own teenage sons, this is—more or less—an accurate portrait of Sandra Vaughan, funeral arranger/conductor, four months old. And she has already started to thrive, in this quirky environment of light and shade where death is the daily business of life and where her air of kindly authority is so appreciated by the mourners who pass through the doors.

A celebrant performs the funeral, but Sandra produces it, creates it, puts all the oddly shaped pieces into place. She helps prepare the body, blending make-up into cold skin until it resembles the face in the photo provided by the family. She shepherds the mourners through every stage of the funeral's organisation and execution; keeps a watchful eye from the back of the room where she solemnly stands by the door like a lighthouse; leads the procession over soft grass to the new-cut grave. She brings the full force of her perfectionism to every detail of the funerals she conducts like symphonies. With the money she is earning, she pays for Rick's daughter to go to a private school.

Carefully placing the newsletter in a drawer, she turns to open a bottle of wine and tells Rick, 'I adore this job, love it with a passion.'

'Good on you, darl,' Rick says as he grabs her car keys off the table and goes out for the night.

When making small talk with her mourners, Sandra will mention that she started this job 'later in life', which is true in its own way. She is only in her mid-thirties but she has lived and grown old and died in her previous, secret lives. Now, in these 'later' years, she starts changing to become more authentically herself. Her make-up is toned down, her clothes are toned down, her voice is turned up, her concerns are broadened and the road spools out before her. She breezes into work each day in a power suit looking impossibly gorgeous. She is slim and willowy and so golden blonde that she appears, in photos from this time, to have a halo. By the time Rick finally leaves her for one of the women he has been cheating with, a woman in a wheelchair who is about to come into some money, Sandra has set her sights higher.

Craig comes up to the office from the mortuary down the road to help carry a coffin or speak to the boss but lately it seems that he's there more than usual and stays longer than necessary. Craig is skinny but strong, his freckled face is perpetually tanned and his thin lips hover above his perfect teeth in a cynical sneer. It was months before she had any reason to say more than a few words to him but she catches him staring at her all the time and she can tell when he's doing it because it feels like a burning arrow. Lately, she's started staring right back; it's become sort of a game. One Friday evening, when everyone stays back for beers and then fish and chips, he laughs, watching her sip white wine on the boss's knee, admiring the way she teases the old man whom everyone else defers to. Later he strolls into her office, where she is tipsily packing up her bag to go home.

'It doesn't quite match,' he muses, walking too slowly around the room, pretending to admire the framed print she recently hung on the wall. He stops at her desk and squints at her through his dark blonde fringe. 'Something's not quite right. A beautiful blonde like this, flirting with an old cunt like that. What's not right here?' he wonders. She smiles, says nothing. She shoulders her bag, pushes her chair in and, just before she walks out to her car with her heart racing, she plucks her silver pen out from between the vases on her desk and writes her phone number on the palm of his hand.

When Sandra tells me about 'The Hot-Friggen-Dog' or 'Johnny

Hotcock from the Funeral Home Who Was Absolutely Gorgeous', she is referring to Craig. Craig looms large in the Pantheon of Pankhurst; saying his name still gives her a visible boost. Even now, tonight, if her sleeping pills allowed her to dream, she would dream of Craig. He remained the love of her life long after she married George.

She met her husband when she buried his wife. That was the one-liner she gleefully tossed out like a black streamer over the course of their fourteen-year marriage. Alfred George Pankhurst was a grandfather in his early sixties when he arrived at the funeral home, his shirt as grey and as wrinkled as his last image of his wife's hands. An image that haunted him less and less the more he looked at the golden goddess showing his friends to their seats as Pachelbel's Canon played in the background. He had believed his life was over on that day when, really, it was beginning again.

George starts ringing Sandra, seeking her good counsel. Could she, possibly, help him with this or that? He's so new to life as a widower. At his request, she drops in to see him at Mackay Rubber, where he is an export manager, and soon he asks her out and it starts to feel like she's walked into a movie: the chairs pulled out and the doors opened, the champagne and the cocktails, the wine and 'fine dining', the managers who come over to shake George's hand, his 'first class manners', the way he walks, always, on the outside of the kerb, keeping her protectively tucked in.

Sure, he's a little overweight and balding and red from drink and far too eager. Sure, his thirty-year marriage just ended and she is only six years older than his son and eight years older than his daughter. But he is also a sweetheart and a gentleman and safe and competent and respectable. He even looks handsome in his suit with his remaining hair slicked back. And each time she gazes into his eyes she falls in love. Not with him per se, although she will remain loyal to him in her own way until his death. She falls in love with the idealised image of herself reflected back at her: the blonde bombshell; the career woman; the perfect homemaker; the good mother; the equal partner; the loved wife. She falls in love, finally, and over and over again, with herself.

When George asks Sandra to marry him, her reaction is to freeze. *Fuck. I've got in over my head. What am I going to do? I've got to tell him what the story is here.*

'Look,' she says. 'I've got something I have to tell you but I don't know how to tell you.'

'OK,' George replies, confused, then crestfallen, then terrified. But Sandra can't find the words. At first it feels like she lost them, as if they rolled away like a coin on the floor. But then she realises that she never had them to begin with. 'We'll go to the doctor's, OK? And I'll talk to the doctor about how to explain it,' she says.

George's stomach seizes up and he struggles to even get the question out. 'Have you got cancer?' he whispers.

'No no no no,' Sandra says with reassuring dismissiveness. 'I just need to talk to my doctor.'

She makes an appointment for that afternoon. George drives her there and drops her off and though it's still pretty early he probably goes for a quick drink before he circles back to wait for her in the car out the front, newspaper on his lap, unopened.

Inside, after Sandra waves away the doctor's concern about what might be the matter, he sits back in his chair and listens while she explains about George. 'So how am I going to tell this dude? He's got no idea at all what's going on,' she says urgently.

The doctor thinks for a moment. 'Well, just tell him that you're transgender, that you've undergone "gender transformation" or "reassignment". That's a bit softer than saying you've had a sex change.'

As she gets back in the passenger seat, George searches her face and pleads with her to just tell him what's going on. But Sandra asks him to drive to her thinking spot at the beach. She says she'll tell him there.

When she is older than George is on this day, she will still remember precisely how to get to this small spot on Beach Road, right at the end of Charman Road, where she sat so many times and let her mind churn like the water.

George parks and they sit in the cocoon of the car, and he looks at her looking at the horizon.

'George,' she says finally. 'I've had gender reassignment.' She braces for whatever comes next, which she's pretty sure will be a punch in the mouth because that's what has happened before, with others. But there is only silence.

'Well, George, what do you think about that?' she prompts, turning cautiously to look at him.

'So,' he says, clearing his throat and pushing his palms onto his thighs, thick fingers spread wide on the dark material of his trousers. 'You're…ah…tellin' me you want to be a, ah, a lesbian now?' he asks uncertainly.

'No, not quite,' Sandra replies with a small smile. She tries again. 'As I *appear* is not how I was *born*, you see?'

'Huh,' George nods, genuinely trying but absolutely failing to understand.

Sandra takes a deep breath. 'George, I weren't born the way I look. I was born in a *different form*, OK?'

Now she braces again, expecting that punch. Steeled, she squints at the water for what feels like 'a fucking eternity', listening for movement. But still, nothing.

'Well?' she demands, tight with tension, twisting towards him now with raised eyebrows.

But George is only quiet. He looks very small in that moment and, despite the stubble and the wrinkles, despite the jowls and the wiry white hairs in his eyebrows, she could have seen with perfect clarity, had she been looking for it, the baby boy born to a farmer and his wife over half a century before. He sits very still with his hands hanging from the wheel of his hot car parked at the edge of a deep sea. He smells of alcohol and cologne and soap and sweat. He smells familiar now. And she knows that however he cuts her she will miss him.

'Well,' he says, clearing his throat and starting the car. 'I met Sandra. And I fell in love with Sandra. And that's all right by me.'

Mrs Pankhurst. Long after they eventually separate, long after George passes away and their marriage is bureaucratically 'cancelled' on the grounds of her sex, unamended on her birth certificate, Sandra will keep a photo from their wedding displayed on the small table by her front door. She will also keep her married name. That is who she was for well over a decade and also who she was always meant to be: not George's wife, necessarily, but sufficiently normal, as a woman and as a person, to be deserving of love.

'I've got a new lease on life!' George brags to his colleagues around the table at the restaurant after introducing them to his beautiful new wife. 'We're thinking about buying a pram!' And though she laughs lightly and smiles through the meal and the cheese platter and the brandies, Sandra explodes once they are alone in the car.

'A pram, for fuck's sake?! GEORGE! Fuckin' stop this circus! You're making it worse, you know! Don't *do* this,' she yells.

'What?' he says, tipsily tapping the key around the ignition. 'You're getting upset over nothing.' She takes a big breath and lights a cigarette. It's the same thing he did before they were engaged, when he took her to the picnic at Ballam Park to meet his family. His kids were there, some cousins as well. George kept parading her around like a show pony and mock-complaining to everyone about

179

Sandra pushing him down the aisle. Even after she took him aside and said gently, 'Now George, don't do that, that'll come back to bite me. Tell them the truth. You're the one who's hassling to marry me!' But he kept it up and kept it up until she downed the rest of her drink and stormed off to the car with him running after her like a puppy.

'Don't you ever do that to me again, George. Don't you ever fuckin' insult me. *You're* the one who's pushing to get married. I don't give a fuckin' rat's arse whether you want to marry or not. I don't need to be fuckin' married!' she spat, her face bright pink from anger and fear and humiliation.

That had all sorted itself out, but here he was again tonight, exuberantly running his mouth, embarrassing her while intending only the opposite. She stares through the windshield, focusing on the road home, fading from bright to black and back again as they speed between streetlamps and the headlights of oncoming cars. Of course, she thinks with an audible snort, he'd have to be a little bizarre to be with someone like her anyhow.

But it's much more familiar than that. George, too, loves gazing at himself in the mirror of their marriage. There he is young again. But unlike the first time he has the career and the house and the financial security of a lifetime of work behind him. There he is powerful, virile, attractive; his drinking is celebratory, his health is fine, his wife is gorgeous, she desires him and he is worthy of her desire. So while George knows that Sandra was assigned male at birth, that she fathered and then had to leave two children, that she worked as a prostitute for a decade and that she survived a brutal rape, he also un-knows each of these things.

Her past does not simply go unmentioned, it is erased entirely through the allusions to their putative babies. And while her deep anxiety is triggered by such comments, she also craves the suspension of knowledge that underlies them. It is, she thinks, her best chance at a normal life. Though it is lonely and crazy-making and unsustainable, the redemptive power of magical thinking is, also, an offer of sanctuary: a gift each gives the other. 'I met Sandra. And I fell in love with Sandra. And that's all right by me.'

When she agreed to move in to George's triple-fronted brick veneer family home her terms were straightforward. 'Your furniture has to go. I'm moving in with my furniture and we'll rearrange the joint, we'll change it,' she told him. She has a wall knocked down to open up the lounge area and spends 'more than the house is fucking worth' on drapes for the large picture windows that look out onto the street. She spends hours landscaping the lawn, kneeling in the front garden. The old lady next door, who was so unwelcoming towards her at first, finally comes around; tells her with a soft smile that she has transformed the house, so dark and dormant during the drinking that dominated the final years of George's first marriage, into 'a real home'.

These are the days when she sits at the breakfast bar where the late afternoon sun hits the fruit bowl and the immaculately cleaned bench, flipping though the local paper while listening out for the sound of George's car; when she hears the deep purr of his engine pulling up outside and runs out to open the gate for him to drive through; when she closes the gate behind him and runs up to kiss him and then runs back inside to fix him a Scotch before they sit down to the meal she prepared. These are the days when she regularly throws lavish dinner parties for his work colleagues and the clients he entertains from overseas. These are the days when they don't need her money, so George asks her to quit the funeral home and travel with him on his frequent business trips.

Sandra applied for her first passport at the age of thirty-six, eight months before she was married. This required her first to change the name on her birth certificate to Sandra Anne Vaughan, although the sex said (and, when I met her, still said) male. The fact that a passport was issued to 'Sandra Anne Vaughan, F' is, therefore, not to be underestimated.

Repeating this process less than a year later in order to have her documents changed into her married name was fraught. It was complicated by the lack of consistency in relation to her name and her sex across the rest of her identifying documents. It was also complicated by the fact that marriage was (and is) legally understood to mean the union of an opposite-sex couple. It required hiring an expensive lawyer who wrote elaborately to the Registry of Births, Deaths and Marriages brandishing Sandra's successfully registered marriage certificate, hoping that the bureaucrats would not look too closely at the birth certificate underlying it. Again, she was successful.

Still, she is extremely nervous and self-conscious on her first flight overseas; she is 'paranoid', unsure how 'convincing' she looks to the officials who stamp her passport, terrified of being an embarrassment to George. *That's the problem with being put on a pedestal*, she thinks to herself as they start the descent into Hong Kong. *You're too frightened to fucking move or you'll fall off.*

There are never any problems at the airports or at any of the hotels when they travel to Asia and America. But though she tries her best to unfurl and be a lady of leisure, she is bored and restless, crackling with unspent energy.

She meets George in the freezing lobby of their hotel in Bangkok where he leaps up from his martini to help her with her shopping bags. He signals for the waiter: 'Two more, please. Good man,' and then he gives his wife his full attention, smiling wetly at her with his thick lips. 'New dress? Let's see.'

She waves the request away. Then she leans forward, rests her elbows on her knees and clasps her hands together. 'There's only so much travel I can do, George,' she sighs, exasperated. 'There's only so much shopping I can do, so many lunches I can do.' His forehead pleats. 'We need to buy a business,' she concludes. She has been thinking of a boutique, picturing herself as a lady in a shop.

George remembers seeing an ad in the local paper before they left; the thought that had pecked through his mind like a bird crossing a road. 'Let's buy a hardware store.'

'Huh.' Sandra is nonplussed. Then she is intrigued.

North Brighton Paint & Hardware on Bay Street, the main shopping strip in Brighton, would become Sandra's launch pad. As co-owner she was instantly embedded in the daily life of one of Australia's wealthiest suburbs. Though she lived at the edges in a neighbouring suburb, Brighton was where she spent her time. These customers were her community, their concerns were her concerns, their values were her values, their legitimacy was her legitimacy.

'Sandra Pankhurst became the credible person. George made me credible,' Sandra explains. 'George treated me like I was a princess, like I was somebody, someone to respect, someone to treat nicely. He gave me belief in myself and the strength in myself to realise that I could have a better path in life. He was there at that time to make me realise that I could be whatever I wanted.'

The executive director of Transgender Victoria, Sally Goldner, once told me about speaking with 'a trans woman who survived the St Kilda street scene from the 1970s and she said that you had two choices for work: the parlours or the drag shows. The chances of getting any other job were virtually zero. There was that instant limitation of potential'.

In this context, the self-propelled rise of Ms Sandra Anne Vaughan is so remarkable that, despite Sandra's belief that George 'made her credible', I have to be extremely cautious about overestimating the impact of her marriage. It is true that upper-middle-class Australia in the late 1980s would not have automatically opened up to Ms Vaughan. However, before she even met George she had already secured, thanks to her own skill and intellect, an adequately paid and profoundly satisfying 'straight' job. Had she never met him, Sandra could have worked at the funeral home long term and made a future for herself. Or her deeply restless and ambitious nature could have propelled her towards bigger opportunities. But the *perceived* impact of her marriage on her subsequent choices is not in doubt: 'I was important for the first time in my life.'

Welcome to the world, Sandra Pankhurst, President of the North Brighton Chamber of Commerce! Newsprint from October 1992 shows Sandra dressed up for a Halloween street party: a ringmaster in striped Lycra tights, bowtie and tails, arms raised triumphantly like Nadia Comăneci. In clippings, quotes and photos from that period President Pankhurst, placard in hand, leads the resistance of local traders to the expansion of the retail behemoths. She appears at charity balls and promotional events. She is chairwoman of the Brighton Police Community Consultative Committee: launching a new register for senior citizens to discourage their social isolation; pictured at a fundraiser for at-risk youth. In 1996 Oprah Winfrey comes into possession of Sandra's résumé as Sandra writes to her exuberantly proposing a series of fundraising shows Down Under.

Disappointingly, Oprah fails to respond but still, these are the years when, for the most part, whatever Sandra wants to do or be is limited only by her own energy—and that feels boundless, only increased by everything she takes on. You can see it happening in the pages of the *Sandringham-Brighton Advertiser* and the *Bayside Times* and the *Bayside Shopper* and the *Moorabbin Standard*, among the ads for private schools and custom-built wardrobes.

From this local news archive Sandra emerges gradually and then fully as from a chrysalis. Sandra is Small Business Owner, then Leader of the Small Business Owners. She is Chairperson,

Spokeswoman, Hostess, President, Politician, Philanthropist. She is interviewed, photographed, quoted. She is. She tells people that owning the hardware store is teaching her about the technical side of things, 'how things work and how they fit together'. But what she is really learning is how well she fits into the Order of Things.

It is always hot in December but this year the heat is unbearable. Still, she smacks open the screen door to leave the air-conditioned house and sit alone on the burning bricks of the back steps, pumping her damp silk blouse to cool herself down. Convinced, these last weeks, that she must be going through 'an early change of life', she is overwhelmed with heat and dizziness and her growing resentment about the fact that no one ever helps her cook or clean.

She has always tried to make sure that Christmas each year is 'like Disneyland' for George and his children and their children, who rush in from the car calling out to her, 'Nana!' She invites his friends and his cousins. For the first few years, she spent days planning and shopping and cooking a meal for thirty people.

But this year, something is different; a switch has been tripped. She's having trouble keeping her mouth shut about the disrespect shown by Neil and Anita towards her and their father, who now pokes his head through the door.

'You all right, love?' George asks, perspiration glistening on his upper lip.

She turns and gives him a hard look. Closing the door behind him, he smooths down a cowlick that no longer exists, waits for her to explain.

'They live the life of Riley,' she hisses, whipping her head back to stare straight ahead. They let themselves into the house and take paintings off the walls, take whatever they want, and the way in which George handles this has become a point of tension in their marriage. She turns around again and looks at him in warning.

'George, respect begets respect. These kids do not respect you. You can't keep trying to please *them* all the time. I'm your wife, you put me first.'

'You know what?' George says. 'We're not going to celebrate Christmas in this house anymore. You go to so much trouble and they won't even lift up a plate and put it on the sink. We're not doing it anymore.' Shrieks from the grandchildren playing with their new toys in the living room float outside.

From then on, they go away each year to somewhere new, starting with Lake Como. This solves the immediate tension around the holidays but does little to promote family accord.

George is many things to her: husband, friend, lover, business partner, drinking partner, father, child, teacher, companion, consultant, co-worker, supporter and, truly, a love of her life, though it cannot be said that he is *the* love of her life, because Craig is. So while she has no plans to leave George, she does tell him with some regularity that an emergency committee meeting has been called, what a bother, but to eat the leftovers in the fridge and no need to wait up, it's no use both of them being tired, OK? Then she drives over to Craig's place. Other times, Craig rides over on his motorbike when George is at the hardware store.

They are lying on the couch early one afternoon when she hears George's car pull up outside.

'Shit,' she spits, twisting off the couch and grabbing Craig's shoes. 'Hide! Hide!' she urges, as though the force of her voice could pick him up and deposit him in the closet with the vacuum and the winter coats.

'I'm fuckin' not hiding for anybody,' Craig says, sitting up on the couch and crossing his arms over his bare chest with exaggerated insouciance. Down the hall, a key crunches in the lock and the front door opens. George pads heavily towards them on his way to the kitchen. Instantly, Sandra fills the living room doorway, arms reaching upward, bottom poking to the side for maximum coverage.

'Ah, you're home early, love,' she yawns to George standing in front of her and directly facing, though he can't see it, the back of Craig's head resting against his formal sofa. 'I was just having a little nap before I do the shopping.' She takes his arm and gently leads him towards the kitchen where he locates the papers he forgot to take to the shop that morning. 'Now what would you like for dinner? I was thinking a nice beef bourguignon to go with that red you bought...' She keeps his eyes focused on her as they retrace his steps down the hallway. She gives him a kiss goodbye for the first time in months, waves, shuts the door and returns to the living room.

'Remind me never to trust you,' Craig grins, lying back down again. 'You're too convincing a liar.' Her hands are still shaking as she pours herself a Scotch.

# Marilyn

The roses growing around Marilyn's small house are long untended, growing wild and heavy in a neighbourhood of weekend-washed cars and tidy front lawns. This is the first and only hint you get from outside: a visual dissonance so slight as to be, maybe, nothing; one string out of tune on one instrument in an orchestra. And while many of the houses that need Sandra proclaim their problems—the rusted bathtub full of bowling balls in the front yard, the door hanging off its hinges, the solid smell of cigarettes that hits you like a falling brick—there are, equally, many other houses where the signs are more subtle. The permanently drawn blinds, the uncollected mail, the car that never moves; look, now, and you will start to notice them everywhere. But sometimes all you get is a couple of overgrown rose bushes, waggling their long, thorny fingers in the breeze as if to say: you may come this close, but no closer.

After calling Sandra to request a house clean, Marilyn neither answered her phone for a few weeks nor returned Sandra's numerous messages. But they finally managed to connect and Sandra arrived today with three of her cleaners.

Sandra is in high spirits this morning. Lately she has been

concerned with a vitamin C skin serum, whether her contract for police work will be renewed, the trouble a friend is having with her teenage son, whether she might have sleep apnoea, how—if she does have sleep apnoea—the required breathing equipment would ruin the look of her bedroom, missing the early-bird registration for the annual Hoarding and Squalor Conference, how bloody infuriating it is to deal with VicRoads who threatened to hang up on her if she continued swearing, a lovely thank-you card she received from a client and what kind of psychopath laid the carpet in her new office inasmuch as it's clearly three shades darker than the room it was supposed to blend in with. She is meticulous in this regard, as she is in her work, where the prospect of not perfectly completing a task horrifies her more than anything she could ever encounter as part of a trauma job.

'I'm a high achiever,' Sandra explained to me once. 'I have to get a high result and if I don't, that's more damaging to me than having to deal with this crap all day.'

One time, I asked Sandra about the most disturbing job she ever did. 'There are a few jobs that stick in your mind,' she conceded. 'Like, there was a guy, for example, after a Melbourne Cup a few years ago. What took him over the edge I don't know, but it was more the *way* he went about killing himself. It was with tree loppers and bricks. So the pain threshold that he went through was quite mind-blowing. And you look at the slash of blood all over the room—has he cut his toes off? Has he cut his cock off? What's he done? And he's walked around the house as well. Then when you get to the stairwell, even though there's no blood, there's this sense that something isn't right. And I didn't know what it was. So we started to lift the carpet, and it's full of maggots underneath. I went, 'Oh my godfather!' It just *blew* me away, the amount of maggots down the stairwell. That played on my mind. 'Cause if I didn't have that sixth sense of something, what else would I have left to chance?

And that would've gone badly against my name.'

Sandra likes to show me her 'before and afters', photos on her phone from jobs recently completed. 'This is in Caulfield. Mould,' she explains as we stand outside Marilyn's house. 'This is the stovetop; the rats and mice.' She swipes through more photos. 'Look at the mould. It's pretty unreal, isn't it?' Swipe, swipe. 'Ah, that's a suicide, sorry.' She hurriedly swipes past two photos of a black puddle. 'That's the end product.' Proud swipe. 'That's the end product.' Proud swipe. 'End product, end product, end product.' Each room is meticulously clean, shiny to the point of caricature. 'That's two days of work. I think that's pretty good. Oh, I've gotta show you this, just so you can have a laugh,' she says. 'This is a little dog in a teddy bear outfit.'

Sandra's mode is no-nonsense kindness when she walks through Marilyn's cream-coloured front door. Marilyn does not look her age. Though she walks slowly, with the aid of a gliding walker on which is balanced a gin and tonic effervescing in the early morning light, her face is smooth and her tone is archly playful. But then you look closer and you see, before you register that she is in her mid-seventies, that she is simply not well. Her skin is as light as the white hair that shoots out in short bristles above her face. With her stomach swollen round and her pale lips and her finger left quivering in the air while she pursues a forgotten word, Marilyn looks like a dandelion whose seeds are about to blow away. But she directs Sandra and the cleaners around her kitchen with the clipped commands of someone used to being in charge. When she tells me she was a schoolteacher, I am not surprised.

'I had to go into respite care, in the retirement village, when I was really sick,' Marilyn explains as Sandra pats her shoulder reassuringly. 'I basically became one of the staff,' Marilyn snorts, raising one eyebrow, 'the old dears didn't know whether they were Arthur or Martha...' Marilyn waves her hand dismissively; her nails—like

Sandra's—are artificial and supremely long. They have been recently painted a dazzling shade of purple.

Thirty years ago, Marilyn bought this house for herself and the two young children she raised on her own. She was a working single mother then, is a self-funded retiree now, and, despite being shot through with cancer and arthritis, has no plans to leave. I look around at the spacious living room and the kitchen where the fridge door is propped open. I ask whether it is broken.

'No,' Sandra answers breezily on Marilyn's behalf. 'It was too full and she didn't have the strength to open it, so things have gone a little bit tacky in there.'

'How long have you had the trouble with the fridge?' I ask.

'It must be about three weeks, perhaps longer,' Marilyn answers vaguely.

Starting at the front door, the foyer is thickly planted with white plastic bags full of groceries in various states of decomposition. For at least a few weeks, Marilyn has had the physical and mental energy to drive to the supermarket, to select from the shelves, to make small talk with the cashier who arranges someone to help load the bags into her car, to drive home and to schlep the bags from her car through her front door. But Marilyn has not had the energy to make the final transfer of the groceries from the foyer to the kitchen. And even if she could have summoned this strength, she wouldn't have been able to fit anything new into the fridge because it was already full of rotting food which she didn't have the energy to clear out. So Sandra's crew are now cleaning the fridge and the kitchen, swiftly, efficiently and to the arrhythmic percussion of cutlery and crockery. Every few minutes, one of 'the girls' hauls a huge black plastic rubbish bag out the front door and over the lawn, where she hefts it into the trailer attached to the back of the STC van parked on the street.

Life here looks to be less in crisis than surreally interrupted. You get the feeling that someone simply pressed the pause button with the shopping just waiting to be put away and the kettle mid-boil in a house with nobody home. The problem here, then, is subtler than many Sandra normally handles. Milk has curdled and plants have died in these tastefully appointed rooms with their carefully framed photos. Though the house appears generally tidy, three cleaners are working frenetically in the kitchen, hauling bag after bag after bag of rubbish outside. This house, like Marilyn with her beautifully manicured hands, is not its surfaces.

Sandra suggests that Marilyn and I chat in the formal living room, which will let the cleaners move freely through the hallway. Marilyn rejects this suggestion, citing a problem with the height of the sofa, and leads me instead down a dim hallway to her bedroom. She snails along, chanting, 'The more I walk, the better I'll walk.'

Marilyn's bedroom floor is streaked with dirt and strewn with junk mail. There are plastic laundry baskets overflowing with paper and clothes and food and random household items that you must negotiate in order to cross the room. The smell is bad but not over-powering and in this respect it is better than nearly all of the houses Sandra works in; there are top notes of dirty skin, rotting fruit, dust, industrial cleaning products, shit. Marilyn's bed lies beneath different strata of paper (magazines, TV guides, flyers, legal documents, unopened mail) in which various items have become lodged: a Tupperware container of yellow liquid that she later explains is from a can of peaches, a milk carton standing upright, a box of crackers, a can of insect repellent, and a jumble of other stuff including a plastic bottle of cream, five boxes of paracetamol, bags of chocolate and an unopened soap and lotion gift pack. Her many pillows have no cases, and both they and the bedspread are yellow with dirt or age.

Entirely unselfconscious about the state of the room, Marilyn makes her way slowly around the bed and waves for me to open the drapes covering one wall, explaining that she always keeps them closed. I tug at the heavy orange fabric and sunlight filters over the potted gardenias sitting on the patio, through the spiderwebs layered over the dirty glass and into the room, where it washes over Marilyn stepping out of her slippers and hoisting herself back into bed. There is a large pile of slip-on shoes next to the bed: lemon yellow sandals, turquoise clogs, pristine purple sneakers. Marilyn leans over the ball of her stomach, straining to spread her lavender robe over her legs, and then settles back, Buddha-like, against her pillows. I sit, sideways, on the bed next to her.

One of the cleaners comes in and starts wiping down the walls and floor in the small en suite bathroom while Marilyn tells me about the cancer she was diagnosed with in 2014 and how the drugs she was put on exacerbated her arthritis and depleted her oestrogen, causing her to experience something like menopause for a second time, which was 'not awful, but inconvenient and uncomfortable'. The physical sequelae of these painful and debilitating illnesses are presented as the reason why she presently requires the help of Sandra to clean her house.

'And then, last Christmas, things started to go downhill,' Marilyn sighs. She pulls the lavender robe up to her face where red capillaries burst across her cheeks like faint fireworks. Her eyes peer up and over the top of the fabric for a moment; they are very large and very round and for a moment they are the eyes of a child.

Marilyn has two adult children. Though quite different in personality, they are both clearly intelligent and she lists their accomplishments with pride. Equally, however, when she speaks about them it is mostly with cutting judgment and a sense of having been wounded: the warmth present when she talks about previous housecleaners is missing when she discusses her children. While Marilyn usually spends Christmas Day with her younger son and daughter-in-law and their children, they told her they would be celebrating with the wife's family that year. This left Marilyn feeling as though she 'didn't really fit in'. So she arranged to go to a restaurant with her older son, who has 'never ever married', and who lives an hour and a half away. That son had planned to spend Christmas morning with his girlfriend, so he could only join Marilyn for lunch. He didn't come over until 2 p.m., at which point Marilyn was feeling 'very discontent'. Marilyn and her son were 'the last to arrive' at the restaurant and despite the fact that there was still a surprisingly abundant spread of both hot and cold foods on offer, 'the damage had been sort of done'.

To understand the nature and extent of this damage, you must also understand a number of other things. First, Marilyn devotes a room in her house to the appurtenances of Christmas and there she keeps many rolls of Christmas-themed wrapping paper, Christmas-themed rugs, strings of Christmas lights, at least one artificial Christmas tree and 'lots of Santas' including one who is 'life size but with beautiful clothing'.

Second, among the various sweet treats rotting on her bed this morning is a basket fashioned out of chocolate, to which she relatively recently treated herself expressly because it was something her parents would purchase for her from Darrell Lea each Christmas of her childhood. While it still tastes the same, she laments the fact that they used to be 'so much bigger' and came with a tiny chick inside— inexplicably excluded from the modern iteration.

And you must understand that, aside from the two boys she raised by herself after her husband took off with his girlfriend when they were toddlers, Marilyn is alone on this rock floating in space. So the hours spent alone from, and including, Christmas Eve until 2 p.m. on Christmas Day in the year she was diagnosed with cancer felt not just long but absolutely agonising.

'From then on I just went downhill with depression, my arthritis got worse and about three months ago I really hit rock bottom,'

Marilyn says, toying with a wooden back-scratcher she has dredged up from under a pile of magazines at her side. In Marilyn's en suite bathroom, where the cleaner is working, there is a sloping mound of empty tonic-water bottles and cask-wine boxes that reaches from the floor to the height of the pink basin. On the bench, near Marilyn's toothbrush and Crabtree & Evelyn talcum powder, is a jar of pickles and two cups of instant noodles with silver forks sticking out at odd angles. The cleaner is bent down, scooping rubbish into a black bag.

'I just wanted to go to bed and stay in bed. I didn't want to get up. I had no reason to get out of bed. I have always had pets, but not at that stage. I knew that is not the time to get a new kitten. November is the time to go looking for a kitten. Not only that, I questioned whether I was really capable of looking after anything. I was so depressed. I went to my GP, and he doubled my antidepressant medication and my anti-inflammatory for the arthritis because I was in so much pain.'

I ask Marilyn whether she has told her sons about her depression. She says no.

'I don't want them worrying at all. I use the word "harassing" me, but they don't harass me. When I let things get out of hand, I don't let anybody in the door. I just did not want to do anything. I just lost interest and enthusiasm. Some days I could sleep all day and sleep all night. I used to hide the phone so that it didn't wake me up. You can see the magazines that I haven't even read. I had no concentration, no enthusiasm. I would just get up and take another sleeping pill.'

I look at the empty file holders on the far bedside table and a neatly labelled box of folders from the 1990s on her floor. I wonder how many times the house has fallen into this type of neglect, whether it has been a struggle over her life or a relatively recent phenomenon. 'When would you say that it became harder for you

195

to be as organised as you usually are?' I ask.

'It gradually got worse, got to the stage where I just did not want to do anything, nothing at all, just stay in bed all day,' she answers.

During this period, as per their usual practice, Marilyn spoke to her sons on the phone at least once or twice a week. 'Usually about what they have been doing, what I have been doing, and if I have not been doing anything, I just say, "It's been too cold to go out today," which is not an untruth, I can tell you. It's been hideous this winter.'

Sandra breezes into the room with a smile and stands with her hands on her hips, assessing what needs to be done while fighting to regain her breath from the walk down the hallway.

'Do your sons know that Sandra is helping you today?' I ask.

'Not today, they don't. They did last time and that was soon after I was diagnosed with cancer,' Marilyn responds.

'That's right, yes, and your dog had just died; the love of your life,' Sandra says gently. Marilyn wanted to have her older son over so she could break the news about her cancer.

'I said, "I can't let him in because the place is a mess,"' Marilyn explains. 'I had not had help for about twelve months, and I was starting to not be able to do things that I would have liked to have done. I did not want to let my son in because he has always threatened that if I cannot look after myself…'

'She goes into a home,' Sandra finishes.

'So Sandra came in with her team for a day on the Friday, and they cleared the decks,' Marilyn says. 'And I had my son over on the Sunday.' That clean involved removing from the floors a foot of rubbish and accumulated faecal matter from the dog that has since passed away. I ask Marilyn whether she experienced any depression after her husband left her with two young children.

'I don't remember being depressed then. That was such an upheaval in my life that I had to just keep going,' she says.

Sandra goes to check on how the kitchen is progressing. When Marilyn talks, her eyes seem to adjust their point of focus, as though she is only sometimes looking outward. When they are out of focus, so too is her face; her mouth slackens, as does her chin, her eyebrows hang low and her breathing slows. There is then a slight delay with her speech as though she is struggling to hear or struggling to take a full breath in order to respond. This makes her appear much older.

Something else I notice about Marilyn is her sheer intelligence; it is undeniable from the breadth of her frame of reference, the size of her vocabulary and the architecture of her phrasing. Marilyn is quick, she is droll; at the height of her powers she would have been exceedingly intimidating and for much of her life she has probably been the smartest person in the room. She is so naturally authoritative that it takes me too long to recognise that Marilyn is an unreliable narrator.

It is not possible to judge how much the state of Marilyn's home is to do with her current physical illness and related depression and how much may be due to a more entrenched type of mental illness. While her explanations are circumstantial, there are also strong indications of true hoarding, severe squalor, alcoholism. Marilyn is perfectly lineball. But in the end, what does it matter? Pain is pain is pain is pain.

'I'm a bit out of breath today,' Sandra says, coming back into the bedroom, smiling as she violently sucks in air, her chest pumping rapidly like a fish on the bottom of a boat.

'Now don't you do too much,' Marilyn warns, shaking her finger at Sandra from the bed. The undersides of Marilyn's manicured nails are grey with dirt. 'I don't want to have to pick you up off the floor.'

'Oh God, leave me there, love!' Sandra says, waving her concern away. She pushes aside a pyramid of unopened mail from the corner of the bed and plonks herself down next to Marilyn. Retrieves two pillows from under the rubbish on the bed, both of them visibly dirty, pumps each one like an accordion, flings them against the headboard and reclines against them, crossing her long legs over the side of the bed.

'She looks better than I do,' Marilyn says to me.

'Full of Botox and filler,' Sandra says with a theatrical sigh, nonchalantly picking up a sealed envelope from the top of the pile she displaced, squinting at the sender and then employing one exquisitely long French-manicured nail as a letter opener. Extracting a phone bill from two years ago, she places it on the bed next to her and throws the envelope into an empty rubbish bag near her feet.

'Just think of Jane Fonda,' Marilyn says solemnly.

'She looks fantastic, doesn't she?' Sandra inhales reverentially. 'I think she's seventy-eight.'

'And look at Joan Collins,' Marilyn says.

'She is plastic upon plastic; you could call her Miss Tupperware,' Sandra says, pulling out another bill and adding it to the last.

'If she had one more facelift, she would be wearing a beard,' Marilyn deadpans.

'Or talking out of her arse,' Sandra adds, chuckling. Sandra is queen of the one-liners. She once said to me, 'I always felt like I had to be the court jester. It's probably an illusion or a mask that I put on to be accepted by everyone, masking myself to be comfortable with people.'

Another bill goes on the pile, another envelope gets stuffed quickly into the bag. Again and again and again. This is Sandra's gentle genius: the trauma clean that she is at this moment both overseeing and actively progressing looks and feels completely desultory. Everything she is doing appears incidental to the schmoozing going on between her and Marilyn. Anyone who glanced in at this scene would see only two friends, completely at ease, having a natter. They would not know that Sandra has calculated a precise timeframe in which she will clear the room around Marilyn; that she intuitively knows exactly how far she can push Marilyn to throw out what is broken, useless, rotten or infested; that she is keeping one eye on the employee disinfecting the stained bathroom surfaces; and that she is aware of how much progress her other two cleaners are making in the kitchen.

As she inspects another unopened envelope, Sandra's gift is to appear as though she is simply keeping her hands busy, the way someone would pick the label off a beer bottle on a lazy Sunday afternoon at the pub with friends, when she is, in fact, expertly negotiating a logistically complex emotional minefield. At her most effective, it will look like Sandra has completely forgotten that she is at work. And this is because part of her has.

'Have you got a phone bill to pay? What's the date of this?' Sandra says, holding up a sheet of paper, alarmed.

'No, it's all by direct debit,' Marilyn replies, waving it away.

'OK. While I'm sitting here, I'm going to put these newspapers in the bin,' Sandra says lightly, gesturing to one of the myriad stacks of gossip magazines populating the bed.

'Hang on, have I read that one?' Marilyn asks pointing to one of the covers.

'Pick out which ones you have read,' Sandra suggests, selecting a magazine and contemplating the cover. 'What about that Jen? Finally getting married. And having twins,' she marvels. For the next few minutes, Marilyn specifies which magazines can and cannot go into the recycling. Under one of the cleared magazine piles, Sandra finds a miniature stylus and mentions to Marilyn that it's the same as the one she uses for her phone. Marilyn explains that she doesn't like using it but that she has trouble operating her phone without it.

'If your nails are too long, you can't press the screen properly,' I offer.

'It's impossible that nails are *too long*,' Sandra snaps, and I adore her. 'OK, this is an old tax receipt for something you bought at an electrical store...'

Sandra's phone rings. 'Good morning, Sandra speaking. Hi Jesse, how are you? I tried to ring you this morning because the Dean Street property...It has been flooded, the wood has all puffed up, so that will have to be taken out. Then it's also got to be treated for cockroaches and you're probably better off to get Housing to get that done because they get that at a cheaper rate than what I will, because Prozac—maybe I need Prozac—Propest, yes, they've got the government contract, so they get it done much cheaper...Yes, there are major holes in the walls...Right, because that girl that lived there, we've done her several times, I think she's a patient at the psychiatric department...I don't know whether the bed is damaged... All righty, I'll work on that tonight and get that over to you tomorrow. OK darling...thank you, bye-bye.'

Sandra opens a TV magazine from 2012 with Ronn Moss on the cover. 'That is it. Gone with the wind. Ridge is out,' she sighs, reflecting upon his face. 'I watch *The Bold and the Beautiful* every day.'

'Me too,' Marilyn says.

For Sandra, watching *The Bold and the Beautiful* is an act of mental hygiene that provides her with the type of sanctuary others might get from taking a holiday or a walk or some deep breaths. She picks up another magazine and reads out the headline, '*Love in the Boardroom*...Huh!' She peeks inside, momentarily losing herself, before casting it, too, into the rubbish bag.

'Be careful what you throw out there,' Marilyn warns.

'OK, I will,' Sandra promises.

'Because there is my will and testament there,' Marilyn says.

'Oh, good, I'll just change it and put my name on the bottom, shall I?' Sandra smiles and then squints to read the small print on a receipt. 'Now this is...*As seen on TV...pure silk...Kelly's Kloset Cold*

*Shoulder Embellished Kaftan…*Shit!'

'Have a look at it!' Marilyn urges with pride, pointing towards her walk-in closet opposite the bed.

'Is it one of the Katherine Kelly Lang ones? Oh you *bitch*,' Sandra says, hurrying over while explaining for my benefit that, in addition to playing the role of Brooke on *The Bold and the Beautiful*, Ms Lang captains her own line of kaftans. Over the sound of squeaking hangers, Sandra's muffled voice calls out, 'Hang on, you've got two!' Sandra appears in the doorway holding two kaftans aloft. 'They're gorgeous and they would flow lovely over the body,' she muses, appraising the jewel-coloured silk between her fingers.

'This is when I was feeling good last spring,' Marilyn says, motioning towards the kaftans.

Sandra returns the garments and settles back on her side of the bed, where she starts investigating a stack of documents. 'That is from the lawyers; that's your will, is it?' Sandra asks, holding up the papers.

'Yes, those are the ones I want,' Marilyn replies. One corner of the bed has now been cleared and tiny mites are jumping around on the fabric.

'You've got bugs on your bed,' Sandra says matter-of-factly.

'They don't seem to do any harm,' Marilyn answers, and turns to the pile of mail that Sandra has prepared for her to sort through. 'I've got mail here I haven't even bothered to open.'

Having cleared more space on the bed, Sandra now finds another silk kaftan crushed against the bedspread. She tries to smooth the deep wrinkles out with her palm, reunites it with its belt, arranges it on a hanger and swoops it back into the closet.

'Have you got a leak in your roof?' Sandra asks with concern as she emerges, pointing at a tea-coloured stain on the ceiling next to a fan wearing a grey wig of dust on each of its blades. 'I reckon you've got a cracked tile, and you've got water coming through.'

'No, it's been that size for about three years.'

'OK. I'd better give that fan a clean, it's looking a bit gruesome there,' Sandra says. She then hefts a plastic laundry basket up onto the bed and starts considering its contents. I ask Marilyn what she likes to read.

'*The Six Wives of Henry VIII*—I'm a bit of an expert on Henry VIII,' she says. '*Elizabeth I*...It just fascinates me. I used to be an avid reader, and I've got piled up there *Bleak House* by Charles Dickens, which is about that thick,' she says, gesturing with her purple-tipped fingers, while nodding to her bedside table on which there are no books, thick or otherwise, amid the various air fresheners and alarm clocks old and new.

'What about TV?' I ask, gesturing to the enormous screen opposite her bed.

'Oh yes,' Marilyn agrees with some enthusiasm. 'I love my television.'

'You weren't watching *Last Tango in Halifax*?' Sandra asks, looking up from the laundry basket.

'No. I saw *Last Tango in Paris* and I thought it would be a bit like that,' Marilyn says with disappointment.

'It's actually quite interesting,' Sandra replies. In addition to regularly watching a broad range of TV shows, Sandra reads the papers every day, both state and local, and also enjoys magazines about cooking and interior decorating. She is, she says, 'not a book reader', but if she was, she would gravitate to biography. 'I love the Packer story; I love Bondy; I like Gina Rinehart. I like how these people think and how they get ahead,' she told me once.

Motioning towards her bathroom, Marilyn says, 'Once the fridge is cleaned out, there are a couple of jars of stuff in there to put in it.' Sandra nods and asks for permission to dispose of some of the food on the bed.

Permission is denied. 'No. Those are all things I bought at the supermarket today,' Marilyn answers. This seems unlikely, but not impossible. Sandra accepts it and pushes on.

I once asked Sandra about how physically demanding her work was. 'I do come home exhausted from a day of hoarding, I am *absolutely* wrung out,' she answered. 'Because there's constant bartering and getting them to agree but trying to turn it that it's their idea and not my idea. You've got to be very manipulative to a degree.'

'So, it's actually the people who are alive that are more problematic?' I asked.

'Oh, bingo. I'd rather a dead body any time.'

A bird sings outside the bedroom window. A cleaner from the kitchen comes in to ask Sandra a quiet question. 'We are slowly getting there,' Sandra nods, turning her attention back to the papers on the bed. 'I'm just making sure there's nothing in there, but I think it's just bullshit letters,' she says, moulding the pile into a neat brick and then flipping through it. 'Standard letters...urgent action, shareholders, payment dividends...do you need that?'

'Yes,' Marilyn responds and picks up another flyer. 'Community conversations...spotlight on mental health. That's me!' she smiles.

'Yes, me too, I get a guernsey,' Sandra says wryly. She picks up a grey plastic lid lying on the bed.

'That goes on my NutriBullet, that is not to go in the dishwasher,' Marilyn instructs regally.

'They're doing everything by hand in the kitchen,' Sandra reassures her.

Marilyn finds a letter from a social group of 'professional business people' she used to regularly attend. 'At the moment, I've put my membership on hold because to go and sit in an unreasonably cold church hall...' she explains. 'When the weather gets warmer, I will think about pulling myself up by the bootstraps. We always have Christmas in July.'

'And she's a Christmas junkie here,' Sandra says.

'I'm a Christmas tragic,' Marilyn allows.

'This year her aim is to have all the family here for Christmas, because she missed last Christmas,' Sandra explains lightly. 'Yes, that's her goal. We are setting goals to keep us on the go.' Rule of Pankhurst: small, achievable goals.

'Even if we don't have lunch here, or even if everybody brings something,' Marilyn adds and then urges me to go get a good look at her Christmas room. This is the other bedroom, into which it is impossible to walk because of the sheer volume of items stored there. While it is true that Christmas decorations and various rolls of wrapping paper are visible from the doorway, Christmas is not readily identifiable as the distinguishing theme. There are just piles of appliances and electronic items and pet products and cardboard boxes stacked on top of each other, entirely obscuring the floor and forming a swampy situation that reaches halfway up the walls.

'Isn't it a Christmas extravaganza?' Sandra bubbles when I return. I can't tell if she's humouring Marilyn or if, from her higher vantage point, she saw more than I could. She moves around to Marilyn's side of the bed, stopping to transfer a large Ziploc bag full of brightly beaded jewellery from the floor to a shelf in the closet. She then drags out a pink shopping bag from behind one of the drapes, removes from it a small cardboard box and briskly swipes a layer of dust off the lid and into my hair.

'That's my darling dog. Jojo,' Marilyn says.

'Oh, Jojo's ashes,' Sandra nods.

'I don't know where they go but I want them. The ashes are being cremated with me,' Marilyn says, rearranging her robe over her legs.

'Yes, my two dogs are up in my bedroom,' Sandra says, referring to Mr Sparkles (1 January 1995 – 17 June 2010) and Miss Tilly (5 September 2000 – 9 February 2011), resting now in their fine wood boxes with brass nameplates on a shelf across from her bed.

She pauses for a moment to think. 'I'll put them behind the TV so they're in the room with you.'

'Oh, good.'

'Now what have we got in here?' Sandra asks, peering into another large paper bag and removing another cardboard box. 'Christmas presents, hey?'

'That's my cat. Her name was Aurelia,' Marilyn says. And then, peering closer: 'Oh no…it's a vase.'

Sandra removes and opens a third cardboard box.

'Ah, here we are, Aurelia!' Sandra exclaims. 'I'll put the two animals together.'

'Thank you,' Marilyn says. 'She was a beautiful cat. She used to sleep with me every night.' Sandra starts coughing from the dust. The cleaner comes out of the bathroom with a huge bag of rubbish. 'Now don't you try to lift that,' Marilyn warns Sandra.

'I won't,' Sandra promises as the cleaner pushes the bag into the hallway. Sandra starts sorting through another packed washing basket on the floor and Marilyn instructs her to keep a few unopened wall calendars from previous years and a broken attachment for a garden hose. The cleaner returns and asks Sandra if any of the other bathrooms will need a clean.

'No, that's OK. Only this one gets used, and it's just, of course… the…accidents…here, so use some Amsolve to clean that up,' she says, referring to the industrial stain remover touted by its marketing materials as equitably eliminating *carpet stains caused by orange juice, soft drinks, wine, blood, and protein-based foodstuffs such as milk, egg, ice-cream and chocolate*. It also successfully removes faeces, a significant quantity of which streaks the bathroom floor.

Marilyn vigorously motions to the cleaner to hand over a plastic bag full of deliquescing apples and oranges extracted from the bathroom. 'Thank you, my love,' Marilyn says sweetly as the cleaner hands it over. 'I'm going to throw these out for my possums.' She peers inside the bag with approval and then hangs it from the handle of her walker. The smell is nauseating.

'You've got bags and bags of paperwork here,' Sandra says, looking around the room with her hands on her hips. 'We're going to have to sort all this out, rather than keep it for the sake of keeping it. We'll go through and see what is to keep and what is not.'

'All right,' Marilyn agrees.

'We will start with this pile,' Sandra says. She peels a single sheet off the top. 'Now that is from your lawyer, and the lawyer has got to stay, yes?'

'Yes.'

'OK.' That sheet is placed to the side and another is lifted. 'The bank?' Sandra asks, holding up a statement.

'Yes.'

Sandra peels off a water bill. 'This?' she asks.

'I don't know, what's the date?' Marilyn asks.

'These are all from 2012, so they're no good to you. I'm thinking that most of this is quite old by now,' Sandra says, paging through the stack.

'Just chuck it,' Marilyn says.

'Yes, be gone with you!' Sandra intones, dumping the pile into a rubbish bag and swiftly pulling it into the hall before Marilyn changes her mind. 'Gone with the wind,' she says, returning. The cleaner emerges from the bathroom with a jumbo-sized plastic bottle of orange juice which both Marilyn and Sandra confirm needs to be thrown out. I ask Marilyn if she enjoys living alone.

'Yes, I'm quite happy with my own company,' she answers.

'Did you ever want to get remarried?' I ask.

'I didn't have time for that,' Marilyn answers quickly. 'I just did not want to. Anyway, once bitten, twice shy...'

'You see, I like to live on my own,' Sandra agrees. 'I couldn't stand to have to cook or clean or do anything for anyone. There is an independence to living on your own. You can shit the bed if you want or you can live it up on the town!' She nudges a bunch of reusable bags into a large, fluffy pile and nods at the cleaner who has emerged from the bathroom with another two bursting bags. 'So what is the next thing on your agenda? What are you going to do between now and Christmas? What is your next goal?'

'When I get some nice warm days, I am going to gradually walk around the block, taking it bit by bit,' Marilyn says.

'Bit by bit, slowly.' Sandra nods.

I ask Marilyn if she feels OK with driving herself to the supermarket or to get her nails done.

'Yes, I'm fine,' Marilyn says. 'I'm slowing down a bit, though.'

'That's the fear, when you feel you cannot drive anymore, that you'll lose your total independence, and that would be freaky,' Sandra commiserates, touching on Marilyn's great fear, which is also her own.

I ask Marilyn if she's starting to feel a bit like her old self again.

'Yes, and I know I will feel even better tomorrow because Sandra has been here,' she replies. Despite excavating these rooms, and seeing that many of the layers predate Marilyn's cancer diagnosis, Sandra remains faithful to the view that Marilyn's situation was caused by her recent physical ill health.

'We need to change the way we look after the elderly people who have worked all their lives,' Sandra says as she sorts through another basket. 'I think people who've worked and paid taxes all their lives should be getting some sort of dispensation from the government, so that someone comes in, checks on them or makes sure that their needs and things are met.'

Whereas Sandra's only family is her sister-in-law, who lives in another state and whom she sees only rarely, Marilyn has two adult children. Marilyn's relationship with her children, however, is such that this level of squalor has, on at least two occasions, built up gradually, like a mountain range, without their knowledge. She can stay in bed for a week or more without that fact coming to their attention. A phone service calls her each morning between 8.00 and 8:30 a.m. to check that she is alive. ('My son organised that for me.')

I do not know what happened in this house over the past thirty years. I do not know when Marilyn started drinking. Though Marilyn takes control of her isolation by putting a protective spin on it, I do know that disconnection on this scale has long antecedents, that it metastasises over time. So perhaps the surprise isn't that her sons are here so little; the surprise may be that they are still around at all. But regarding the question of whether Marilyn has been abandoned with or without justification—and the true meaning of the white grocery bags carpeting the foyer like unmarked graves—the most satisfying resolution may lie in Sandra's complete lack of interest in the answers.

'Now tell me, how long are you going to stay here?' she asks, adding some letters to the pile that Marilyn has promised to go through later. 'As long as you can?'

'As long as I can,' Marilyn says.

'What would make you move?'

'A stroke, but even then I'd be screaming all the way out of the door.'

'Would you consider one of those retirement villages?' Sandra asks.

'Yes, if I feel I am not coping.'

'You'd have to downsize,' Sandra says.

'But how do I choose what I don't need?' Marilyn asks. And despite the weight of the question, which is the weight of the world, Sandra is, as always, breezily pragmatic.

'Well, how many lounge suites do you need? You'd still have a guest room, but your Christmas decorations would be buggered...'

Sandra examines a photocopy of an official record. 'The Australian Imperial Horse…' she reads.

'That was my great uncle. I thought he was killed at Gallipoli. It turned out he was killed on the Western Front after they left Gallipoli,' Marilyn explains. She mentions also that her father fought in the Second World War.

'Did he survive?' Sandra asks.

'Yes, minus one big toe. He dropped a drum of petrol on it and ended up in Alice Springs Hospital for six months,' Marilyn replies.

The cleaner joins in from the bathroom. 'My husband's grand-father was the same. He chopped off three fingers when he came back. Isn't it funny? They go to war and nothing happens to them until they come home.'

I think of Marilyn's years of being a single working mother raising two children by herself. Of the unrelenting pace and of her endurance, and of what happened, eventually, as the pressure eased off. I ask Marilyn whether she had a happy childhood and she tells me that she did. 'We weren't very rich, but I didn't know the dif-ference,' she says.

Sandra nods in agreement. 'We were all pretty well equal then. There weren't the multi-rich, and if there were, you didn't really know about it because there wasn't the media presence that we have now. Everyone was the same.'

'Our town had one car,' Marilyn recalls.

'They still had the shit-carters in those days, because you didn't have sewerage,' Sandra adds. 'That's where the old saying comes from: as flat as a shit-carter's hat.'

'I think ours used to carry it on his shoulder,' Marilyn muses. 'The baker delivered every day. The milkman came in the wee small hours and we used to leave the bottles out with the money, in front.'

Sandra nods. 'We didn't have refrigerators. Everything was either in brine or in the meat safe.'

'No, we had an ice chest,' Marilyn says.

'Oh, you were rich,' Sandra teases as she stretches out her legs full length on the bed, turns to lie on her side and rests her head in her hand like she's at a sleepover party.

'We used to have a little Asian man who would come along with a wagon that was drawn by a horse. He sold fruit and vegetables,' Marilyn explains. 'Every now and again he would get a little jar of ginger from China and give it to Mother. She thought that was just wonderful.'

'The simple things in life,' Sandra murmurs in a strange, soft voice, gazing dreamily now up at the ceiling, staring through it and back in time. But while Marilyn is participating in a shared remi- niscence between two women of a similar age, Sandra is merely borrowing the warmth of someone else's memories. Feeling their softness for a few moments, like the expensive silk dresses in the closet. At the age when Marilyn was taking a curious look at a jar of Chinese ginger, Sandra was stealing food and wrestling to open the can as her teeth rotted. But the age difference and the geo- graphical difference and the economic difference and the emotional difference all fall away before Sandra's social dexterity, and this is not a trick, it is a wish.

'But that's just chitchat,' Marilyn says and the spell is broken. 'How are my clothes going? The ones I want picked up?'

'Have not got there yet,' Sandra answers. 'We are doing the other fridge as well. I thought we might as well get both fridges out of the way and then you'll have a clean slate.'

'OK, you're the boss,' Marilyn says. 'I'm planning on having you back again.'

Sandra goes to check on the kitchen. I stand for a moment to stretch my legs and reposition myself in my small clearing on the bed. The pile of magazines and food boxes that I had pushed aside to make room for myself shifts precipitously, revealing a few bugs that look like millipedes crawling around on the quilt. Sandra returns. 'We've sorted out all the shopping,' she says, referring to the bags by the front door. 'A lot of it was past its use-by date, so we've given that the flick.'

'I feel as though everything is not revolting and out of hand, and beyond my coping with it. All I have to do is be determined to never let that happen again,' Marilyn says.

And while we all know that is not the solution to this problem, I wonder whether having Sandra here today is a sign that Marilyn is out of control, or a sign maybe that she is actually still very much in control: living her life exactly the way she wants—eating pickles in the bathroom and drinking gin in the morning, watching TV in bed and calling in Sandra to clean up when the mess gets too great; in control even of losing control. And yet.

'What was the reaction from your sons when you told them about your diagnosis last year?' I ask.

'The younger one was quite upset about it. I told him over the phone. The older one...after Sandra had been out the first time, I had him around here, instead of me going to his place. I said, "Look, I'm afraid I've got a bit of bad news for you, I've been diagnosed with cancer." His immediate reaction was "We'll get through this together, Mum."'

I think about Marilyn's eyes going out of focus as she drives to the supermarket, how she steers the shopping trolley down the bright aisles, clutching the handle like her walker. How she supervises the employee who carries the white plastic bags to her car, carefully drives those bags back home, carries them inside and leaves them by the door to rot. I think of the dull popping noise a tranquilliser makes as you fumble it out of a near-empty bottle, the pasty bitterness it leaves on the tongue when swallowed in haste without water. I think of how a body with cancer maintains itself on a fuel of alcohol and sugar. Of a phone ringing and ringing and Marilyn's voice saying that it's been too cold to leave the house. The moths that spiral up into air like ash from embers when the quilt is adjusted. The odd sensation of rolling over onto a can of insect repellent; whether that discomfort is something you might try to ignore, like a full bladder on a cold night. I think of Marilyn closing herself into herself and willing herself to sleep as the sky purples, drains clear and darkens, eventually, again.

Sandra takes a call, then announces that she's off to do a quote for another job. She will be back soon to make sure everything is finished correctly. Marilyn nods and fares her well. Then she hefts herself up from her bed and walks me out slowly, inching her way down the hallway, which is lined, on both sides, with photographs of her forebears—her great-grandfather in shirtsleeves, her parents on their wedding day.

I search in vain for a photo of Marilyn in full flight; an iron-tongued warrior in silken finery and bold beads. But such a photo would just be another proof, like the faces looking down from these walls or the pets in their funeral boxes, that the staggering difference between what we were once and what we are now is, sometimes, as true as it is false. I leave down the front path, past the STC trailer overflowing with garbage, and the roses—bright, still, under their wild tangle of leaf and thorn.

# 14

Between chairing and meeting and speaking and networking and fighting off competition from giant retailers, Sandra is also running a struggling small business seven days a week. Working under this pressure, and this closely with George, who just wants to retire already, means that they have 'a few tumultuous times'. She has, for instance, picked up the cash register and hurled it at him at least once. For the most part, however, the centre has held.

George's heart is dying and his liver is dying. His business is dying and his marriage is dying. His children are alienated and his house is about to burn down. But there is a time before when it is still possible to un-know most of this; when he can press a hot washcloth up to his face, rub shaving cream onto red-warm cheeks, zip the excess off his lips with one thick finger and shave in slow strokes to reveal skin that feels new; when he can thread his shrinking arms through a navy sports jacket and take his still-younger wife out to dinner; when he can drink a Scotch followed by a bottle of red and feel, for a few hours, like himself again.

They are defeated, in the end, by Goliath. North Brighton Paint & Hardware cannot compete with Bunnings. Suddenly, two people who have worked their whole lives and become used to a certain standard of living are left choked with debt. They call in liquidators but the auctioneer for the day costs them forty thousand dollars. The debt opens up like a sinkhole. It swallows their savings, their cars, their home, George's dignity. He starts drinking more and Sandra starts cleaning houses.

The ad in the local paper says:

> Sandra Pankhurst presents
> *We're Absolutely Fabulous*
> The Specialist in Domestic Duties

The ad and the article that appear alongside it in the weekly Business Profile column are an act of friendship: her contacts at the local newspaper, who have become friends over time, give her the publicity she is unable to afford. *Because 'We're Absolutely Fabulous' is the name of the business it must reflect the opinion of the owner about their service! No point in hiding your light under a bushel! Or so Sandra Pankhurst believes…*

Sandra is described as 'a long-respected member of the community, working as a funeral director and shopkeeper as well as serving as President of the North Brighton Chamber of Commerce', and quoted as saying her business is going so well that she's seeking more employees. Within three months, she is managing a staff of twenty cleaners.

She strides through the door of their rented unit waving the new edition of the local paper. 'They printed it!' she calls out triumphantly. George, dozing in front of the television in his robe, looks up briefly but says nothing. The tension they have ignored for years, clinging to the edges like rising damp, is more palpable these days. Her ring clinks on the bench as she spreads opens the paper and reads her letter to the editor out loud across the room:

On Monday, I attended a prospective councillors meeting at Brighton Town Hall. It was a shame that there was such an air of aggression. We should have used the time to get to know each other because we could be working for the same cause— the welfare of Bayside citizens. Running for the council should not be a matter of power games, but of serving the community.

She looks up expectantly but George has closed his eyes again, appears to be dozing. Her cheeks burn. 'What were *you* doing when you were my age, George?' Sandra asks him. He says nothing. 'You were wheeling and dealing and travelling the world! Let me do what I need to!'

She grabs her keys and her handbag and slams the flimsy door shut behind her, leaving behind a silence so heavy it deserves a place in the Book of Things Which Can Be Seen.

Her campaign slogan is 'Sandra Pankhurst, Fighting for Community' and she repeats it, on an endless loop, to everyone who walks down Bay Street as she smiles and presses her bubblegum-pink flyer into their hands. It features her photo, cut from a shot taken with George at a dinner party, a short résumé and her campaign statement:

> I live and work in the Clayton Ward with my partner George who fully supports my candidature. I also currently run my own business but before this George and I were the proprietors of the North Brighton Paint & Hardware. I am an energetic, community-minded person and I understand the concerns and needs of the local area well.

After the polls close, she stays up drinking Scotch with the television turned up, trying to stay away from the phone while the votes are being counted. An early tip from the scrutineers has her in the lead, but the official call comes in at midnight. She has lost the seat by a small margin. Sinking, she makes small talk anyway, chatting for a while before hanging up.

'Fuck. It was because of the mistake in the phone number I put on the flyer. I know it,' she sighs, turning to George. 'Apparently the guy who had the phone number is pissed off because his phone has not fucking stopped.'

'You tried your best, that's all you can do,' George says, not managing to sound despondent.

She ignores his tone and pours another drink. On the one hand, she couldn't really have afforded to live on a councillor's meagre stipend of two hundred and fifty dollars a week; on the other, she's pissed off because her pride is hurt. She takes her sleeping pill and gets up at six o'clock the next morning to run Red Cross Calling with a smile covering her face, before going to clean houses.

'It's a nightmare on nickels and dimes,' she says to Craig as he parks at the drive-in, his son in the back seat in pyjamas.

'The hourly rate isn't bad,' Craig says, fiddling with the speaker through the window.

'Yeah, but see, in an eight-hour day, you can only earn six bloody hours of money, because you gotta travel between house to house. And people want general house cleaning on a nickel-and-dime budget,' she says. She's never slept easily but this keeps her up at night. Lately she has been thinking about something new, toying with it in her mind: a gap in the market she observed from their days in the funeral business. 'Anyway, it'll be all right. There's gotta be a way around it,' she sighs, putting a hand on Craig's thigh as the movie starts.

When she turns her phone back on as the credits roll, she is flooded with increasingly frantic messages from George. He's returned home to find that their house has been robbed and when

Mr and Mrs Pankhurst

Craig

The President of the North Brighton Chamber of Commerce, 1990s

Sandra with members of the STC team, 2007 PHOTO: DAVID CAIRD / NEWSPIX

Sandra Pankhurst at home, Frankston, 2016 PHOTO: DAVID KRASNOSTEIN

he couldn't reach Sandra for two hours, he became terrified that the same people who ransacked his home had harmed his wife.

'I'm just out with friends,' she reassures George when he answers halfway through the first ring.

'Get your arse back here now!'

She turns to Craig as he starts the car, pensively putting one long nail up to her lips and trying not to smile. 'Do you think I should go home or not?' she asks softly, careful not to wake the child.

'Ah, you better, you better,' he chuckles.


The first trauma clean comes through contacts at the funeral home. She enlists a girlfriend and they work seventy-two hours straight. When she sees the state of the house, she is aghast that people can live like this. There are rats running down the hallway and empty bottles shoved deep into holes in the walls. Every cupboard is stuffed with empty beer cans and the floor is black with filth. They pull up three different layers of rotten flooring from the kitchen.

She will remember this first trauma job in granular detail. How naive she was about what the work required, physically and mentally. How poorly she estimated the cost. How the extra five hundred dollars she negotiated from the client was nothing for what they went through to get the last layer of flooring up, because not only was it stapled to the floor, it was also glued. So they had to cut the linoleum and pour boiling water over it and wedge spades under-neath to try lift it. Every time they hit a rivet it jarred against their hands, leaving them red and swollen.

George opens the door for her when he hears her car pull up. She drops her purse on the kitchen counter, struggles to open a bottle of white wine.

'How'd it go?' he asks.

'Hands are killing me. Clients were very happy with the end job, so they fuckin' should be,' she snaps. 'I'm going to bed.'

Her hands take a long time to heal. George has never seen her so down. She still goes out every day to continue her domestic cleaning jobs. It takes months, though, for her to reconcile herself to the trauma cleaning; the fact is, it is the highest-paying option she has, and it is work that she can, yes, actually do.

Finally, she embarks on the technical research in earnest; places a large order for chemicals and equipment; registers the name All Trauma Cleaning for the new business she will run out of their garage.

When their house burns down, Sandra blames herself. She had a bad feeling about leaving the cleaning cloths in the dryer. Sorting through the wet ruin of their rooms, she finds that some things have survived in the charred cupboards and closets, though not unscathed; photos have been melted against the glass of their frames, everything stinks of smoke.

With the payout from their contents insurance, the couple move to another rental unit. And though she tries her best to make this one, too, into a proper home, there's something wrong with George. His alcoholism. His poor health. The loss of his business and his triple-fronted brick-veneer house and his cars and his savings and his neighbourhood and his retirement and his sweet, blonde wife who used to listen out for the sound of his car. Now in his mid-seventies, George is becoming increasingly sick and small and dependent. He doesn't want to do much—isn't able to do much—and his need to keep his wife by his side only pushes her further away.

In the background, like music or heating or the smell of the fresh-cut flowers, there had always been Craig and the sustaining certainty that, one vague day in the future George would no longer be around and they would be together. That certainty doesn't go away just because she hasn't seen Craig recently. Their relationship has always been 'on again, off again', less because he is the type who refuses to commit and more because her gender 'played with his head'. Regardless of that, Sandra has always told herself that she would not leave George, that she would do the right thing by him. But by fifty, something changes for her.

She feels increasingly limited and constrained; she is resentful. It is not only that George is autumnal, and she is (comparatively) vernal; that he has grown to need her more as she needs him less. She is tired and busy and stressed earning the only income that supplements his small pension, and when George tries to tell her what she should do, or what he would like them to do together, she feels this as an unjust encroachment on her autonomy. 'You'll never own me, George,' she warns. And while George's grasping for control will become, through repetition, the explanation for her leaving, it does not accurately reflect the cause. Having lived so long without the true gift of family—unconditional love—she is not equipped to take on the true burden of family—unconditional sacrifice. Ten years in a marriage of partial intimacies has not changed this. She has no desire to play 'nursey nursey'.

George moves in with his son near Brighton Beach and Sandra moves an hour down the coast where she scrapes together enough to put a deposit on 'a shit shack in Mornington, in the housing commission area'. When she isn't working she knocks down walls, landscapes the small garden, decorates inside and out from 'all the garage sales under the sun'. This is when, as she finds herself moving slower and slower, the pace as startling as it is frustrating, her health starts to fail her.

George is in and out of hospital. Though they have separated, they remain friends. Sandra occasionally drives an hour each way bringing Tilly, their dog, to visit him. And whenever George is feeling stronger, he drives down to Mornington. Usually he spends the night, he in one room and she in another. This is how I like to think of them; sitting side by side on the back deck under the stars

219

floating in the dark bowl of the Peninsula sky, surrounded by the rose bushes she recently planted. Their livers are deteriorating—along with her lungs and his heart—but for now they are clinking glasses, they are chuckling over the dog's antics or some funny memory or old joke. For now they are OK, despite the fact that this is so much less than either of them wanted: united, still, by all the things that separate them.

When he rings on Friday morning to tell her he'll be coming down, Sandra makes sure that the fridge is 'chock-a-block of alcohol'. Anything George wants to drink, she's already bought it. Still, on that weekend, he insists on more. 'We gotta get some more beer, and some of that new Scotch,' he urges. Closing the fridge, running a dry hand over his white stubble.

'George, surely I've got enough there,' she says, exasperated.

He insists.

'Well, you'll have a skinful,' she sighs, putting her knife down, grabbing a dishtowel and looking around the kitchen for her car keys.

The next morning, she cannot wake him. She rings an ambulance. Three days later George is dead 'and everything goes to shit for a while'.

It is made clear that she is not welcome at the funeral. When she insists on going anyway, she is referred to—only once during the service—as George's 'friend', which she finds deeply hurtful. The next week, she finds out she's expected to contribute to the cost of the funeral.

Sandra and George were still married at the time of his death in October 2003. Their fourteen-year marriage was, however, officially 'cancelled' by the Registry of Births, Deaths and Marriages in 2004. When Sandra told me this, she did not know why it had been cancelled, and she had forgotten both how and when she found out. The registry explained to me that they 'had been advised' in 2004 of her sex reassignment surgery and identified the unamended sex specified on her birth certificate.

The dominant legal definition then—as at the time of Sandra's wedding in 1989 and as I write this now—provided only for marriage between a man and a woman. On this basis, the registry referred the matter to the Attorney-General's office and were instructed to void the marriage. Though it is probable that the registry tried to contact her, Sandra does not remember this happening nor does she remember being told how this specific piece of personal information came to their attention or offered a right of reply. The registry file no longer contains this information, a fact that took nearly a year of repeat inquiries made by Sandra to ascertain.

In any case, the point was moot; it was simply not possible until 2005 to amend the sex on one's birth certificate to reflect sex reassignment surgery. Victoria was the last Australian jurisdiction to allow this change. The legislation that would allow such an amendment—to 'result in fairer treatment of people with transsexualism'[7]—was being drafted by the government in the very year in which it voided Sandra's marriage.

It was a bureaucratic killing of sorts. When, in 2014, her doctor told her to order her affairs due to her precarious health, Sandra needed to standardise her name across her assets and identifying documents. 'I don't really want to go in front of the bureaucrats,' she told me, referring to the registry. 'They're only going to gawk and pass judgment. So I've now gotta go to a lawyer and get my name changed because, as is, I don't exist. Everything—Medicare, seniors card, drivers licence, credit cards, houses—is in Sandra Anne Pankhurst, and yet I don't really exist. But that is what I've been for the last twenty-eight years! I've got to change my name to Pankhurst, otherwise my will can't be settled. And yet I have paid taxes all these years…'

•

She sits safe in the blare of the television with music from the radio overlapping from her bedroom down the hall. But her shoulder muscles are tight and high and a glass of cheap white wine grows warm in her hand in her house under the dark sky. She craved this independence but now she dreads the nights alone. She can feel it, the undulating, whispering silence bearing down on the small square of roof, pushing in on the thin glass of the windows, breaking through to flatten its dry hand across her forehead and her nose and her mouth. When she finally tries to reconnect with Craig she finds out that he died, a month after George, from the cancer he refused to tell her about.

'Yeah. So that was a bit spinny!' she tells me with classic understatement. Be clear. When Sandra says that something was a bit spinny or freaky or eerie, or 'a bit of a rocky road' or 'scary Mary', what she means is that a pit cracked open beneath her feet, dropping her straight into the liquid centre of the earth.

'My heart's really still with Craig and that's why I'll probably never have anyone ever again in my life,' she says with a tight smile. 'I've since spoken to the mother of his child, 'cause we've known each other through the years. She hated my guts. I said to her, "Well, don't be like that, Carla. At least we both have got good taste…"'

I know a little about Craig: he was 'a health junkie', 'a fitness junkie', and a devoted father to his little boy. I know that Craig 'had all the toys': motorbike, jet-ski, four-wheel drive. But like Rick, like George, he remains a shadow.

The more I ask about these men, the smaller they become, compressing gradually into a point of singularity until they simply blink out. Like her ex-wife and her ex-girlfriend, like her siblings and her sons and her drag friends, like Rick's daughter and Craig's son and her stepchildren and her step-grandchildren, like her friends and her employees, these men existed only in relation to Sandra. Their inner lives unseen, their feelings unfelt, their additional dimensions irrelevant; too exquisitely beautiful and dangerous to notice or hold dear or remember.

Though friends sometimes make the long drive to visit, though they fling their buttery leather handbags onto her secondhand dining table and look out of the doors opening onto the deck with its roses and ornamental pear trees, exclaiming, too brightly, 'You wouldn't even know where you are! You'd think you were in Brighton, sitting there!' she is frantically lonely and increasingly unwell and desperate to move.

She is trapped down in Mornington, where she runs the business, now called Specialised Trauma Cleaning Services, from home. The only way she can afford to move anywhere else is to make a decent profit on the sale of the house. But a number of real estate agents have told her that she simply won't get that sort of money. Each time she hears this, she responds, 'Fuckin' oath I will get that money.' She spends all her free time camouflaging the house's flaws. It is 'a house of cards' but she has to work with what she has.

'I've got the photographer turning up at noon tomorrow,' the real estate agent tells Sandra. A 'real fucking bitch', she's added no value so far.

'You'd better fucking cancel him,' Sandra replies tartly, squeezing the phone between her ear and her shoulder as she drives back from a trauma clean in the inner city. 'I told you I wanted *twilight photography*. The house looks best under lights, when it's wet. That makes it look good. That's what I paid for and that is what I'm having.'

An hour later the agent calls back to say that she's managed to move the session to later that evening.

'OK, I might be there a little bit late because I'm getting the last of the plants,' Sandra replies. She is pushing a trolley through the gardening section at Bunnings, looking for the most attractive of the plants on sale.

'You're going a little bit overboard,' the agent laughs.

'If I do anything, I do it properly,' Sandra replies, deciding on the larger of two peace lilies.

When the agent brings the photographer to the house that evening it is as though they are the first guests at a chic, though silent and freezing, cocktail party. Out on the deck the lights are on, candles are lit, plants are arranged tastefully in brightly glazed pots. Sandra is pouring champagne into glasses that surround platters of cheese and smoked salmon, styled with care on the large outdoor table.

Seeing their expressions, Sandra explains curtly, 'This is only for the photographer. The photos need to show that you can *entertain* out here, they need to *plant the seed*.' Struggling to take a full breath, she finishes folding the napkins into crisp white sails. 'This is what will sell the property.' She is entirely unconcerned that they think she is insane.

The house sells the first weekend on the market for more than double the purchase price. She can now afford to buy a unit in Frankston off the plan; just enough left over for the adjustments to the layout that will make the space perfect. With no extra money and no financial safety net, the last thing she needs is for construction on the house to start running behind schedule.

She starts 'ringing around the world to try to find somewhere to live'. Nothing is available. No one steps forward to help.

The caravan park that is, eventually, the best she can find, is cold and run-down. It is unsafe at night. At five hundred dollars a week, it costs more than a mortgage for the privilege of staying there, but it is her only option. She figures that she can put up with anything for a while. Visiting her house and assessing the progress on its construction is her one joy. But it is there that she trips on a piece of lumber and slices her leg open, down to the bone. Skin dangling like a banana peel, she wraps herself up and drives herself to the hospital, where she parks at an odd angle and walks into the emergency room, bleeding on the floor. 'I've got ambulance cover and here I am, driving myself to hospital,' she laughs to the nurse who signs her in.

She is back the next week after another fall breaks her wrist. Though she hides it under jokes, she develops a phobia of walking. She cannot go too far without steadying herself against a wall, clinging on to the back of a chair, a sofa, the edge of a table, whatever is immediately to hand. Then comes the pneumonia that hits her like a meteor and hollows her out like a crater.

Though her impulse is to hide herself away, to heal or die, in her cold caravan like a sick animal, stronger still is her desire to make it home: her unit is, finally, ready. With no other choice, and though it makes her stomach cramp with discomfort, she allows a couple of her friends to see her weakness and accepts their offer of help. The women drive down to Frankston from Melbourne. They clean the mess left behind by the builders. They retrieve her boxes and furniture from storage. They unpack everything and put it away, neatly, in her new closets and drawers.

This 'wild fucking year' culminates, finally, in the loss of her big toe while wrestling a large fern into a stone urn in her 'al fresco area'. Again she wraps herself up, again she drives herself to the hospital. Down the highway she has driven a thousand times before, without ever realising that while everyone is moving at the same speed the trucks hauling the heaviest loads have the most momentum.

'Chop the fucking thing off,' she instructs the doctor.

# Glenda

'Her name is Nefertiti,' Glenda tells me as we stare down at a cat carrier in the overgrown grass of her front lawn. Behind us, on a busted navy sofa on Glenda's porch, four other cat carriers holding four other cats are lined up in a row. It is 9:50 a.m. on the type of grey morning that does Glenda's neighbourhood no favours. It's not really a neighbourhood. It's a strip of houses on one side of a highway facing a strip of fast food places and service stations on the other.

After driving over an hour to get here, I walked through a high wooden fence and into a smell so strong it felt like a slap. On the lawn are about fifteen black bags full of the rubbish that Sandra has already talked Glenda into throwing out this morning. Sandra will be here, working with Glenda, one day a week for the next five weeks.

Glenda is short, maybe sixty. Her hair is white at the roots and the rest of it is the same neon pink as her T-shirt. She is European and when she speaks she sounds like one of my relatives. She should be pink-cheeked, smelling like powder. Stuffing everyone full of cookies. Instead she is completely alone and living in a house full of books and yellowed newspapers and cats and their shit, which for years she has been unable to clean or unwilling to acknowledge so she presses newspaper on top like a layer cake.

The cleaners are working in Glenda's kitchen/living room. It is full of books, plastic tubs of more books, office supplies, appliance boxes, old newspapers and other items, such as a child's polka-dot suitcase, all floating on top of each other like flotsam on a choppy sea. My eyes water from the smell. Sandra leads me to the threshold of Glenda's bedroom where I am immediately confronted by a great wall of similar debris that almost sweeps the ceiling. It is dark and there is only room to peer sideways and down at Glenda's nest—a tiny mattress on the floor not long enough for her to stretch out on. A stack of reading material rests beside it; books, the *Economist*, the *Quarterly Essay*, a pair of gold-rimmed glasses folded neatly on top. The small clearing is in danger of being filled in by the precarious fence of stuff that surrounds it.

Glenda invites me outside for a chat. She leads me past the mewing peanut gallery on the porch and out onto the lawn, near a small tin shed, where she sets up two wooden chairs and introduces me to Nefertiti, lolling in her cage.

Glenda qualified as a dentist and also has a degree with honours in psychology. She worked for years as a grief counsellor. In addition to a plethora of short courses and certificates, she has completed a professional writing and editing class and she has pursued, as I have, a postgraduate degree in law. She was involved for many years on a television program that interviewed people 'who had a personal and professional vision for a better future'.

She tells me, 'You are those people I used to interview.'

Roles are starting to blur; I am losing altitude and things are getting messy. Which is, yes, the whole point of sitting in her yard. Sandra has pointed out to me many times that hoarding does not discriminate on the basis of income or intellect.

'You look on the wall, Director of this Hospital or Head of this Company, and you think, "What incident happened in your life? Or did someone leave you and leave you emotionally scarred, and you couldn't deal with it?" Like, there's so many fragile things can just twist you and turn you,' Sandra once said to me. 'By the grace of God, it could be me. So I'm not going to judge anyone. These people were mentally strong, they were high achievers. So, you don't know. None of us know what tomorrow's got in store.'

Glenda mentions her honours thesis and I ask what it was about.

'Ah, back then, it's not me anymore but that's your journey...' she replies, swatting the question away. And I commiserate, mentioning sheepishly how irrelevant my own honours thesis seems in retrospect.

She elaborates, dismissively, 'It was about how anxiety affects your attitudes and your being able to perform. I can't remember more...'

Sandra walks up to Glenda holding a wicker basket overflowing with miscellanea: a shower cap, a free anti-virus CD, a contraption to give a dog a pill.

'I've made an executive decision,' Sandra announces. 'This is shit.'

They giggle. 'But some of them are not shit,' Glenda says, still laughing.

'Oh, tell me what,' says Sandra.

Glenda holds up the CD. 'This is not shit.'

'Are you gonna use it, really?' Sandra coaxes.

Glenda nods. 'Yes. Tonight.'

'Oh, you liar,' Sandra scolds, causing Glenda to break out again into giggles. 'This thing's going to the shithouse, I'm telling you now, this is going to buggery.'

'This is going to the neighbour,' Glenda counters.

'Well, tell her she can jump in a lake,' Sandra smiles, backing away with the basket, hoping to add it to the pile on the lawn that is big but not nearly big enough.

'She might, really, because she has brain injuries. So I cannot tell her that. You can tell her,' Glenda says, before explaining how the dog-pill machine works.

'Hmm,' Sandra says and then asks what the CD is.

'Free software!' says Glenda.

'Oh, bugger, throw it out!' says Sandra, 'You've got more than you can poke a stick at.'

I point out that you can download it for free. Glenda says she doesn't know how to do that, which I don't believe even before she asks me if I know the Linux operating system.

Glenda mentions how much she and Sandra laughed last week, 'You know how you are tired and you crack up? We couldn't stop bloody laughing. That is much better—laughing than crying. And sometimes you do both at the same time!'

After a period of estrangement from her husband, Glenda spent his final days with him while he was dying in hospital. Then she developed a flu 'like a big kick' in the chest. For three months she couldn't cry. 'I became wooden,' she says. A few months later she started to feel a 'delayed grief reaction', but it was too painful. So she went to school. 'I did so many short courses,' she laughs. 'That's my way of calming down and staying focused. This is my drug, this is how I survive. It didn't affect my ability to study.'

I think back to my own delayed grief response, after my mother left. When it became clear she was not coming back. I think back to the years when I barely left my room, when the pills I took each day for anxiety and depression made the light hurt my skin and my hands tremble too hard to hold a pen. How I devoured books, lying in the foetal position in the dark until my hips hurt against the mattress. How much I needed the desolate predictability, the safeties of stillness and solitude. Beyond distraction or entertainment was just the perfect permanence of the written word and the camaraderie embroidered in its silence.

Eventually Glenda gave herself permission to grieve. 'I got a little kitten, she's twelve years old now, and I put it next to me on her blanket. I slept, I woke up, I started crying, I'd stretch out and there was her warm, purring body and I'd fall asleep again.' That cat now has ten siblings. 'I was able to integrate the grief in my life. But it's amazing to come out the other end. That's why I'm surviving this situation too, otherwise I wouldn't be here,' Glenda says.

She is referring to the reason Sandra is here today. The narrative is as messy as her house but it appears that Glenda has been on a downward spiral, at least since losing her husband in 2001. She bounced between private rentals and public housing, until five years ago she ended up in the unit she currently occupies, which is intended as temporary housing for women in crisis.

'All the nightmare started since my husband passed away 'cause I was by myself and then I had to go onto the disability pension because of chronic fatigue, fibromyalgia, carpal tunnel syndrome, all this, osteoarthritis and because of the ongoing trauma of being up in the air for years. I had to find support on my own, there's no one I can ask to talk on my behalf. And post-traumatic stress now...'

Her eyes well up. And then it starts to rain, so she drags our chairs inside her minuscule tin shed and arranges them between plastic boxes of books and piles of bulging rubbish bags. We resettle ourselves over a thin puddle of cat vomit. Case workers from the housing organisation work with the tenants, stabilising them so that they can move on to longer-term housing, for which they are fast-tracked.

However Glenda perceives this therapeutic approach as a siege. She has used her intelligence to fight every step of the process. Of the first attempt to move her on, she says: 'I ended up in the foetal position for months. Disgusting, evicting someone...they knew from day one that I am a widow, and all my medical conditions, and I've got no one, no family...'

At first I feel indignant on Glenda's behalf. Then, as her narrative expands, so too does my awareness of the bags bursting with yellowed newspapers around us and the cat vomit pooled at our feet and the smell of shit everywhere, and I realise that my feeling is more accurately empathy for the pain.

There are two Glendas. There is the Glenda who tells me, 'You don't really stay in a transitional property for five years...' And there is the Glenda who cites perceived technical violations by the housing organisation as justifying her continued occupancy. There is Glenda the grief counsellor and psychology graduate, who finds it 'interesting when you can observe yourself as disassociated from what you are feeling'. And there is the Glenda who tells me that the explanation for her current state is structural: 'If you haven't got space to put your stuff in, what are you going to do?' When she calls her house a 'third-world slum' she is referring to the lack of built-in wardrobes, not the faeces on the floor.

I cannot diagnose Glenda, but she is just ill enough and just autonomous enough to be the type of client that housing services—with the best of intentions—do not have a solution for. Glenda was simply refusing access to anyone who visited, leaving the organisation with a choice between breaching her and rendering her homeless, or letting the property persist as a threat to public safety. This is why Sandra is vital: not merely the work she is doing here today, but the way she is doing it.

I can't prove that anything Glenda has told me is correct. You can make up your qualifications and you can tell a story through the lens of fear and pain until it is distorted beyond reality. But you cannot make up the fact that you own a copy of *Life and Fate* by Vasily Grossman because I can see it lying in a plastic bin beside me. And because books, certain books, are a shibboleth, I feel more proximity to Glenda than distance.

I change the conversation to the books around us. 'I think this is a normal, admirable, amount of books,' I confide, knowing that Sandra would have my head. I see *Papillon* by Henri Charrière. Of it, and Viktor Frankl and her reading preferences generally, Glenda says, 'Anything which shows the human strength under the most appalling circumstances helps me to survive.' And I want to say, 'Me too!' I want to explain about my dark room and shaking hands and how the road back starts in thick forest. But I realise that such a conversation will not be possible because we are dwarfed by this gargantuan smell of shit and because, to one of us, it is a question of inadequate storage.

We exit the shed and head back to the house and I think of how a documentary I once saw used landscapes on earth to explain different planetary environments. How this stunned me, that the Arizona desert looked so like the surface of Mars.

As Sandra walks me back to my car, Dylan hurries out after her. He whispers to her that Glenda has started reopening bags on the lawn. The smell made Cheryl vomit and Glenda is getting upset. Sandra hurries back inside to return to the necessary business of cauterising. 'That's what happens when you open the bags that you agreed to throw out,' she sighs as she goes.

On the long drive home in the rain I think about Glenda's books and the wingspan of Marilyn's beautiful sentences and the bewilderment of Dorothy's neighbour with her soft protest: 'But she's such an *intelligent* person...'

I think, again, about my own lost decade, the darkness that swallowed me whole, not when my mother left but when it became clear just how much she had taken with her. I think about my tremors, my migraines, my years of days asleep; years of minutes as infinite as they were unbearable. The weight loss that turned my spine into an abacus and my clavicles into bowls. The unrelenting intrusive thoughts that everyone else would now leave too and the thousand ways in which I was worth leaving. I think how, in a world keeling like a ship, there was also my father. My father, who I saw when he popped his head into my dark room before he left for work in the morning, and when he checked in during the day and when he returned home at night. And before he cooked dinner, and after it was cooked, and then once again when he invited me to watch some TV or to have a cup of tea with a cookie or to go on a small walk with him, maybe?

I call him from the car and ask him about his morning, tell him about mine.

'What kind of hoarder was she?' he asks.

'Books and cats, mainly,' I tell the man who loves his cats and who I know is now actively considering his extensive book collection.

'What's the difference between a private library and a book hoarder?' he wonders.

We are both silent before chuckling and answering in unison: 'Faeces.'

But the difference is this phone call. And the others like it I could make. And how strong we are when we are loved.


I'm not sure I will ever be able to tell you, exactly, how Sandra has made it through. It is true that there is no Table of Maims when it comes to trauma; what chips some people like a mug cracks others like an egg. But that's an observation, not an explanation. I believe it has something to do with her innate calibration: an inherent and unbreakable conviction that she, too, is entitled to live her one best life. I believe it has much to do with the emotional machinery she has jettisoned in order to stay afloat. That is the buoying wonder and the sinking sadness of the particular resilience of Sandra.

Sandra who, even after three years, I fall in love with anew each

233

time I listen to her speak; Sandra who makes me laugh until my cheeks hurt; Sandra who called me her angel. Sandra who takes my breath away with her great kindness towards those she works with so fleetingly; Sandra who cannot notice me in a photograph of two people or ask after me when I'm ill or say my last name. Sandra who wrote it down for me clearly in her notes, 'No old friends', and, also, 'Can't connect to people on personal level'. Sandra who agonises; who won't reconcile, and who then, sadly, does.

# 16

To return to her childhood home, Sandra drives her sleek white 'Missibitchi' past the Footscray drill hall where she was forced to participate in cadet training with the other young boys. It is now a performance space used by a women's circus. She drives past St John's Primary School, where she was routinely caned across the knuckles and where ninety-five per cent of the students now speak a language other than English at home, past a green footy oval that used to be just a big hole in the ground. She drives past meticulously renovated Edwardian homes that are selling now for close to one million dollars until she crosses a date line where the cottages get a little shabbier and the streets get a little narrower and, by the time she pulls into the dead end of her childhood street, it feels like we have driven back through time.

The house facing Sandra's childhood home, the one her grandparents lived in, is as immaculately cared for now as it was then: freshly painted and blooming and neatly clipped. But Bill and Ailsa's old house slumps on its small plot of dirt like a body exhumed, recognisable but rotting.

There it is, behind a low brick fence that has cracked into three separate sections and which threatens, at any moment, to tumble over: a single-fronted weatherboard cottage. Under the drooping porch roof, a large window with the curtain drawn looks blindly out onto the street, a milky cataract beneath a paralysed eyelid. Ailsa's beloved front garden is all brown weeds that come up to my knees. The glass of the thin window running down the side of the front door is broken; boxes and rags have been piled high inside in a poor attempt to stop the gap.

We try knocking. No one is home. So we walk down the long driveway where Bill would struggle sloppily with his car each night and, as we pass along the length of the house, Sandra looks over the tall fence. 'That was Barbara's room. That was the boys' room. That was my room.' The top half of 'the bungalow' is visible, just, from where I stand. Back near the front of the house, we peek around the other side. We see only one window, broken; a hole into the house in the middle of winter.

'It's a fuckin' dump,' Sandra says, less in a tone of resentment and more in the spirit of clean appraisal. This is exactly the type of property that she is called upon to clean.

We get into her car and she takes me on a tour of the neighbourhood. To the eternal drone of her news radio station, she points out Sims grocery store where her mother shopped, her primary school, a number of government houses she has been contracted to clean and the tiny flat in Swan Street where her father interrupted her eighteenth birthday party to try to kill her.

'I wonder if we could go in and see the nuns?' she smiles as we pass the convent where she used to help out after school. She reconsiders: 'They might spank me for changing sex.'

I ask her what it feels like to see these places again.

'I'm OK with it now. I wasn't when I first came back here. I was crying my eyes out. There were just so many bad memories and I wanted to get away,' she says, steering back to her street. Tapping on the car window with a pink-lacquered nail, she points with some enthusiasm at a house near the corner and says, 'The lady in that house here, she died in the toilets at Myers.'

As Sandra parks outside her old house again, a short woman with frizzy blonde hair and a teenage girl, both laden with shopping bags, shuffle past the car and through the gate of the house across the road.

'Here are the people that live in Nana's house!' she says, crackling with excitement. 'Let's go talk to them.' She pops open her seatbelt and launches herself out of the car with the brisk vigour of someone much healthier.

'Hi, I just want to introduce myself. I'm Sandra Pankhurst,' she says, smiling, gasping a little as she walks up to the woman and shakes her hand. 'I used to live in that house sixty years ago.'

The woman squints up at Sandra through her Transitions, dark in the glare of the sun.

'OK, yes,' she nods eagerly, waiting for Sandra to continue.

'I was just wondering, do you know any of the history around the area?' Sandra asks.

'Tell you what, the person to ask would be Nancy,' the woman advises, with a lisp and a slight stutter. She calls out to her daughter to go on inside with the shopping. 'I'll come with you.'

'OK, darls,' Sandra says, and we stroll to the house next door.

'Nancy's mum lived here for years. Nancy's had a heart operation,' says the woman, chatty now. And then, oddly: 'Do you know anybody from Geelong who lives at the end of the road?'

'No, not Geelong,' Sandra says, taking the non sequitur in her stride.

'Simon,' the woman says.

'My brother, Simon? He's dead now. But he didn't live in Geelong,' Sandra corrects her.

'Nah,' the woman says as we climb the steps to Nancy's front door. 'This one was alive.' She rings the doorbell.

'Hi Nancy! It's Debbie!' booms the neighbour as the door is opened by an old woman with short brown hair.

'How are you doing?' Nancy says formally, standing in her white-carpeted foyer.

'Pretty good. Are you well?' Debbie inquires.

Nancy nods. 'Do you want to come in?'

Before Debbie can answer, Sandra is introducing herself in a loud, breathless voice. 'I used to live over there, sixty-odd years ago. My mother, Ailsa Collins, has died, and my brother, Simon, has died, and my Aunty Sullivan used to live in there.' She twists to her left and points behind her. 'I'll give you my card.' She grabs her wallet and pinches a card out between her long nails. 'This lady lives in my Nana's house.' She motions to Debbie.

'What was her name?' Nancy asks.

'I can't remember her name now, it's so long ago,' Sandra answers.

Nancy nods. She tells Sandra, 'After Nana died, Ailsa's daughter moved in.'

'Did my sister move into that house?' Sandra asks with brief interest. 'When Mum died—I was excluded from the house many years ago when I was sixteen or seventeen—apparently my sister wanted to turn the house into a shrine, but the boys said it's got to be sold. They had a fall-out and never spoke.'

Nancy and Debbie are looking up at her wordlessly. There is so much of the story and it comes gushing out, contextless and disorganised, sloshing in and over itself in big waves and small eddies from Sandra's pink-frosted lips. 'No one knows where my sister is, but she married some Asian gentleman and moved. My brother Christopher is now a wheeler-dealer, and my brother Simon who was in the army is dead. And so there's me left.'

'Right, because I know the family there,' Nancy says very slowly, nodding towards the house. 'I know they were Ailsa…'

'Ailsa Collins and Robert Grifford Parker Collins,' Sandra confirms eagerly, stumbling, as always, on her father's second name, which is Griffith.

'I can only remember Ailsa,' Nancy says.

'It was always well painted, I remember that,' Sandra says.

'I remember that too, I do. It was a lovely house,' Debbie nods.

Sandra turns and looks at a large house a few doors down. 'Bonnie Sullivan lived there, and then they pulled the house down. Her house was green.'

'That house there is on two blocks, so there were two houses there, I think,' Debbie says, looking in the same direction.

'Right,' Sandra says. 'So much changes.'

Throughout this conversation, Nancy has remained coolly formal whereas Debbie, with her rapid-fire nods and eyes wide behind the Transitions, which have cleared in the deep shade of the porch, has now come on board.

'Nancy, do you remember that fellow that come knocking on my door not long ago?' Debbie asks suddenly. 'Is that part of the same family?'

'Yes,' Nancy says simply. And though Sandra is a few moments away from realising it, standing there half-listening to this irrelevant aside, the architecture of her world is about to be drastically altered.

'Simon,' Debbie says, remembering his name again.

It's been circling like a bird, this shape that now lands on me, heavily. I look up at Sandra to see whether she felt it too. But her mind has been trained for so long to ignore certain forms. So I say the words softly for her: 'Maybe, is it your son?'

'Ohthatcouldbemyson!' Sandra exclaims.

'He came knocking on the door with his mother. She had dark hair. He works in a surf shop,' Debbie says, giving Sandra the first piece of information about her child in forty years. 'Where are all the surf shops? In Torquay or one of them, yes.'

Then she turns to Nancy. 'Tom is still very sick,' she says.

'Has he gone to work today?' Nancy asks.

'Yes. He shouldn't have but anyway he did,' Debbie replies. 'My husband got really sick,' she explains to Sandra. 'He got a brain infection, so he's pretty sick.'

Sandra nods sympathetically. 'Did Simon leave a contact number or anything?' she asks.

'He left you a card,' Debbie says.

Nancy goes to look for it. I ask Debbie if she remembers what Simon was asking about that day.

'About the same things you are,' Debbie says.

'Wow. Isn't that amazing,' Sandra marvels.

'You don't see him?' Debbie asks.

'No,' Sandra says. 'I'll tell you the situation. I used to be their father. So that's why things are the way they are.'

'OK,' Debbie says neutrally. 'You know what? I get it now.' She gives a series of small nods that make her curls bounce. 'And you know what? He said that.'

'Did he?' Sandra asks.

'Yes, he did,' Debbie answers.

'So he is looking,' Sandra says, stunned.

'He is definitely looking,' Debbie confirms.

'Isn't this amazing,' Sandra says to herself.

'He's desperately looking,' Debbie adds.

'I've wanted that, but you see, when the divorce came through I wasn't allowed to talk or touch them,' Sandra explains.

'OK,' Debbie says, nodding rapidly.

'And so all these years I haven't gone. I've got a photo of them in my bedroom: my two boys. Everyone says to me, "Why don't you contact them?" and I said, "Because I'm not allowed to, by law." But I would welcome them to come into my life if they want me to,' Sandra says.

'I'm sorry, I didn't keep it,' Nancy apologises, returning to the front door.

'Oh bugger,' Sandra says.

'It was one of them surf shops, so go along to one of them and you'll see a Simon,' Debbie says soothingly. 'Even if you have to go to all of them. It was Torquay. I'm pretty sure he said Torquay.'

'Yes, excellent, thank you. We'll do a bit more research,' Sandra says.

'He was a nice boy, wasn't he?' Debbie says, turning to Nancy.

'Oh yes,' Nancy agrees.

'He was very happy, sociable,' Debbie continues. 'And he had two children, I think he said.'

'Wow!' Sandra says.

'Who do you think Simon is?' Nancy asks sweetly, having missed this part of the conversation while she was searching for Simon's card.

'He's my son,' Sandra answers. 'I'm the eldest Collins boy.'

Nancy nods politely. 'But if Simon is your son, wouldn't you know what he is doing?' she asks.

'No, because we were estranged. Because I was his father,' Sandra explains.

'I know there was trouble in the family,' Nancy says, very slowly.

'You would probably have been one of the ladies of Les Girls? Nah, I'm only joking,' Debbie chuckles.

'Yes, I was at one stage,' Sandra smiles.

'Really?' Debbie is delighted. 'We'll have a little bit of history about our house!'

Sandra thanks Nancy and says goodbye.

'Listen,' Debbie says eagerly as we walk back to the car. 'You will catch up with Simon because he does work at that surf shop.'

'How long ago was it when he was here?' Sandra asks.

'It was about six months ago. See, it was not that long ago!'

Debbie says as we stop outside her house. 'I'd invite you in, but Tom, my husband, is sick.'

'That's OK, darling,' Sandra says.

'Renee's doing her eBay,' Debbie says. 'Renee is a special needs, you know.'

'We deal with special needs kids all the time because of the type of business we're in,' Sandra says. And then, like a mantra: 'We do industrial cleans for people who cannot quite deal with their cleaning. We do that plus crime scene, plus meth labs and assisting people with home help.' There are very few things that Sandra does not take in her stride but even when she is absolutely reeling, she is always willing to discuss her work. It is grounding for her: a solace.

'Do you know what you should do? You should go to Torquay, go to one of them motels and just stay one night and just have a really good look. He's definitely there, and he does look a bit similar to you. He does, I'm not just saying that,' Debbie says. 'I'm happy for you anyway.'

'Thank you,' Sandra says. 'It's been a long time. Because of the family law court.'

'I'm just going to ask this question: what made you do it?' Debbie asks, peering up into Sandra's face.

'It's just, I felt…' Sandra starts and falters. 'I decided I wasn't going to contact the children because I thought it would be child abuse if I did. As far as I know their mother told them that I was dead. Now, how do I turn up?'

Debbie nods. 'My mum passed away. She committed suicide in front of me, so that is something I'll never forget. That was really damaging.'

'Very damaging!' Sandra says.

'She had a nervous breakdown. My dad was an alcoholic and them days, they drank, drank, drank. Eight kids in the family. He used to hit her a lot. I saw most of it.'

'That's ghastly,' Sandra says.

'So that was pretty bad,' Debbie says. 'I'm sure you'll find him because I know he works in one of them surf shops. Like I said, he runs it or manages it.' Debbie wishes Sandra luck and walks up her driveway and into her house.

Slamming the car door shut, Sandra sits back for a moment against the cool, black leather and looks out the windshield, stunned. 'I always thought in my heart of hearts that Simon would come back to me.'

I suggest that she might find him on Facebook.

Taking out her phone, she opens the Facebook app. 'Let's have a look. I wonder if he's called Simon Collins or Simon Hughes?' she says, considering the possibility that he might have taken on his mother's family name.

She starts with her own former surname. Clicks on the first search result. Looks down at a face the same shape as her own, smiling her smile. It is, unmistakably, the face of the older baby in her silver frame grown into manhood.

'Wow. Yes...' Sandra says with soft wonder at his face and the feeling, and the feeling of having the feeling. And her next impulse is as strong as it is reflexive: to write to him, to run to him, that very second because, like the house to our left and the house to our right and the drill hall and the primary school and the people shopping at Sims and the way Debbie's stutter gets a little worse when she talks about her mother, the fact that everything has changed, changes nothing, really, at all.

'How do I contact him?' she asks.

17

A wall has been unexpectedly knocked down in Sandra's house and she doesn't quite know yet how she feels about the way the new space looks; doesn't know if she can live there. Still, in the second week of September, one week after learning that Simon was actively looking for her, Sandra writes to him, by hand, in her elegantly slashing script with its letters that look like arrows rising and falling. She explains her choices, neither apologising nor seeking forgiveness, and invites him to contact her if he still wishes. She signs it, *Respectfully, Sandra.* Then she folds herself into an envelope which she posts to the address a friend has tracked down for her and she waits.

'Have you heard back from Simon?' I ask during the second week in October.

'No reply,' she says, too casually.

A week later, I ask again.

'No,' she says lightly. 'I'm not even thinking of it. What will be will be. If it comes, then I'll deal with it then. No good pre-thinking, I've got enough on my plate.'

Although she comes across as ambivalent, she is actually just pre-emptively damping the pain of rejection to come with compensatory thoughts about the continuation of her peaceful, predictable life. Double-bound by the fear that her son will not reply and the fear that he will, she puts the anxiety of waiting and the associated 'what if' thoughts into a box. Locks it. Turns her mind to matters more immediately at hand: hiring some new employees, organising a fundraiser for domestic violence, the maintenance of her office suite, inviting her local federal member to the 'official launch' of those offices, and getting to the bottom of 'the fucking seizures' that have been afflicting poor little Moët Chandon, who went downhill suddenly 'after her grooming last Saturday'. While this looks the same as the cognitive technique of mindfulness, and though it serves some of the same purposes, it is different in texture and effect.

Sandra's truest emotions are buried in tombs sealed with curses. Denial, distraction and excision are fundamental physical laws in her universe. They are the coping strategies that have allowed her to maintain forward momentum and, along with self-medication, they have been her only coping strategies. So while they are about as useful to the maintenance of intimate relationships as a broom is to brain surgery, they have allowed her to keep going and to find moments of peace along the way.

In Sandra's universe, walls come down and wrinkles fill out, the members of her friend-family and the facts of the past are entirely interchangeable; everything is always becoming better. But life is an unforgiving medium and the hand of the artist leaves traces that cannot always be erased. Starting with Simon's visit to Birchill Street before us, there are signs, now, that the past is gaining on her.

One day after work she stops in at a random pub in a neighbouring suburb with one of her employees for a knock-off drink. She's never been there before but she thinks she recognises the dour-faced woman behind the bar.

'Now, where do I know you from?' Sandra asks.

'You won't be happy when I tell you,' comes the reply.

'Oh?'

'Anita Pankhurst.' George's daughter. Her stepdaughter for fourteen years whom she hasn't seen since 2003. Sandra steps away.

Soon after, Sandra is admitted to hospital for a problem with her retina and, to her vast annoyance, is required to spend the night. There are three other beds in the room to which she has been assigned, and one of those beds is occupied by her ex-wife, Linda.

Because Sandra and I and Linda and nearly six million other people live in a state that covers an area of 237,629 square kilometres, the chances of this are sufficiently remote that, when Sandra texts me from the hospital with this news, I wonder about the drugs they are treating her with. That is when she sends me a photo that she has surreptitiously taken on her phone of someone who is, as I know from our mutual and separate Facebook stalkings, undeniably Linda. This is also when she texts me with the confirmation that the nurse has just called out Linda's full name, which has not changed. Sandra remains silent, but still, she is being drawn back.

Sandra started her day, as always, with the television news. This morning it told her that a woman in her seventies had been stabbed to death in her home. Her home happens to fall in Sandra's catchment and, allowing the usual buffer for the forensics team to finish, she reckons she should be getting a call about the clean soon. Until then, she is free to drive a friend to the doctor and to try to source a particular type of Italian tea that she's recently discovered. So she is having a perfectly normal day when I ask her how she would feel about me talking to her ex-wife.

'Go for it,' she replies, saying that it might give me a different perspective on things, which would be valuable.

'Is there anything you would prefer me not to tell her?' I ask, admiring how mellow she sounds.

'I don't care. I really don't give a rat's arse,' she says, too harshly.

So I contact Linda and go sit in her kitchen and listen to her talk about Pete, her ex-husband and the father of her children. Like her sons, and unlike Sandra, his surname is still her surname. Linda speaks entirely without animosity although she remembers to the cent, forty years later, the amount of money she received each week from the government to try to feed, clothe and shelter herself and their two toddlers: an amount of money that was always a blanket too small, so that something paid for meant something forgone.

She's in her mid-sixties now, still working, and she inadvertently mentions something to me that indicates she worries about her superannuation. She returned to work much later than she wanted; every time she tried to leave the boys at child care the older one would vomit with anxiety.

'Simon was vomiting every day. It was only a trial to get him used to it,' she explains. 'The welfare, in them days, used to come and check on you all the time. They said, "What are you doing?" and I said, "I need to get money. I've got to go back to work." They said, "What do you think we give you a pension for? So you stay home. One parent has already left. They need you here with them."'

In Linda's kitchen I meet Pete, the bearded, smiling golden god, the husband, the father, the friend, in the photo albums she has stacked high. These are the photo albums that went missing one day and that she found squirrelled away in the garage by her teenage sons, who had sat there in secret, looking for answers in the books of their father. I see the wedding and the red-accented bridesmaids and groomsmen, the small house in Benjamin Street. I see Pete renovating the front with Linda's dad. I see the christenings, the Christmases, the baby sprawled naked on Pete's chest and how father and son beamed at the camera. I see the toys donated by the Salvation Army and the smiles of each boy holding up an Ernie and a Bert.

And though Linda feeds me warm custard tarts and proudly

shows me photos of her grandchildren—though Linda is excellent at putting one foot in front of the other—when I ask to use her bathroom and forget which door she said, I choose one only hesitantly, as though I might walk through it and into a molten river of pain that would sweep me away forever.

Sandra calls the next day to find out how it went. She acts, again, blasé but I can tell that she is steeling herself. I report back that I'm now able to fill in a few blanks. For instance, she did have a wedding reception after all. It turns out she did all the cooking for it, got fresh scallops from the fisherman next door and everything turned out beautifully. 'Hmmm!' she marvels. And: 'I can't remember, but that sounds about right...'

I tell her that she did attend the births of both of her sons. And that Ailsa helped Linda only a little, and then abandoned her completely when she became pregnant to her new partner, six years after being left. 'Mmmm,' she says. And then there is a uniquely strange sound, at once extraterrestrial and intimate. Sandra is crying.

She didn't mean for them to go through any of this, she says. There is so much she cannot remember, she says, so much she has lost. And though she still knows so little of the narrative, perhaps the facts are secondary to the feeling of it, coursing, now, down vestigial pathways I had thought long atrophied. For one wisp of a moment, the sounds she is making come down the line in an ecstasy of sorrow, and the image I've had so many times—of a majestic ghost ship doomed never to make port, pelagic, forging through every latitude on wind and tide, fearless because empty—evaporates. Then she sniffs, and tells me about the new office premises she is about to sign the lease on and how much she adores her new car.

Simon's text pops up on Sandra's phone like a kiss behind the ear. He would love to see her, is overjoyed that she made contact, has been looking for her forever. He respects her courage, is looking only towards the future. The reason he didn't respond sooner was that the letter went to the wrong house. After more than two months of waiting for his reply, another of Sandra's girlfriends took matters into her own hands and, without consulting Sandra or knowing why Simon had not responded, tracked down his contact details and called to inform him that 'his father' was trying to get in touch.

Simon was receptive and enthusiastic, luckily. He holds no grudges. Nathan not so much. Sandra's younger son was not included in her letter because he did not come looking for her. So she is intent on respecting that fact, which also dovetails with her own hesitance, given he was so young when she left.

Waiting for the weekend she will finally meet Simon, Sandra is on top of the world. At the same time, however, this excitement has disturbed the soil in which she has rooted herself so neatly. The happy anxiousness she is now experiencing feels the same for her as acute anxiety, and it has left her exhausted. She is nervous about what will be said and what will be expected of her and how this will all pan out moving forward. She has great trepidation about the many difficulties and awkwardnesses and expectations that may arise should she, suddenly, be reintegrated into family life.

These worries are not alleviated after her initial meeting with Simon and his partner, even though it goes wonderfully. Nor after she meets her beautiful grandchildren. These worries are there, in the background, though her tone is lighter when she speaks about her family ('It's just so loving.'). These worries lurk at the back of her mind when she spends the weekend at Simon's home and when his family come to her house and when he starts not calling as often as she would like and when she has no clear answers to the question of how much she should mix in when family problems arise and how much to bring up the past and what the future will look like.

About this, I am initially not only unsympathetic but pretty delighted. Many of these problems are all the same problem and that problem is the messiness of love and of family. And why, I ask her, should she be exempt?

But months pass and it becomes clear that any relationship with her sons will take much more time and also, probably, professional help to work through the deep wounds of the past. This state of affairs has inflamed the enduring subterranean shame, the defensiveness that she has carried about leaving her children. Both of those children are now very different men with similar faces; it is the face of their father: folded down the middle, just between the eyes, where the individual pains have shoaled together, blocking out the light.

Sandra's sparsely populated personal life is not perfect but it is perfectly ordered and relatively peaceful. This has been the compensation for the pain that she suffered with her family of origin, as she told me in one of our first conversations.

'You still love them, you still want to be accepted, everyone needs to be loved and blah blah blah blah blah…but in some respects, I appreciate it now, because it's made me tough, it's made me resilient, it's made me think, "I don't give a fuck." And I don't *need* to have family. I have my sister-in-law and my brother, who I didn't really have that much to do with when he was alive. My sister-in-law used to push for us to have contact, but it's just that I've never had them, so I don't really need them. I have good friends, who I appreciate, but if they did the wrong thing by me'—she clapped her hands loudly—'I wouldn't bat an eyelid to turn around and say, "See you later!" I don't have that bonding that I need to have people in my life.'

When Sandra wrote, in her first letter to Simon, *I do not regret leaving you and your brother and your mother as I was so unhappy with myself and my life at the time and I had to do what made me happy*, I believe she was not talking about 'happiness' per se but the fact that she had passed a 'clinical threshold' in which persistent uncertainties about her gender had become a struggle so intense it felt like the most important part of her life.[8] But the more contact she has with her sons, and the more we discuss her feelings about this reconnection, the more I come to believe that the point was not just inelegantly expressed; it was insufficiently felt.

'Has this affected your will?' I ask in reference to her small estate.

'No,' she replies. 'I've already told them that my will has been finalised. It's all going to the university to fund scholarships in my name.'

At this, it silently pops open inside me, like the boot of a car into which one might fit the universe: anger.

So loudly does it scream, this anger that I haven't felt towards her before, as it hurls itself against the locked door of her emotion; this anger which screams that it isn't about the money but about the act of connection and concern, of care and responsibility that it would represent to her children, or to Linda. So loudly does this anger scream inside me—this anger of, and for, the abandoned child—that I forget—for weeks, I forget—my one task: to listen for the truer sound.

My anger is Sandra's Scotch. It is her wine, her sleeping pills, her years of speed and 'mandies make you randy', her denial, her forgetting. These are the ways we numb the pain of vulnerability, but emotion cannot be selectively numbed.[9] If we are too good at it for too long we will numb our ability to form true connections, with ourselves and with others, which is the only thing we are here for—if we are here, glued to the same crumb busily suspended in infinity, for anything at all.

Social researcher Brené Brown explains that we need 'excruciating vulnerability' in order for meaningful human connection to occur. That is, we have to overcome our fear that we are not worthy of such connection and allow ourselves to be truly seen.[10] Sitting in, and with, our vulnerability we can move towards empathy—feeling, not merely *for*, but actually *with*, others—and form true connection. Or sitting in, and with, our vulnerability we can move away from empathy and towards shame—that deep fear that if we are truly seen, we will be found undeserving of human connection. Which is to say that shame 'breeds fear, blame, disconnection'; it 'absolutely unravels our relationships and our connections with other people'.[11] And shame was, repeatedly, the only type of vulnerability that Sandra was allowed to have.

When they denied her food and soap and love, when they tied her to the clothesline the better to beat her, when they shut the door on her once and forever, Ailsa and Bill moved her towards disconnection. The members of the Victorian Government who passed and preserved laws against 'homosexuality' and wearing women's clothes moved her towards disconnection. The members of the Victorian community who supported those laws, actively or with silence, moved her towards disconnection. The Victorian police officers of the 1970s who threatened her, the men who paid to beat her and to fuck her, her rapist and her girlfriend's killer and the bureaucrats who voided her marriage all moved her towards disconnection. The people who, even now, legislate and police and 'pick' her gender, move her towards disconnection.

So you see, despite the great and wondrous energy that Sandra manages to generate, she requires the lion's share for herself, just to keep breathing. She cannot conceive of emotional or financial generosity towards her children or Linda in the ways I wish to see. And yet she has given me the means to understand her reaction: compassion. As she has said: 'I think it's a drive for me that everyone deserves it because I deserve it as well.'

Compassion, Brené Brown explains, is the expression of 'a deeply held belief that we are inextricably connected to each other' by the bonds of shared human imperfection, of suffering and of love and of goodness. If we make the vulnerable choice to connect with empathy—to be vulnerable, excruciatingly so, in order to access that in me which has suffered as you are now suffering—we bring compassion alive by communicating that bond, so others know they are never alone.[12]

From her parents' garden to the nuns' convent, from the massage parlours to the funeral parlour to the dark homes where people with hardly any human contact wait to die, Sandra has spent her life enthusiastically being of service to others. There is deep love in Sandra but, despite all the desperate strangers she has so greatly helped over her lifetime, it has not yet begun to be truly expressed.

How do we form true connection? By being terrified to tell our story and by doing it anyway.[13] When Sandra agreed to speak with me she was finally, and for the first time, ready to tell her story. But by that point, she was no longer able to remember it. So I have done my best to give it back to her. And my choice to view her darker aspects in their full context is not merely the just choice of perspective; it is a tool for daily living, a gift of worthiness and belonging that I give not just to Sandra.

Sandra, you exist in the Order of Things and the Family of People; you belong, you belong, you belong.

Sandra's house in Frankston is about an hour's drive from the house where she grew up, but the distance is more appropriately measured in astronomical units because, really, it is further than driving to the Sun. The light in her small home is always beautiful and, rather than perfect tidiness, the overwhelming impression given by the space is one of healthy harmony. The tamed clutter (a kitchen corkboard pinned with cards and flyers, dog brushes in a basket under the coffee table, the tchotchkes crowding the cabinet in her bedroom) functions like vines in the margins of manuscripts, attesting to the life of the orderly text within.

The sense of harmony is equally a function of the various styles she has effortlessly wedded in each room; there are tartan pillows and Chinese vases, an open French provincial sideboard stocked with colourful ceramics, an intricately wrought silver dining table for six, framed lithographs of tweedy Victorian gentlemen, heavy wooden sculptures on sleek marble stands in the foyer, a standing liquid silver loop that looks like a Brancusi. There are birds in her space: painted, stuffed, hewn from wood, etched in glass. There is a vintage-style French poster of an ad for cognac above her couch, a Marilyn Monroe print keeps watch over her desk and by the door she keeps two tiles featuring classical Indian portraits so fine they appear to have been painted with an eyelash.

I will go on. The harmony in Sandra's home is also a function of the way the space feels: the energy of it, if I may say that without hating myself. In addition to the sunlight that suffuses the whole house like chamomile tea, washing over your eyelids in a way that makes you yearn for a little nap, there are beautifully arranged flowers both artificial and real, pleasingly plush carpets and deep sofas to sink cosily into. There are overstuffed chairs with footrests and fluffy hand towels and woven baskets full of Donna Hay magazines. There is perfumed hand soap, cable TV and a clean fridge covered in magnets with impressionist art reproductions and snappy slogans like *Queen of Fucking Everything* and *How about a nice big cup of shut the fuck up.*

I will go on. The harmony in Sandra's home is also a function of the fact that when you stand in her foyer with its framed photos, it is 2016 but it is also 1989 and you are smiling at George smiling at Sandra and, nearby on paper as he was in life, admiring Craig's good looks. When you walk from her bedroom towards the kitchen, as she does each morning to make her coffee, her baby sons smile out from their silver frame and it is 1974 again and she herself smiles out from between her older sister and her baby brother and it is also 1958.

I will go on. The harmony in Sandra's home is most of all

a function of the fact that, while life is inescapably messy and discordant, its beauty is in the end a question of proportion. Sandra can tell the Story of the Green Lounge Suite a thousand times and never lose the triumph of that couch—so long that two of her could lie on it full length to watch *The Bold and the Beautiful* together—which she bought before the house was even completed and which she placed in storage while she waited anxiously to move in. She wasn't sure if it was the right size, but 'when it come, it was just like *Hallelujah*'—she snaps her fingers—'it just fit into place. I was so blessed.'

And this is everything, really. Though her health has stabilised for now, Sandra never breathes with ease and she lives with a significant risk of developing liver cancer. If she is caught anywhere silent for too long, the Old Fear comes lumbering, comes swiping down at her with its dark paws, comes knocking her down and around. Sandra has chronic insomnia and bouts of vertiginous insecurity; she is quick to love, quick to give and, when she feels she has been wronged, quick towards the rage and rejection that are the converse of that defensive sweetness. Sandra has financial worries and family worries and subterranean pain that surges inside her like a great ocean in the earth's deep mantle. She is hypervigilant, which robs her unjustly of energy she could use better elsewhere. She has spells of deep exhaustion and deep distraction, lungs that clench on her like fists and skin that rips like paper; she has a memory that has betrayed her, erasing the good with the bad.

But the opposite of trauma is not the absence of trauma. The opposite of trauma is order, proportion; it is everything in its place. It is one long green couch in a sunlit corner, looking like it was built for the space and waiting for you. It is an act of wilful seeing, a conscious choice about perspective. A bronze jaguar head guards a bedside table in Sandra's guest room, its veneer melted off by the fire that swept through her rental unit with George. That is not why she keeps it. That is not its story, that is just something that happened to it once. She displays the jaguar now for the same reason she purchased it originally: she likes the way it looks. Here, in this home, in this light, the worst parts of Sandra's past still prowl but they are forced to concede room to the good memories and the new plans and the life lived and living which take up much of the space now.

Sandra's unit extends out onto the back deck where she lost that toe. The deck is protected under its own glass roof, but just enough breeze blows through to remind you that, while you can knock down walls and change your addresses and the topography of your face, there is also much you cannot control. There are plants there and chairs with waterproof cushions and speakers through which she can play CDs and sip her Scotch while listening to Celine or Whitney or Madonna or Mariah or Babs or Bette. But regardless of what is playing and what noises it is drowning out, the deck is dominated by an eight-foot-tall Classical-style figurehead of a woman mounted on one wall.

Seeing this piece in a shop, Sandra tried, using the bulldozer of her charm over a period of two years, to bargain the owner down on the price. The owner would not budge but Sandra bought it anyway because she 'had to have it'.

The figure is plaster, but looks like she was carved from stone. Under her arms, which are crossed protectively over her head, her eyes are lowered and her chin is tucked into her chest. Naked from the waist up, her long hair flows over her breasts. She was actually assembled from two pieces, though I cannot tell where one piece ends and the other begins—which is probably, yes, an act of wilful seeing: a choice about perspective.

She reminds me of you, my friend—as if I needed it, I think of you so often. She reminds me of all the times everything told you to stop fighting and just sink, and how, with your eyes locked on the horizon, you simply refused. She reminds me of the sheer distance you have covered, inch by inch. Of the staggering weight of everything you have carried with you and everything you have lost. She reminds me, this magnificent warrior who is infinitely more than her pieces, that life may break others like a wave on a prow.

But that is not how Sandra Pankhurst is going out.

# ACKNOWLEDGMENTS

I would not have been able to understand the many worlds in which Sandra Pankhurst lived without the insights provided by the following people and the access to materials provided by the following institutions. I am gratefully indebted to each of them: the woman called 'Linda Collins' in this book, Pat Balfour, Margaret and John, the STC Services staff, Simon Ceber, Doug Lucas, Terri Tinsel, Sandra's friends and sister-in-law, Lois Greig, Sally Goldner at Transgender Victoria, Nick Henderson at the Australian Lesbian and Gay Archives, the research archivists at the Manuscripts, Archives, and Rare Books Division of the New York Public Library who guided me through the vast LGBT periodicals collection, the librarians at the State Library of Victoria and at the Victorian Supreme Court Library, the many contributors to the Facebook group 'Lost Gay Melbourne' and Elaine McKewon for her significant and captivating study, *The Scarlet Mile: A Social History of Prostitution in Kalgoorlie, 1984–2004* (University of Western Australia Press, 2005), which gave me an intricate web of historical detail in which to situate Sandra's personal experience. In addition,

I am thankful for the time taken to identify and retrieve records by Victoria Police, the County Court of Victoria, the Supreme Court of Victoria and the Victorian Registry of Births, Deaths and Marriages.

My deepest thanks to the following people:

The editors at *Narratively* for publishing an early incarnation of this story. Hannah Ozer for getting the ball rolling.

Josie Freeman, Daniel Kirschen and Heather Karpas at ICM Partners and Karolina Sutton at Curtis Brown for believing in this book from the very beginning, for their good guidance and for their efforts on my behalf.

Michael Heyward, the talented crew at Text Publishing and Mandy Brett, editor and human extraordinaire, who sees the beauty in the 'dark velvet'—thank you seems very small in return for all that you have done, but here it is: thank you.

My early readers, for their valuable time and wise counsel: Paul Chadwick, Declan Fay, David Krasnostein, Patricia Stragalinos, Charlie Pickering, Alexandra Bowie and Nina Collins.

Norma and Jack Krasnostein, Ruth and John Krasnostein, the Stragalinos family, the Pickering family, the Berger family, Tony Jackson, Nina Bilewicz, Laura Chasen, Lee Kim, David Philips, Caren Silver, Fran Brooke, Kris Smith, Emily Fishman, Gaby Wolkenberg, Sarit Musat, Emily Mars, Nina Collins, Lisa Kentish, Roslyn Borg and Joanna Kahn for their wisdom and their warmth and for making it possible, each in their own vital way, for me to write this book.

For the type of unbounded love and support without which books do not get written: my father, David Krasnostein, who is my hero and guide; my stepmother, Patricia Stragalinos, whose positivity and beautiful sense of perspective always inspire me; my brother, Josh Krasnostein, who is wise and hilarious.

My husband, my person, Charlie Pickering, for everything, forever. And to our great joy, our beautiful child, for opening doors in my house that I never knew were there and for filling them only with light.

This book is dedicated to the indomitable Mrs Sandra Pankhurst for her bravery and her sheer strength. 'My life is a book,' she said to me on our first day together. Sandra, you were right. I will be forever honoured that you let me write it.

# NOTES

1 Vivian Sherman quoted in 'Transsexuality: An Interview with Vivian Sherman' (1975) *Gay Liberation Press* 2, 49.

2 For this idea of 'great preparation', I am indebted to Alfred Kazin. See Alfred Kazin, *New York Jew* (Knopf, 1978).

3 This image is Susanna Valenti's: see 'Susanna Says' (1961) 12 *Transvestia* 1.

4 Michael Hurley, 'Aspects of Gay and Lesbian Life in Seventies Melbourne' (2011) 87 *LaTrobe Journal* 44, 58.

5 Elaine McKewon, *The Scarlet Mile: A Social History of Prostitution in Kalgoorlie, 1894–2004* (University of Western Australia Press, 2005) 1.

6 Brené Brown, *The Gifts of Imperfection* (Hazelden Publishing, 2010).

7 Victorian Parliamentary Debates, Legislative Assembly, Second Reading Speech, 22 April 2004, 790 (Robert Clark, Attorney-General).

8 Harry Benjamin International Gender Dysphoria Association, *Standards of Care for Gender Identity Disorders*, 6th version (2005).

9 Brené Brown, Shame & Empathy (https://www.youtube.com/watch?v=qQiFfA7KfF0).

10 Brené Brown, The Power of Vulnerability (http://www.ted.com/talks/brene_brown_on_vulnerability).

11 Brené Brown, Shame & Empathy (https://www.youtube.com/watch?v=qQiFfA7KfF0); Brené Brown, The Power of Vulnerability (http://www.ted.com/talks/brene_brown_on_vulnerability).

12 Brené Brown, *The Gifts of Imperfection* (Hazelden Publishing, 2010); Brené Brown, Brené Brown on Empathy (https://www.youtube.com/watch?v=1Evwgu369Jw); Brené Brown, Boundaries, Empathy and Compassion (https://www.youtube.com/watch?v=utjWYO0w1OM).

13 Brené Brown, Shame & Empathy (https://www.youtube.com/watch?v=qQiFfA7KfF0).